BTEC Tech Award

DIGITAL INFORMATION TECHNOLOGY

Student Book

Rob Cadwell

Alan Jarvis

Published by Pearson Education Limited, 80 Strand, London, WC2R 0RL.

www.pearsonschoolsandfecolleges.co.uk

Copies of official specifications for all Pearson qualifications may be found on the website: qualifications.pearson.com

Text © Pearson Education Limited
Typeset by PDQ Media
Original illustrations © Pearson Education Limited 2018
Picture research by Integra
Cover illustration by KJA Artists

First published 2018

19 18 17 16
10 9 8 7 6 5 4 3 2 1

British Library Cataloguing in Publication Data
A catalogue record for this book is available from the British Library

ISBN 978 1 292 20837 4

Acknowledgements
The authors and publisher would like to thank the following individuals and organisations for their kind permission to reproduce copyright material.

Text
The publisher would like to thank the following for their kind permission to reproduce their material.

(Key: b-bottom; c-centre; l-left; r-right; t-top)

p. 78 Crown Copyright: Link from Office for National Statistics. Contains public sector information licensed under the Open Government Licence v3.0.

p. 91 Link from Data.World, Inc.

p. 91 Link from The World Bank.

p. 91 Link from data.gov.uk. Contains public sector information licensed under the Open Government Licence v3.0.

p. 128 Crown Copyright: Link from GOV.UK. Contains public sector information licensed under the Open Government Licence v3.0

p. 187 Gemalto NV: Link from Breach Level Index.

p. 195 Link from Information Commissioner's Office. Contains public sector information licensed under the Open Government Licence v3.0.

p. 198 Recycling Guide.org.uk: Computers, http://www.recycling-guide.org.uk/materials/computers.html

p. 198 Link from UKPower.co.uk Limited.

p. 198 Sibelga: Link from energuide.be.

IOS is a trademark or registered trademark of Cisco in the U.S. and other countries and is used under license, 12, 146; Mac and macOS are trademarks of Apple Inc., registered in the U.S. and other countries, 31; iTunes, iPhone and iPod are trademarks of Apple Inc., registered in the U.S. and other countries, 148

Google: Courtesy of Google 21c, 111t, 111c, 116br, 118t, 118b, 123t, 123b, 124b, 145c

Microsoft corporation: Courtesy of Microsoft Corporation, 33b, 90, 92t, 92b, 93, 94t, 94b, 95, 96, 97t, 97c, 97b, 98, 99t, 99b, 100t, 100b, 101t, 101b, 102, 103t, 103b, 105, 106, 107t, 107b, 108t, 108b, 109t, 109cl, 109cr, 109b, 110b, 112, 113, 111t, 111b, 112, 113, 114, 115t, 115b, 116br, 117t, 117b, 122b, 124t, 125, 126t, 132

Photographs
The publisher would like to thank the following for their kind permission to reproduce their photographs.

(Key: b-bottom; c-centre; l-left; r-right; t-top)

123RF.com: Kaspars Grinvalds 7c, Ewelina Kowalska 11t, Scanrail1 12bl, Famveldman 24t, Shtanzman 50b, Shtanzman 50b, Highwaystarz 85tr, Maridav 146bl, Andreypopov 156b, Andriy Popov 158t, Rawpixel 168tr, Scyther5 173c, Andrey Popov 174b, Pixinoo 178cl, Aleksey Boldin 179tr, Kjetil Kolbjornsrud 182b, Georgejmclittle 204b, Maxxyustas 210b. Wavebreakmediamicro 213cr; **Alamy Stock Photo:** Kevin Britland 8c; **BananaStock**: 228 cl; **Pearson Education:** Naki Kouyioumtzis 133br; **Shutterstock:** Violetkaipa 3, Syda Productions 4t, James W Copeland 9c, Belushi 15cr, Seyyahil 18b, Alhovik 23b, Andrey_Popov 60l, Watcharakun 71, Pete Saloutos 73cr, Anna_Zubkova 75b, Bacho 77b, Fujji 80bl, Matej Kastelic 83tr, Rawpixel.com 84b, Wavebreakmedia 104b, NAN728 134b, Chanpipat 139, Georgejmclittle 141t, Ye Liew 142bl, Ye Liew 142bl, Elnur 146tl, You can more 146tc, Vovan 146tc, Bloom Design 146tr, Jolypics 146bl, Vasabii 148b, Monkey Business Images 149t, Jmiks 151t, ScottMurph 153tr, Vectorfusionart 155t, Rawpixel.com 157t, PureSolution 160cr, iQoncept (c) 162bl, Ken Schulze 163bl, Andrey_Popov 167tr, Rawpixel.com 169cl, MaverickLEE 175t, Brian A Jackson 177t, Noppawan09 178cl, O.Bellini 178cl, Arka38 180bl, Rawpixel.com 181cr, Huguette Roe 186b, Rawpixel.com 190t, Balefire 192b, Georgejmclittle 196cl, Anton Gvozdikov 200c, Telnov Oleksii 201tr, Pandpstock001 208t, Route66 212b, Sam72 215t, Sean Locke Photography 228 cr

Cover images: Front: shapechare/iStock/Getty Images, Back: Plume Creative/Getty Images

All other images © Pearson Education

Contents

Contents

About this book

This book is designed to support you when you are taking a BTEC Tech Award in Digital Information Technology.

About your BTEC Tech Award

Congratulations on choosing a BTEC Tech Award in Digital Information Technology. This exciting and challenging course will introduce you to the digital sector. By studying for your Award you will gain the important knowledge, understanding and skills that are the foundations for working in this area. This will include many of the skills that are used by professionals on a day-to-day basis, such as project planning, designing and creating user interfaces and keeping data secure. You will also learn about virtual workplaces, cyber security and legal and ethical issues, with the opportunity to apply these in realistic scenarios.

How you will be assessed

You will be assessed in two different ways. Components 1 and 2 are assessed through internal assessment. This means that your teacher will give you an assignment brief and indicate to you the deadline for completing it. The assignment will cover what you have been learning about and will be an opportunity to apply your knowledge and skills. You teacher will mark your assignment and award you with a grade. Your third assessment (for Component 3) will be an external assessment. This will be a test that is set and marked by Pearson. You will have a set time in which to complete this test. The test will be an opportunity to bring together what you have learned in Components 1 and 2.

Additional resources to support Component 2

Some of the Activities in Component 2 require students to create a spreadsheet. To save time these spreadsheets can be downloaded from our website www.pearsonschools. co.uk/techawardDITsupport, and are clearly marked within the relevant Activities.

About the authors

Rob Cadwell

Rob is an experienced secondary school teacher and head of department. He has seen how digital technologies have developed and changed during this time. Rob believes that digital technologies give young people essential skills that they need to be successful in lots of different areas of learning and employment. Rob has written many exam papers in the past and has also developed a range of teacher resources.

Alan Jarvis

Alan has over 20 years experience as an IT lecturer in FE and has contributed to many BTEC textbooks and teaching materials. He also works as a trainer, examiner and standards verifier. Alan has worked with IT apprentices and is keen to see young people develop the skills that will support them into employment.

How to use this book

The book has been designed in a way that will help you to easily navigate through your course. Each component from the course is covered in a separate chapter that makes clear what you are learning and how this will contribute to your assessment. There are opportunities for you to test your understanding of key areas, as well as activities that will challenge and extend your knowledge and skills. You will get the most from this book if you use each feature as part of your study. The different features will also help you develop the skills that will be important in completing your assignments as well as preparing you for your external assessment.

Features of the book

This book is designed in spreads, which means that each pair of facing pages represents a topic of learning. Each spread is about 1 hour of lesson time. Your teacher may ask you to work through a spread during a lesson or in your own time. Each spread contains a number of features that will help you to check what you are learning and offer opportunities to practise new skills.

Getting started A short activity or discussion that will introduce you to what you will be covering in the lesson.

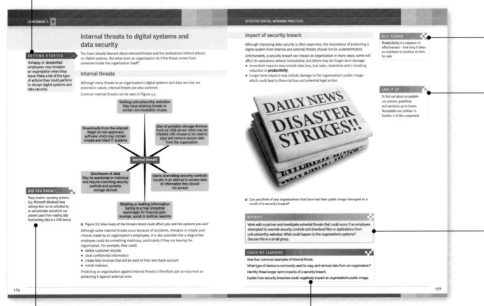

Key terms Important words or terms are defined.

Link it up This indicates where what you're learning about is covered in another part of the course.

Activity These will help you learn about the topic. You may be asked to work in pairs, groups or on your own.

Did you know? These include interesting facts that relate to what you're learning about.

Check my learning This is an opportunity to check back over what you have learnt. It may be a discussion or homework activity.

At the end of each learning aim there is a section that outlines how you will be assessed and provides opportunities for you to build skills for assessment.

Checkpoint This feature is designed to allow you to assess your learning. The 'strengthen' question helps you to check your knowledge and understanding of what you have been studying, while the 'challenge' questions are an opportunity to extend your learning.

Take it further This provides suggestions for what you can do to further the work you've done in the practice assessment.

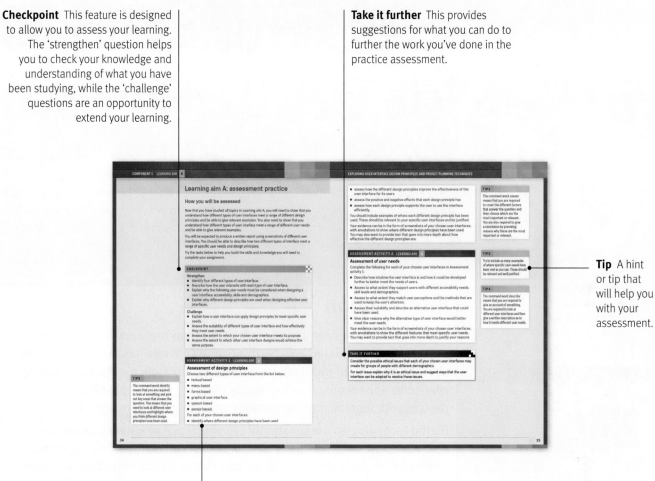

Tip A hint or tip that will help you with your assessment.

Assessment Activity This is a practice assessment that reflects the style and approach of an assignment brief. In Component 3, tasks in the assessment activity features will be similar to those you should expect in your external assessment.

COMPONENT

01

Exploring User Interface Design Principles and Project Planning Techniques

Introduction

Digital technologies are used by individuals and organisations. However, have you ever wondered how hardware and software has been designed to allow humans to interact with their devices? Have you ever thought about why items appear onscreen in the way that they do? People often use their devices without realising the complex study that has gone into their design.

Digital technologies are constantly evolving. Each new development opens up a new project that needs to be completed. The ability to manage these projects effectively and develop devices that meet our ever-changing needs is crucial for hardware manufacturers to keep up with their competitors.

In this component you will learn the different principles that can be used to design effective user interfaces and apply appropriate project planning techniques to create a user interface that meets user requirements.

LEARNING AIMS

In this component you will:

A	Investigate user interface design for individuals and organisations
B	Use project planning techniques to plan and design a user interface
C	Develop and review a user interface.

Introduction to user interfaces

A **user interface** is the software that sits between humans and devices. It allows the user to operate a device to carry out tasks.

What is a user interface?

A user interface is the **software** that you can see when using a device. It allows you to respond to a device by entering information. This can include using a mouse, keyboard or touchscreen. You can now also use sound with some modern devices, where you enter commands by using your voice.

◻ What user interfaces are you familiar with?

Human features

Humans are the individuals that use a device. A device can be used by a small group of users within an organisation or by millions of users across the world.

Users may have different:
- **accessibility** needs – for example, some users may have visual needs and may need some parts of the user interface enlarged. Other users may have hearing needs and may need to read text rather than listen to text being read aloud
- skill levels – for example, some users may be able to operate a user interface on their own. Other users may not have a lot of confidence using digital devices
- demographics – for example, users may be different ages and therefore have different experiences of using digital devices

Software features

Software is the part of the user interface that allows the user to enter commands into a device. This is usually something that the user will see or hear such as:
- menus – for example, a user may select an option to change the brightness of the screen or to change the font styles in word-processing software

- forms – for example, a user may enter details of a person into their contacts list or enter their payment details when buying products online
- voice – for example, the device may read parts of the screen aloud for a user who has accessibility needs.

Human to device interaction

Humans and devices obviously work in different ways, so careful planning needs to go into designing how the two will interact. When designing a user interface, you need to consider all user needs and the features of the device.

Example uses of user interfaces

User interfaces are installed across a vast range of different devices. Table 1.1 gives some examples of devices with user interfaces.

▪ Table 1.1: The different applications of user interfaces

Type of device	Definition	Example devices with a user interface
Computers	These are general computers that are used within the home or workplace.	• Desktop computers • Laptop computers
Handheld devices	These are small devices that are usually portable.	• Digital watches • Smartphones
Entertainment systems	These are devices that are often used in the home for leisure activities.	• Game consoles • Home cinema systems
Domestic appliances	These are devices that are used to complete household tasks.	• Washing machines • Microwave ovens
Controlling devices	These are devices that are used to control other devices automatically.	• Burglar alarms • Central heating systems
Embedded systems	These are much smaller computer systems that sit inside a larger system.	• Car automatic braking systems • Aeroplane autopilots

ACTIVITY

1 Think of different devices that you often use. In pairs, discuss your experiences of using these devices. You should include:
- what tasks you have carried out on the device
- what methods you used to interact with the device
- how successfully the device understood what you wanted to do.

2 Column 3 in Table 1.1 lists example devices with a user interface. In pairs, list other example devices for each row in the table.

CHECK MY LEARNING

What is meant by the term 'user interface'? Give three features of a user interface. Describe three different example interactions with a user interface.

Basic user interfaces

There are many different types of user interface. In this lesson you will explore text-, forms- and menu-based interfaces.

Text interfaces

A text interface works by the user entering specific commands with the keyboard. When these have been entered, the user interface will then respond.

Features of text interfaces

- The user interface is made up of text and does not contain any graphics.
- The user enters commands with a keyboard.
- The user interface will respond instantly with an output.
- Text interfaces do not require powerful hardware as they don't contain graphics.

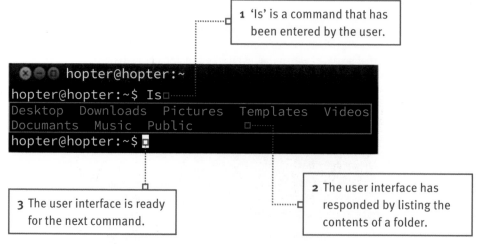

1 'ls' is a command that has been entered by the user.

3 The user interface is ready for the next command.

2 The user interface has responded by listing the contents of a folder.

◘ Figure 1.1: How would you feel if every device you used had a textual interface? What impact would that have?

When would text interfaces be used?

Text interfaces would be designed and used by experienced users who know all of the commands. They are often used by computer technicians when trying to solve problems with computer systems. This is because they are quick and can go directly to a specific location rather than going through lots of different menus.

Form interfaces

A form interface works by the user entering information using various **form controls**.

Features of form interfaces

- The user interface usually takes up a small part of the screen.
- It allows the user to enter information.
- It includes labels so the user knows what the different parts of the form means.
- It uses form controls such as buttons, tick boxes and drop-down lists to enter information. These are often used to input data into a database.

When would form interfaces be used?

Form interfaces are used when you know what kind of data you want the user to enter. For example, if you want to add a friend to your contacts list, you will enter their first name, surname and telephone number. Form interfaces are also used when data needs to be inserted into a device in a specific order. For example, when buying a product online you select which product you want and then how many you want.

Menu interfaces

A menu interface is a way of selecting options by clicking on a graphic on the device screen.

Features of menu interfaces

- The user interface displays a list of options for the user to select.
- It can pop down, pop up, pop across or take up the whole screen.
- It can be cascading, which means when the user selects an item, another sub menu can appear.
- All options listed within a single menu are usually related to each other.

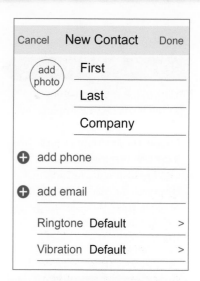

■ Figure 1.2: When was the last time you used a form interface? What was it for?

1 A list of options will appear on the screen for the user to select.

2 The user selects the option they want by pressing a button.

■ Why do cash machines use a menu- rather than a text-based interface?

When would menu interfaces be used?

Menu interfaces are used when the user is either not experienced with using devices or is not expected to type in specific commands using a keyboard. Menu interfaces are also used when there is only a small range of options that the user can select.

CHECK MY LEARNING ■ ■

Poppy has bought a smartwatch. Would this have a text-, forms- or menu-based user interface? Discuss this with a partner and justify the reasons for your choice.

ACTIVITY

In pairs, find an example of a text-, forms- and menu-based user interface.

1 For each user interface, explain its suitability for the task it is being used for.

2 Find four example uses of each type of user interface.

3 Give three benefits and drawbacks of each type of user interface.

Complex user interfaces

User interfaces that are easier to use are often complex because they need powerful hardware to make them work. This is because they have more features that allow users to interact easily with the device.

Graphical interfaces

A graphical **user interface** allows users to interact with devices through icons and other visual features.

Features of graphical user interfaces
- It's a visual interface and therefore made up of graphics.
- Users can **navigate** around the user interface logically.
- Contains icons for users to select with the mouse or touchscreen.
- Contains menus to display options for the users to select.
- Requires powerful hardware as it has to process graphics containing millions of **pixels**.

☐ A graphical user interface used within Microsoft Windows. What other graphical user interfaces are you familiar with?

When would graphical interfaces be used?

Graphical user interfaces are common in everyday devices that have a wide range of uses such as PCs and games consoles. They are used when the functions of a device cannot be limited to a menu. They are also used when the interface needs to be easy to use, therefore allowing users to interact with a device on their own.

Sensor interfaces

Sensor interfaces have commonly been used within the home, but this technology is increasingly used in our personal devices.

Features of sensor interfaces
- They have built-in **sensors** that are constantly monitoring what is happening around the device.

KEY TERMS
Navigate/Navigation is how a user works their way around the software.

Pixels are the smallest dots that make up the screen on our devices. An image is made up of millions of pixels.

KEY TERMS
Sensors detect and respond to the environment around them. They can be responsive to heat, light, sound, movement or patterns.

- When a certain condition has been met, the interface will automatically trigger something to happen. For example, an alarm may sound if the sensor has detected somebody inside a house.

When would sensor interfaces be used?

Sensor interfaces are used when actions performed by a device need to be automatic. For example, a smartphone may automatically unlock when it detects the correct facial features of the user. These types of interfaces have little physical human interaction.

Speech interfaces

Speech interfaces on devices are becoming increasingly popular in the home and respond directly to voices and sound.

Features of speech interfaces
- They allow users to input commands using their own voice.
- They use a built-in microphone that will listen for the user to say different commands.
- They often connect to the internet to find out information.
- They respond to the user through speakers.

◩ Have you ever talked to a device? How well did it understand you?

When would speech interfaces be used?

There are many reasons why speech interfaces may be used. They can be used when users may not always be able to use the mouse or keyboard to enter commands. They are also increasingly being used to make the interactions between humans and devices feel more natural.

ACTIVITY

In pairs, find an example of a graphical-, sensor- and speech-based user interface.

1 For each user interface, explain its suitability for the task it is being used for.

2 Find four example uses of each type of user interface.

3 Give three benfits and drawbacks of each type of user interface.

CHECK MY LEARNING ◼◻◼

Describe two ways that a self-service checkout in a supermarket could make use of a graphical-, sensor- and speech-based interface.

Choosing a user interface

When choosing a user interface for a device or task, it is important to consider carefully different factors to ensure the chosen user interface is suitable. In this lesson you will learn the different areas that you should consider before choosing or designing a user interface.

Performance

The performance of a user interface is important as you need to consider how quickly it allows you to complete tasks. For example, a restaurant will get busy around lunchtime and therefore the user interface will need to enable the restaurant staff to enter customer orders quickly. This means that they will be able to serve customers efficiently and make more profit.

User requirements

The primary reason for user interfaces is to allow the user to complete tasks using a device. Therefore, you need to consider what tasks you want to perform and then consider how well the user interface performs them. It's sometimes difficult to find a user interface that will meet all your requirements. You may need to consider which requirements are the most essential and consider which user interface best meets these requirements.

Ease of use

A user interface may be efficient at completing tasks; however, if the user is not able to operate the interface easily, then they may not engage with it. If the user interface is not easy to follow, then users may choose alternative programs. You need to consider if you will be able to operate the user interface and where you can get support if you need help. The user interface needs to be **intuitive**. This means even if someone has never used the interface before, they should be able to predict how it works and navigate it with ease.

User experience

Different users will have varying levels of experience using devices. Therefore, when choosing a user interface, it is important to look at what features it has and determine how familiar features would be to users or where they could seek additional help from. A user may decide that an interface is appropriate for them if they can instantly recognise different items on the screen. Another user may decide an interface is right for them if there is a simple help menu to guide them when using new features.

Accessibility

Some users may have accessibility needs, including visual, hearing and speech needs. Developing a user interface that will meet the needs of all users is very difficult. You need to consider if the user interface already meets the user accessibility needs or if it is customisable to meet them. For example, a user may have sensitivity to screen brightness or have colour blindness.

ACTIVITY

Can you see the numbers in the circles below?

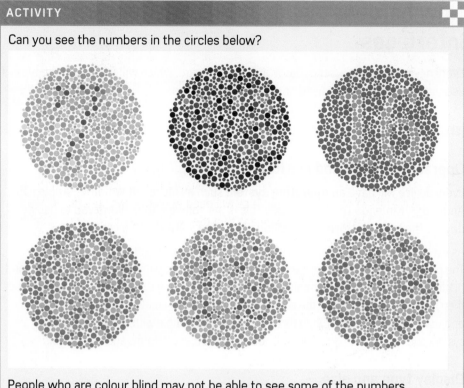

People who are colour blind may not be able to see some of the numbers. Research the different types of colour blindness to find out which colours you should avoid using together.

Storage space

The amount of storage space will often determine what type of user interface can be used and what features it will have. There needs to be a careful balance between storage space and ease of use.

- A graphical user interface is very easy to use but it requires a lot of storage space. This is because it tends to be more complex and has to store a lot of files.
- A speech-based user interface is easy to use but requires a lot of storage space as it has to store every possible human word with different pronunciations.
- A text-based interface, although not very easy to use, only takes up a very small amount of storage space.

ACTIVITY

1 123Laptops is a company that manufactures laptop computers. They have a helpline for customers and receive thousands of calls every day. The company has 100 members of staff and some of them have accessibility needs. In your groups, decide which four factors you consider to be the most important when choosing the user interface that all staff at 123Laptops will use. Justify why you have chosen each factor.

2 A doctor's surgery collects data about new patients. In your groups, discuss which four factors you consider to be the most important to the doctor's surgery when choosing a user interface. Why may they be different to the factors for 123Laptops?

CHECK MY LEARNING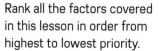

Rank all the factors covered in this lesson in order from highest to lowest priority.

How hardware and software affect user interfaces

Every device will have a set of hardware and software, which will impact on the type of user interface that can be used and what features it has.

Impacts of hardware and software on user interfaces

Operating system and platforms

Every device will have an **operating system** such as Microsoft Windows, Apple iOS, Android™, Nintendo DSi™ or Linux®. This is the software that allows you to use a device. The term **platform** is a method of running software on a computer.

As user interface is software, it has to be developed using programming code. The programming code that is created must be compatible with the operating system and platform. If you create programming code that the operating system does not understand, then it will not be able to run the code. For example, if you create a user interface for an app using Apple Developer then this will only be compatible with an Apple operating system such as iOS and therefore will not work on other platforms such as Android.

Display type and size

Almost all user interfaces need to make use of a display, also known as a screen. The size of the display affects the type of user interface that can be used. For example, a small watch screen will probably make use of a menu interface as there will not be enough space to display graphics.

The display type also affects how the user interacts with the interface. If the display has a touchscreen, then the user can use their finger to tap on the options that they want. However, some options such as menu options may need to be made bigger to allow the user to select them without accidentally selecting other options. If the display does not have a touchscreen, then the user will most likely use a mouse to select the options.

Method of user input

Different devices have different ways of allowing users to input commands. This will often depend on the size of the device. Larger devices such as desktop computers often have several ways of allowing the user to input commands. However smaller and more portable devices such as smartwatches and smartphones may only have one method of allowing the user to input commands.

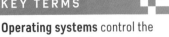

■ What are the challenges when designing a user interface for different devices?

■ Table 1.2: The most common methods of user input

Method of user input	How it works
Keyboard	The user will use either a physical or online keyboard to enter commands such as **keyboard shortcuts**.
Mouse	The user will move the mouse to control the cursor on the screen to select options.
Voice	The user will use their own voice to say what they want to do.
Gesture	The user will carry out a gesture using their hand for the interface to react to. Gestures include tapping, pinching and swiping movements.

Available resources

Devices have internal components that process the user interface so that it can be used by the user. One main component is the **Central Processing Unit (CPU)**. Every time you interact with a user interface, the CPU processes what you have input and then responds back to you. Another key component is the amount of **random-access memory (RAM)** available. While a user interface is being run, it will be held in the computer's memory. The more memory you have, the more features a user interface can have.

The size of the device will influence how much processing power and memory you have available. Generally, bigger devices will have more powerful hardware compared to portable devices.

Emerging technologies

Our digital technologies are always changing. Traditionally, the main way that we interact with our devices is with physical keyboards and a mouse. These lend themselves to textual, menu, forms and graphical user interfaces. All these user interfaces have a visual screen and therefore different design principles have to be used to ensure its design is effective.

However, the way that we interact with our devices is changing as we make increased use of touchscreen technology and use onscreen keyboards and finger presses to select items. Touchscreen technology is not ideal for textual interfaces where the user has to enter commands. Hardware manufacturers are also now starting to make increased use of speech-based interfaces. With this type of user interface there is no visual screen as everything is done by voice.

> ### KEY TERMS
>
> **Central Processing Unit (CPU)** is central to every PC and device. It's the computer's brain and without it a PC cannot function.
>
> **Random-access memory (RAM)** stores the files that the device has open and stores the information from any applications in use.

ACTIVITY

1 In pairs, recreate and complete the table below using word-processing software.

	Desktop computer	Smartphone	Smartwatch
Operating system			
Size of screen			
Type of screen			
Method of user input			
Processing power			
Amount of RAM			

2 Discuss how the hardware and software differs between the three different devices.

3 Discuss how the hardware and software available on each device will impact on the type and design of user interface.

CHECK MY LEARNING

A device has a 5.5-inch touchscreen display. The amount of RAM available is 2 GB. The processor is a 2.5 GHz Quad Core. How will these components impact the user interface?

User accessibility needs

The word 'accessibility' refers to the design of a product for users who experience disabilities. Devices are built with accessibility options so that users can change the way that the user interface looks, feels and sounds to suit their needs.

Accessibility needs

There are many different user accessibility needs to consider when creating a user interface.

Visual needs

Users with visual needs may have limited vision or may be colour blind and not able to see certain colours.

◘ Table 1.3: Dos and don'ts for users with visual needs

Dos	Don'ts
Use colours that effectively contrast with each other.	Don't use colours that clash or lack contrast with each other.
Have an option for the text on the screen to be read aloud.	Don't use decorative font styles that are difficult to read.
Ensure text is large enough to be able to read.	Don't rely on colours alone to get across the importance of something.

Hearing needs

Users with hearing needs may have limited hearing and may not be able to hear everything. They may also lipread when somebody is talking to them.

◘ Table 1.4: Dos and don'ts for users with hearing needs

Dos	Don'ts
Use subtitles for when people are speaking in videos.	Don't rely on just sound without using other methods such as text or graphics.
Write in clear, plain English.	Don't make users read long blocks of text.

Speech needs

Users with speech needs may take longer to communicate when they are talking and may not be able to say or pronounce all words clearly.

◘ Table 1.5: Dos and don'ts for users with speech needs

Dos	Don'ts
Allow alternative methods such as entering commands on the keyboard.	Don't rely fully on the user speaking without using other methods such as using the keyboard.
Allow the user many attempts to say a command.	Don't ask the user to keep saying the same words repeatedly.

Motor needs

Users with **motor needs** may not be able to move all their body. It may take them longer to move the mouse cursor across the screen or use the keyboard to enter text. They may not be able to use these tools at all.

▣ Table 1.6: Dos and don'ts for users with motor needs

Dos	Don'ts
Make sure objects onscreen are large so the user can easily select them.	Don't demand users focus the cursor precisely on a small object.
Allow the user to use shortcuts to speed up tasks.	Don't require tasks to be completed quickly.
Allow the user to use their voice to input commands where possible.	Don't ask users to enter lots of text or click on a lot of objects.

Cognitive needs

Users with **cognitive needs** may need more time when they are completing tasks. They may not be able to spell or say all words.

▣ Table 1.7: Dos and don'ts for users with cognitive needs

Dos	Don'ts
Provide a spell check so users can check their spelling.	Don't use lots of text that requires a lot of reading.
Have an option so the text on the screen can be read aloud.	Don't use complicated language.
Ensure the layout of each screen is consistent.	Don't require tasks to be completed quickly.

KEY TERMS

Motor needs relates to users who have limited function in their movement, muscle control or mobility.

Cognitive needs cover a wide range of disabilities, including developmental delays, learning disabilities, brain injuries and dementia.

▣ What else do you need to think about when creating a user interface for people with motor and cognitive needs?

ACTIVITY

1. Research what the word 'inclusion' means. In pairs, discuss how a user may feel if they have a specific need and are not able to access all areas of the user interface.

You will have read how user interfaces can be adapted for users with specific needs.

2. In pairs, think of other ways that user interfaces can be adapted to support each need. Use the internet to carry out some research.

3. In pairs, choose two programs that serve different purposes. Take screenshots of each program and annotate them to show where they make use of accessible features.

4. For each program, discuss how the accessibility features could be developed to better support users.

CHECK MY LEARNING

A local college has set up an online application form to allow students to sign up to new courses. Describe how the user interface can be adapted for users with visual, hearing and speech accessibility needs.

User skills and demographics

Users will have different skills based on their level of experience with different devices.

User skills

Different users will have different skills. These are summarised in Figure 1.3.

Expert user
- An expert user will have a lot of experience in using a range of different technologies and will be able to use a user interface to complete all tasks.
- An expert user will be able to use technologies confidently and navigate their way around a new user interface on their own.
- An expert user will know instinctively what to do without thinking about it.
- An expert user will be able to predict what a tool/option will do before they select it.

Regular user
- A regular user will have experience of using common, everyday devices and be able to use a user interface to complete almost all tasks.
- A regular user may need help occasionally but will be able to complete tasks on their own after being shown how to.
- A regular user will often be able to navigate their way around a user interface, although they may sometimes need to think about what to do.
- A regular user will often be able to use a 'trial and error' approach in order to complete tasks.

Occasional user
- An occasional user will have some experience of using different devices and will be able to use a user interface to complete most tasks.
- An occasional user may need to complete a task several times before they are able to do it confidently.
- An occasional user may be able to navigate their way around a user interface but may need to think about what they are doing.
- An occasional user may need to attempt a particular task several times before they are successful.

Novice user
- A novice user may have no or very little experience of using digital devices. They may be able to use a user interface or complete some tasks.
- A novice user may need to be supervised by another user with more advanced skills.
- A novice user may need one-to-one support when completing a task.
- A novice user may not know how to attempt to complete a task.

Figure 1.3: What is your skill level?

When thinking about the skill level of a user, it is worth noting that this varies between different devices and programs. For example, the user may be an expert user in one program but may only be a regular user in another program.

User demographics

You need to understand the characteristics of who will be using the device to best design an interface.

Age

The age of a person will be a big factor in determining how much experience and what skills a user will have. For example, a young child will have very little or no experience while an adult will have a lot more experience. Although this factor is changing, there is still a large percentage of older people who do not have the skills to use digital technologies. When you are designing a user interface, it is important to consider the age of the users to ensure that they will be able to access it.

Past experiences

Users' past experiences will dictate what devices or programs they have used before and how much they have used them. When using a new interface for the first time, users will automatically try what they already know from their past experiences. Therefore, it is important to design user interfaces to match users' prior experience. As technology continues to change, it will open up new and exciting ways of interacting with our devices, for example, a virtual reality headset detecting eye movement and input commands dictated by the number of blinks. It is not always possible to keep the design of the user interface the same. However, it is important to keep any changes gradual to allow the user to adjust to the new changes.

Culture and beliefs

Someone's culture has a big influence on their beliefs and practices. This may be their nationality, their religion or the language they speak. These factors should be considered when designing the user interface. For example, if you are designing a speech-based interface then it needs to allow people to speak in many different languages, with different accents and different pronunciations of words.

Certain symbols have different meanings in different cultures – as do colours. A graphic that may be innocent to one group of people could be offensive to others from a different culture. The colour red equates to danger in Europe but is associated with good luck in Asia.

ACTIVITY

When an organisation advertises a job, they will often specify what IT skills are required. Most jobs require employees to use some form of digital devices to carry out their jobs. For example:

- a receptionist in a doctor's surgery may use an electronic booking system to search and make appointments for patients
- a grocery shop manager may use software to create sales charts and graphs.

With a partner, research different jobs on the internet that would require an employee to have expert, regular, occasional and novice computer skills.

Imagine you want to create a program to encourage young people to lead a healthy and active lifestyle. You will create two versions of your program, for children aged 4–6 and teenagers aged 13–15.

1 Discuss with your partner what experiences you think children and teenagers will have of using different devices.

2 Discuss how these different experiences will impact on the design of the user interface.

CHECK MY LEARNING

Make a list of different programs and devices. Would you identify yourself as an expert, regular, occasional or novice user with those programs or devices? Explain your reasons to a partner.

Design principles: visual elements

When designing a user interface, it is important to make use of different design principles to allow users to interact with their devices more effectively.

Use of colour

How you use colour in the design of your user interface can have practical and emotional implications for the user.

Don't use too many colours

You should always try to use as few colours as possible. As a rule, you should use two to three colours on a user interface. Having too many colours on the screen can be difficult to read and make it difficult for users to focus on one area.

Use the organisation house style colours

Each organisation will have their own **house style**. House styles ensure consistency so that customers can recognise the organisation. One element of the house style is what colours will be used. When designing a user interface, it important to use the organisation's house style colours.

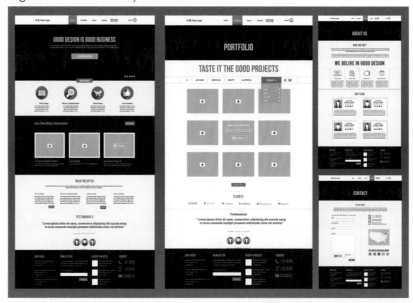

■ Figure 1.4: What three things are the same across these different screens?

Make sure colours don't clash

'Colour clash' is when two different but similar colours are placed on top of each other. When colours clash, one colour is more difficult to see.

Use textures

The word 'texture' is used to define how an object feels in your hand. Every object we touch has a different texture. Trying to create texture onscreen is more difficult; however, different colours can be used to create a certain feeling, mood or emotion. For example, using glossy colours, which look smooth and shiny, are often used to make things look more professional, serious and calming.

Good choice

Good choice

Bad choice

Bad choice

■ Figure 1.5: Do you agree with the colour selections shown here?

We often describe a colour as being warm or cool. Every colour we use tends to lean towards being either a warm or cool colour. You should consider the type of mood that you want to set and then use colours that match that mood.

Use of font styles and sizes

The font is the design of the text used. Your choice of font needs to be clear at all sizes.

Use appropriate font types

When choosing which font to use, it is important to pick the most suitable font for the purpose. There are many to choose from and they can usually be described as 'Serif' or 'Sans-serif'. Sans-serif fonts are a great choice for onscreen text. Serif fonts are better suited to printed text.

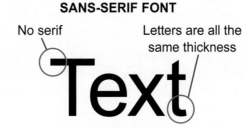

SERIF FONT	SANS-SERIF FONT
Serif — Letters have thin and thick parts	No serif — Letters are all the same thickness

◨ Figure 1.7: Why do you think sans-serif fonts are better suited to reading onscreen?

Avoid decorative fonts

Decorative fonts are usually serif fonts. They are used creatively and are generally designed for small amounts of large text. This is because they can be difficult to read. Some examples of decorative fonts are *Vladimir Script*, *Gigi*, *Edwardian Script ITC*.

Ensure the font style and font size are readable

As well as choosing a sans-serif font which is easier to read on a screen, it is important to ensure that the size of the font is readable. A font size that is clear to you may not be clear to other people. The font you pick should not be too big as this will reduce the amount of text you can fit onto the screen and may increase the amount of scrolling the user has to do.

◨ Figure 1.6: What effects might the use of warm or cool colours have?

DID YOU KNOW?

When you read a word, you don't actually read each letter of the word. Instead your brain recognises the shape of the word. If the first letter and last letter of the word are correct, then you can still understand what the word is even if the rest of the word is spelled incorrectly.

ACTIVITY

The image below shows the initial design for a mobile phone app.

1. In pairs, discuss the extent to which the developer has made effective use of colours, font styles and font sizes. Give reasons for your opinion. Compare your answers with another pair. Do they agree?

2. Using appropriate software, recreate the design and improve the use of colours, font styles and font sizes.

3. Select a website of your choice. Take a screenshot of it and annotate it to show how it has made effective use of colours, text styles and text sizes.

CHECK MY LEARNING

Write a list of dos and don'ts when using colours and fonts in a user interface.

Design principles: text elements

The human brain cannot cope with too much information at once. Therefore, it is important to consider how much information is placed on the screen.

Use of language

When you are designing a user interface, the language you use should be appropriate for the user's needs.

Use language appropriate for the user needs

When writing any text for a user interface, you should ensure that the language of the text can be understood by all users and consider the user's age and their relative experience. For example, a user interface designed for a child will probably have a few short sentences in simple language, while a user interface for an older person may have more text using more complex language.

Don't automatically assume that the user knows something. Users will learn at different paces and some users may forget easily. The language you use should be positive and should encourage users rather than making them feel fearful of using the user interface. For example, if you are designing a user interface that has several screens, don't assume that the user will know that they need to swipe their finger across the screen to move to a different screen.

Use language appropriate for the user skill level

Although it is not always possible, you should try to keep the amount of technical language to a minimum. The complexity of the language should match the user skill level. An expert user will be able to read and understand technical language, but a novice user may not. If the user does not understand the information they may not know what they need to do, which can cause frustration.

For example, here is an initial design for a search facility for a website.

The word 'parameter' may be difficult for some users to understand.

Here is an alternative design that uses simpler language that is easier to understand.

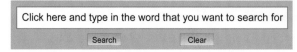

◘ Figure 1.8: Think of another way of writing these instructions that is easy to understand

Amount of information

Too much information onscreen can be difficult to read. Alternatively too little and the user may not understand what they need to do.

Use appropriate information for the task

A good idea is to only include information on the screen that is needed to complete a task. You should explain only one concept on one screen or one area of the screen. If a user sees irrelevant information, they will become confused.

It's important to keep your sentences as short as possible. When giving instructions, you should also keep the language as simple as possible. This will make instructions easier to read and understand.

Make appropriate use of white space

White space is unused space on a screen and can be any colour. The amount of information that is given should be linked to this. If a page has a lot of white space, then it will have more information on it. However, if there is not a lot of white space, then the amount of information given will need to be reduced.

It is important to balance the amount of information with the amount of white space so that the screen does not look cluttered.

For example, have a look at this Google™ webpage.

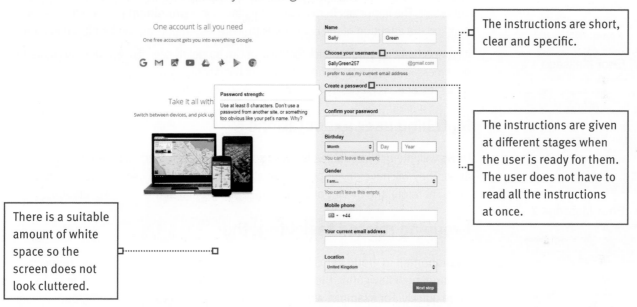

The instructions are short, clear and specific.

The instructions are given at different stages when the user is ready for them. The user does not have to read all the instructions at once.

There is a suitable amount of white space so the screen does not look cluttered.

Google and the Google logo are registered trademarks of Google Inc., used with permission

■ Figure 1.9: Why might short instructions be more effective than long instructions?

Design principles: layout

The term 'layout' refers to where different items on the screen are placed. The placement of items has a massive impact on how easily people can use them.

Consistency

A user interface will often be made up of many different screens. It is important that the way in which the items are placed is the same across all screens. This is because when a user has become familiar with one screen they should be able to use all the other screens within the same user interface.

Placement of items

You need to consider which items on the page are important and which items are less important. The important items should be placed in a **prominent** position as this will demand the attention of the user. Items that are less important can be placed in menus.

It is important that any feedback for the user can be clearly seen. For example, in Figure 1.10, error message 1 is placed in the bottom right hand corner where the user may not see it. Error message 2 is placed in the centre of the screen so that it demands the user's attention.

■ Figure 1.10: Think of other ways to demand the attention of the user on the screen

Matching user expectations

Users will interact with many different user interfaces for many different programs and apps. They will have developed expectations about how the user interface should look. Therefore, the design of the interface should match the user expectations.

Grouping related tasks together

It is important to group items that are related to each other together. This reduces the amount of navigating the user has to do and enables them to complete tasks more quickly. For example, when designing a user interface, you could group all user accessibility tools together. Therefore, the user can review all the accessibility features together rather than having to jump from different places.

Navigational components

The ability to find your way around is one of the most important aspects of a user interface. The user will often start at the homepage of a user interface and then navigate to other pages. It must be easy for the user to move from one screen to another.

Search fields

Search fields are areas of the user interface that allow the user to type in keywords to find something. The user interface will then suggest areas that the user can navigate to based on what they typed in.

It's good practice to have a search field on every screen within a user interface. However, this may not always be possible on devices that have a small screen.

■ Figure 1.11: We automatically associate a magnifying glass with a search

Icons

Icons are buttons that, when clicked, will take the user somewhere within the user interface. Icons will usually have pictures or text to show what the button does.

Breadcrumbs

Sometimes the user will complete a task that involves moving through different stages on different screens. For example, a customer may purchase a product from an online store or complete a job application form. **Breadcrumbs** allow the user to see how many steps need to be completed in total and what step they are currently on.

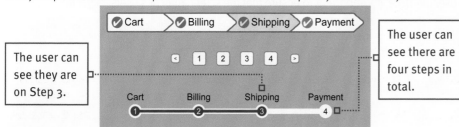

The user can see they are on Step 3.

The user can see there are four steps in total.

◻ Figure 1.12: What other tasks might you complete that could use breadcrumbs?

Input controls

Input controls allow the user to enter data and select options. They are often used on form-based interfaces. Using input controls makes it faster for the user to interact with the user interface. They also reduce the chances of the user making mistakes because there is less typing for the user to do.

◻ Table 1.8: Example input controls

Input control	Description
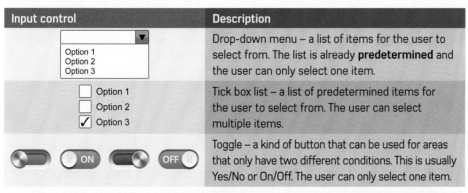 Option 1 / Option 2 / Option 3	Drop-down menu – a list of items for the user to select from. The list is already **predetermined** and the user can only select one item.
☐ Option 1 / ☐ Option 2 / ☑ Option 3	Tick box list – a list of predetermined items for the user to select from. The user can select multiple items.
ON / OFF	Toggle – a kind of button that can be used for areas that only have two different conditions. This is usually Yes/No or On/Off. The user can only select one item.

ACTIVITY

Choose a program or website and take three screenshots of different screens. Annotate each screenshot to show how the program or website has made effective use of layout. You should include the following.

- Which items and features are the same across all screens.
- Where you feel the screens could have made more effective use of layout.
- How well items are placed in prominent positions.
- What navigational components are used to allow the user to easily move around different screens.
- Where input controls have been used and how effective they are.

 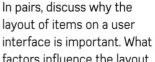

Design principles: user expectations

Users will often get frustrated when they come across something that doesn't work in the way they expect it to. That's because we all have expectations about the way devices and their user interfaces should work.

As a baby, you have relatively little understanding of the world that we live in; you simply react to things as they happen. As we grow older, our brain develops, and we gain an understanding of how things work, including the digital technologies that we use. This allows us to predict what will happen before we do something. Therefore, when developing a user interface, it's important to ensure that the screen matches users' expectations.

▣ From what age do you think children start to expect devices to work in a certain way?

Colour

Humans generally have a perception of different colours and when we see a colour on the screen we are instantly able to determine what it means. For example, people generally see blue as a cold colour and red as a warm colour.

We can use what people think about colours when designing user interfaces.

For example:

Green is used when your interaction with the user interface has been **successful** and you can **continue**.

Amber is used to indicate a **warning** and an error may occur if you continue.

Red is used when your interaction with the user interface has been **unsuccessful** or when you have made an **error** and you need to **stop** and try again.

Symbols

From a very young age we recognise different shapes and symbols and can give them meaning. For example, your teachers in school may mark your work using ticks and crosses. As soon as you see these you instantly understand what they mean.

 Ticks are usually used to indicate that your interaction with a device has been successful.

 Crosses are usually used to indicate when your interaction with a device has been unsuccessful.

New Member Form

First Name:	Lisa	✔
Surname:	Green	✔
Date of birth:	09/10/2098	✘
Type:	○ Peak ○ Off-peak	✘

◘ Figure 1.13: How well do you think the ticks and crosses support the user?

Sound

Humans also have perceptions of sound. Often, as soon as we hear a sound, we can distinguish what it means and then react to it. For example, when a fire alarm goes off, you know immediately that you need to exit the building.

If we hear a sound while interacting with the user interface, we are instantly able to determine what it means.

- If a positive high-pitched sound is played, we instantly know that our last interaction with a device was successful.
- If a negative sharp low-pitched sound is played, we instantly know that our last interaction with a device was unsuccessful.

Visuals

We have learned in this lesson that people instantly form an idea in their head as soon as they see a certain colour or hear a certain sound. However, we can also use visuals such as images and graphics to represent what something does. For example, if we see a picture of a printer, we tend to associate this as being the print button; if we see an image of binoculars, then we associate this with the find button.

LINK IT UP

To find out more about how to use visuals when designing a user interface, go to lesson 'Design principles: intuitive design' in Learning aim A of this component.

ACTIVITY

When you delete a file, a sharp negative low-pitched sound may play to warn you that you are about to delete a file.

1 Think of three other situations when a positive high-pitched sound and sharp negative low-pitched sound may be played while using devices. Explain your reasons.

You want to change your password. A green tick may appear on the screen to confirm that your password is long enough and meets the password complexity rules.

2 With a partner, think of three other situations when green and red may be used to indicate that something has been successful or unsuccessful on the screen. Explain your reasons.

CHECK MY LEARNING

Share your answers for Questions 1 and 2 with the class. Did anyone else have the same expectations as you? Why do you think this was the case?

Design principles: keeping the user engaged

When a user begins to interact with a user interface, it is important to keep them **engaged**. If it is not obvious what they need to do, then they may lose interest.

Grab attention

Sometimes, you need to grab the user's attention. For example, the user needs to be warned if they have made an error when typing into a form.

The following methods can be used to grab attention.
- Pop-up messages – these are messages that appear on the screen to inform the user of something. They are often used to warn the user when an error has occurred.
- Flashing graphics – these are pictures or graphics that flash on the screen. They can be used to help the user. For example, if the user interface has been updated, then flashing graphics can be used to highlight what has changed.
- Sound – these are sounds that are played when you are interacting with the user interface. This could be the shutter sound on a camera, or a round of applause in a gaming app.
- Animations – these are moving images that could be for decorative purposes to improve the look of the screen, to indicate movement from one area of the site to another, or to show the user how to complete a task.

Uncluttered screens

The amount of information and tools on the screen needs to be carefully considered. If there is too much information, the user will have to read more, which may slow them down. However, if there is not enough information, the user may not know what to do, which can also slow them down. Some users are put off as soon as they see lots of text. Having too many items on the screen can make it harder for the user to focus.

Tip text

Tip text gives the user a 'tip' or guidance on what something is. It is often used on buttons to tell the user what the button is called or to tell them what action the button will do. Tip text can be used to give less experienced users guidance without cluttering the screen. Even more experienced users may make use of tip text occasionally if they are using a tool they have not used before.

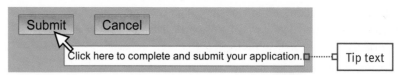

■ Figure 1.14: Where have you seen tip text being used?

Labels

Do not automatically assume that the user will know what every part of a user interface is or how to use it. Labels should be placed next to different items to tell the user what they are. They should be short and limited to one or two words. Long labels can clutter the screen and increase the amount of reading the user must do. Figure 1.15 gives an example of how labels can be used on a forms interface.

Default values

A default value, also known as a predetermined value, is something that is already on the user interface before the user opens it. If an option is popular, then it can be automatically completed to save the user from having to enter it. For example, Figure 1.15 shows a gym membership form for a gym in Liverpool. Most people who use the gym are from Liverpool and therefore the town, county and country have already been completed.

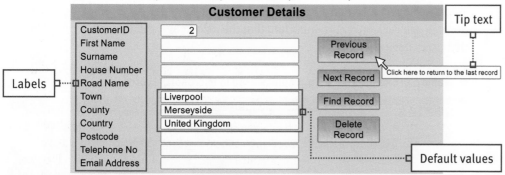

■ Figure 1.15: What form have you completed that made use of default values?

Autofill

LINK IT UP

To find out more about possible risks of autofill, go to lesson 'Data level protection: firewalls and anti-virus software' in Component 3, Section B.

Autofill is when some parts of the user interface are automatically completed with an individual's details that have been previously used and stored on a browser. This tool is usually used on form-based interfaces to reduce the amount of text a user has to enter. Using autofill also increases the accuracy of the text because as the user is typing less text, they are less likely to make mistakes.

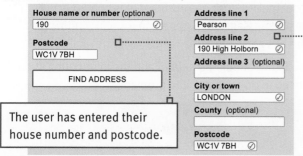

■ Figure 1.16: What other details could autofill complete on a form?

ACTIVITY

1   In pairs, you should each familiarise yourself with a different program or website. Focus on one tool or feature from your website that your partner has not used before. After you have learned how to use the tool or feature yourself, ask your partner to use it without any help from you.

2   Observe your partner completing the task. They should say what they are noticing and thinking at each stage of the task. Make notes about how they found the task. You can include comments on the following.

   • Did they complete the task? If so, ask your partner what features helped to keep their attention on the task.

   • Did they lose their attention? If so, at what point? Ask your partner why they lost their attention.

CHECK MY LEARNING

List three methods that can be used to sustain the attention of a user while they are using a user interface.

Design principles: intuitive design

The word intuitive refers to something that can be used by someone easily without having to think about what they have to do.

Graphics to illustrate what buttons do

When we see an icon image on the screen, we form an idea about what the icon will do when we click on it. It is important that the icon image should match the action that users have envisaged.

◻ Table 1.9: Examples of icon graphics used in Microsoft® Word

Icon	Reason
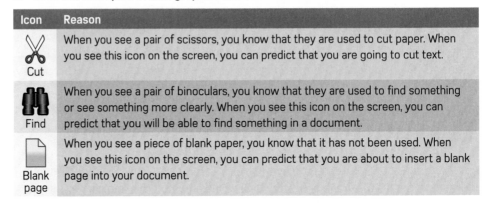 Cut	When you see a pair of scissors, you know that they are used to cut paper. When you see this icon on the screen, you can predict that you are going to cut text.
Find	When you see a pair of binoculars, you know that they are used to find something or see something more clearly. When you see this icon on the screen, you can predict that you will be able to find something in a document.
Blank page	When you see a piece of blank paper, you know that it has not been used. When you see this icon on the screen, you can predict that you are about to insert a blank page into your document.

Helpful pop-up messages

When you need to inform the user that an error has occurred, it is good practice to use pop-up messages. These are messages that appear in a small window with information telling the user what has gone wrong.

When pop-up messages are used, they should be helpful and the information should tell the user exactly what they need to do to correct the problem.

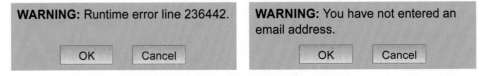

WARNING: Runtime error line 236442.

OK   Cancel

WARNING: You have not entered an email address.

OK   Cancel

◻ Figure 1.17: Which error message is the most helpful and why?

LINK IT UP

To find out more about reversal of actions, go to lesson 'Improving the speed of user interfaces' in Learning aim A of this component.

Easy reversal of actions

We all know how frustrating it can be when we make a mistake and are unable to correct it. User interfaces should be designed in a way that will allow users to return to earlier tasks that they have already completed to make changes or fix errors.

Help features

User interfaces should contain enough help to allow the user to successfully complete tasks. However, novice and occasional users may require more support. Therefore, user interfaces should contain a help feature. This can usually be accessed by pressing a button or selecting it from a menu option.

The help feature should be split into different topic areas for the user to select from. More advanced help features allow the user to type in exactly what they need help with.

For example, on this website, there is a support option on the navigation bar to provide additional support to users who need it.

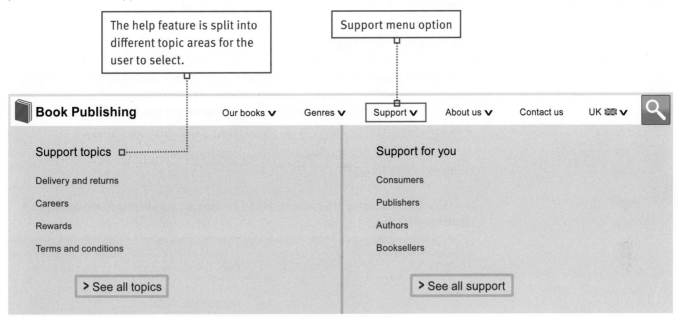

Figure 1.18: Have you ever accessed the help menu on a user interface? How useful was it?

Ensure consistency

Another method of making sure your user interface is intuitive is ensuring that each screen has a consistent design.

LINK IT UP

To find out more about a consistent design, go to lesson 'Design principles: layout' in Learning aim A of this component.

ACTIVITY

1 With your partner, choose some **productivity software** available to you and look at the user interface within the different programs. What features are the same across all programs? What features are different?

2 With your partner, investigate a program within the suite that you have not used before. Would you be able to work out how to use the program based on your knowledge of the other programs you have used? Why?

3 Open some word-processing software. Find out what images have been used for the following tools: copy, paste, print, spelling and grammar. Why do you think these graphics have been used? Are they effective?

KEY TERMS

Productivity software is software that is made up of a suite of different programs such as Microsoft® Office or the Google Drive™ Apps.

CHECK MY LEARNING

We have learned about what the word intuitive means. How can we achieve an intuitive design? Why is intuitive design important in a user interface?

Improving the speed of user interfaces

When designing a user interface, it's important to ensure it's efficient. The efficiency of a user interface is determined by its speed and its accessibility. In this lesson you will learn how to increase the speed of a user interface, which will help your understanding of how to make a user interface more accessible, which you will cover in the next lesson.

Keyboard shortcuts

When we complete tasks using a user interface, it can involve various mouse clicks or finger taps on a touchscreen. However, sometimes it can take a long time to complete a simple task and a lot of time can be wasted, particularly if we are repeating the same actions.

A keyboard shortcut is a way of speeding up tasks. It is when we can press a combination of keys on the keyboard to automatically take you to something or complete a task for you.

◘ Table 1.10: Examples of keyboard shortcuts used across Microsoft Windows and macOS High Sierra

Microsoft Windows	macOS High Sierra	Description
CTRL + C	COMMAND (⌘) + C	Copy the selected item(s) to the clipboard.
CTRL + V	COMMAND (⌘) + V	Paste the contents from the clipboard into the current document.
CTRL + P	COMMAND (⌘) + P	Print the current document.

Reversal of actions

While users are completing tasks on a user interface, it is not uncommon for them to make mistakes and want to reverse or change something they have done earlier. User interfaces should be designed in a way that will allow users to return to actions they have already completed to make changes.

For example, when ordering a product online, before confirming your order, you may wish to return to the 'dispatch address' page to change your delivery address or you may want to return to the 'items' page to delete an item in your electronic shopping basket.

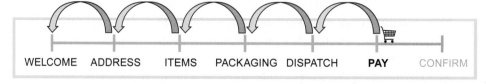

WELCOME   ADDRESS   ITEMS   PACKAGING   DISPATCH   **PAY**   CONFIRM

◘ Figure 1.19: What other reasons might a user want to return to earlier screens?

Informative feedback

It is helpful to allow a user interface to give feedback so the user can see if their interactions are successful. It will give novice and occasional users more confidence to know they are completing tasks correctly. For example, a screen pop-up saying: 'Thank you for your order' would confirm the user's intention to purchase or order was completed. You will also need to consider when to give the feedback and how much. Too much feedback would slow a process down. When you give the user feedback, you should ensure it is informative. It needs to be short, clear and specific.

Distinguishable objects

The user needs to be able to distinguish the difference between each part of the user interface. It can speed up their interaction if they know which areas require them to read something and which areas require them to carry out an action. For example, if the user sees https://www.pearson.com/uk/ then they distinguish that this is a hyperlink that, if selected, will take them to a different location.

For example, here is the design for a table booking screen for a restaurant.

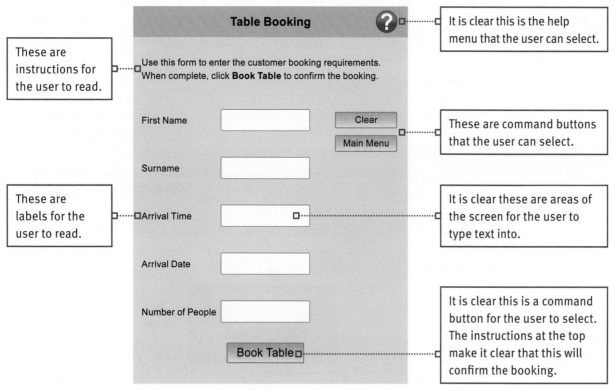

These are instructions for the user to read.

It is clear this is the help menu that the user can select.

These are labels for the user to read.

These are command buttons that the user can select.

It is clear these are areas of the screen for the user to type text into.

It is clear this is a command button for the user to select. The instructions at the top make it clear that this will confirm the booking.

■ Figure 1.20: Think of a user interface you have used. What design features were used to make it easy for you to identify the different objects in the interface?

Reducing the user selection time

The amount of time it takes to interact with a device is made up of thinking time, movement time, selection time and response time. In this lesson you will look at methods to reduce movement and selection times.

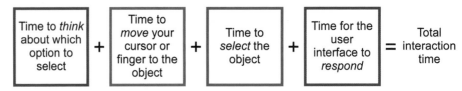

■ Figure 1.21: The factors influencing user interaction time

Appropriate object sizes

The size of the objects, such as icons or buttons will largely depend on the size of the user interface. Objects that are bigger can be seen more easily and selected more quickly; the size of the object can also influence user selection.

It is important that the whole object is selectable. This means the user should be able to click or tap on any part of the object to select it rather than being forced to focus on an area of it. For example, the button in Figure 1.22 is 2 cm high and 4 cm wide. However, the area that the user has to focus their finger or mouse cursor on is a lot smaller.

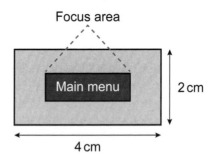

■ Figure 1.22: Why might users with physical or motor needs find it difficult to use small focus areas?

The button in Figure 1.23 is the same size, but the focus area has been increased so that the whole area of the button is selectable. Now the user can focus the cursor or their finger on any part of the button to select it.

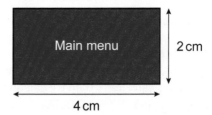

■ Figure 1.23: What keyboard shortcut could you create for this button?

Making the objects and focus areas bigger reduces the selection time. This is because if the user is using a touchscreen, they can tap on the items once. However, if the items are smaller, it may take the user several attempts to get their finger exactly on the item or focus area, increasing the selection time.

Object emphasis

Another way to reduce object selection time is to make objects stand out. This can be achieved using colour, emphasis and font styles such as bold, italic, underline and shadow. You can also make the essential objects bigger. This will allow them to be seen more quickly and selected faster. You can make the options, such as the button to access the help menu, smaller as these may not be needed by all users.

For example, in Figure 1.24 Button 2 stands out more than Button 1 because:

- the size of the button is bigger
- it has a thick border
- the font size is bigger
- the font colour stands out
- bold emphasis is used.

Button 1

Button 2

◘ **Figure 1.24: Examples of emphasising buttons**

Objects can also be over emphasised and therefore distract users. For example, using a large 'add to basket' button may allow users to quickly add items to their shopping basket. However, the 'delete items' button may be smaller and more difficult to find, therefore making it more difficult for users to delete items from their shopping basket.

Group related objects

It is important to group items that relate to each other together. By grouping related items in one area, it reduces selection times because it allows the user to try to guess where a certain tool is.

For example, Microsoft Word groups each of their tools into separate areas. All tools that are related to changing the font settings are grouped together and all tools that are related to changing the paragraph settings are grouped together. Therefore, if you need to use a tool such as the highlight tool, you would be able to guess that this is related to the font settings and be able to go to that area and find the tool faster.

Grouped font tools   Grouped paragraph tools

Used with permission from Microsoft

◘ **How would these groups help someone who has never used this program before?**

Learning aim A: assessment practice

How you will be assessed

Now that you have studied all topics in Learning aim A, you will need to show that you understand how different types of user interfaces meet a range of different design principles and be able to give relevant examples. You also need to show that you understand how different types of user interface meet a range of different user needs and be able to give relevant examples.

You will be expected to produce a written report using screenshots of different user interfaces. You should be able to describe how two different types of interface meet a range of specific user needs and design principles.

Try the following tasks to help you build the skills and knowledge you will need to complete your assignment.

CHECKPOINT

Strengthen

- Identify four different types of user interface.
- Describe how the user interacts with each type of user interface.
- Explain why the following user needs must be considered when designing a user interface: accessibility, skills and demographics.
- Explain why different design principles are used when designing effective user interfaces.

Challenge

- Explain how a user interface can apply design principles to meet specific user needs.
- Assess the suitability of different types of user interface and how effectively they meet user needs.
- Assess the extent to which your chosen user interface meets its purpose.
- Assess the extent to which other user interface designs would achieve the same purpose.

ASSESSMENT ACTIVITY 1 | LEARNING AIM | A

Assessment of design principles

Choose two different types of user interface from the following list:

- textual based
- menu based
- forms based
- graphical user interface
- speech based
- sensor based.

For each of your chosen user interfaces:

- identify where different design principles have been used

TIPS

The command word *identify* means that you are required to look at something and pick out key areas that answer the question. This means that you need to look at different user interfaces and highlight where you think different design principles have been used.

- assess how the different design principles improve the effectiveness of the user interface for its users
- assess the positive and negative effects that each design principle has
- assess how each design principle supports the user to use the interface efficiently.

You should include examples of where each different design principle has been used. These should be relevant to your specific user interfaces and be justified.

Your evidence can be in the form of screenshots of your chosen user interfaces, with annotations to show where different design principles have been used. You may also want to provide text that goes into more depth about how effective the different design principles are.

ASSESSMENT ACTIVITY 2 LEARNING AIM **A**

Assessment of user needs

Complete the following for each of your chosen user interfaces in Assessment activity 1.

- Describe how intuitive the user interface is and how it could be developed further to better meet the needs of users.
- Assess to what extent they support users with different accessibility needs, skill levels and demographics.
- Assess to what extent they match user perceptions and the methods that are used to keep the user's attention.
- Assess their suitability and describe an alternative user interface that could have been used.
- Give clear reasons why the alternative type of user interface would better meet the user needs.

Your evidence can be in the form of screenshots of your chosen user interfaces, with annotations to show the different features that meet specific user needs. You may want to provide text that goes into more depth to justify your reasons.

TAKE IT FURTHER

Consider the possible ethical issues that each of your chosen user interfaces may create for groups of people with different demographics.

For each issue explain why it is an ethical issue and suggest ways that the user interface can be adapted to resolve these issues.

Project methodologies

GETTING STARTED

In pairs, research one IT project that has failed. Share your findings with the class.

In this learning aim, you will use different project planning techniques to plan and design a user interface for an organisation. You will learn the importance of using an agreed set of procedures when implementing a project.

A **project methodology** is how the time within a project is structured and in what order the tasks will be completed. It is important to use a project methodology to make sure that the system you are creating meets the project requirements, and is completed on time and within budget. There are many different project methodologies that you can use. In this lesson, you will look at the waterfall and iterative project methodologies.

DID YOU KNOW?

Around 70% of IT projects that involve creating new hardware or software fail. This could be because the hardware or software does not meet the project requirements or is not completed on time/within the agreed budget. Poor planning, poor communication and not using the correct project methodology are the main reasons why projects experience problems.

Waterfall methodology

A **waterfall methodology** is where the tasks flow in one direction from start to finish. This methodology relies on a lot of planning very early in the project. Once the project has started, the client will have very little involvement. The whole project is delivered to the client at the very end of the project.

The waterfall methodology usually has the following stages.

- Analysis – project requirements are established, including the user requirements, such as what they want the system to be able to do. It will also include how much money is available for the project and the date for completion.
- Design – the look of the new system is created based on the project requirements. It will often include sketches to show the designs of the different screens within the user interface.
- Implementation – the new system is created. In this stage, the programming code for the new system is created along with the user interface.
- Testing – the new system is checked. It will be tested to ensure that it is working correctly and contains no faults. This is where the client will see the new system so that they can try it and give feedback.
- Evaluation – check that the new system meets the project requirements as stated in the analysis section.

KEY TERMS

Project methodology is a term used to define the phases and processes that should be completed within a project and the order that they are completed in.

Waterfall methodology requires one whole task or section to be completed before another task begins. All the project requirements are analysed, then designed, implemented, tested and evaluated at the same time within each stage.

The waterfall methodology is used when the project requirements are extremely clear at the start of the project. It is also used when the requirements will not change throughout the whole project.

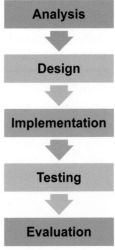

Figure 1.25: Why do you think this methodology is called the waterfall model?

Iterative methodology

An **iterative methodology** is when there is no clear pathway from start to finish. This methodology has a reduced amount of planning at the beginning to complete the project faster.

The client is usually involved at various stages throughout the project. The stages involved in an iterative approach can be seen in Figure 1.26.

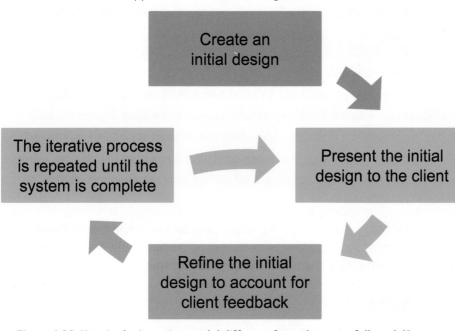

Create an initial design

Present the initial design to the client

Refine the initial design to account for client feedback

The iterative process is repeated until the system is complete

■ Figure 1.26: How is the iterative model different from the waterfall model?

The iterative methodology is used when the requirements in the project are not fully known at the beginning, for example, a school designing a student database at a time when data protection legislation is under government review. It would also be used when the project requirements are likely to change during the project.

Agile approach

An example of an iterative approach is a methodology called Agile. This methodology breaks down the project into smaller parts, which are then completed in priority order in stages of around two weeks each. These stages are called 'sprints'. By doing this, the project is delivered in stages rather than all at the end. At the end of each stage, the client will feed back on what has been created.

Co-ordinating project tasks

KEY TERMS

Task dependencies are the previous tasks that should be completed before a new task can start. For example, Task B depends on Task A and therefore Task B cannot start until Task A is fully complete.

▣ **Table 1.11: The task names, lengths and dependencies**

Task	Length (days)	Dependencies
A	2	-
B	2	A
C	3	B and F
D	2	C
E	2	D
F	3	A
G	2	E and H
H	2	D

KEY TERMS

PERT stands for Program Evaluation Review Technique.

Nodes represent different tasks that will be completed within a project. They will often contain the task number or letter.

Before you start a project, it is important to plan what the tasks are and when they will be completed. When you have done this, you can then monitor your progress during the project to ensure that your project is completed on time.

You are about to plan when each task in a project will be completed. These tasks are shown in Table 1.11. In this project there are eight tasks in total, known as Tasks A–H, and each has an allocated length. The table also shows the **task dependencies**.

You can use visual diagrams to make it easier to understand when tasks within a project will be completed and to monitor the progress being made. These could include Gantt charts, PERT charts and critical path diagrams.

Gantt charts

A Gantt chart uses different blocks to represent the amount of time each task will take. The tasks are usually shown along the vertical axis of the diagram and the amount of time is usually shown along the horizontal axis of the diagram.

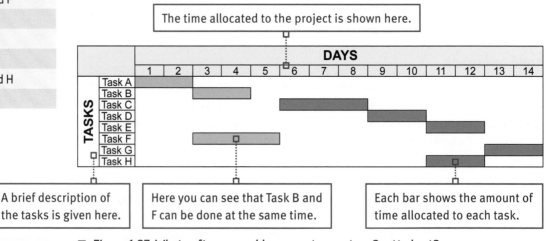

> The time allocated to the project is shown here.

> A brief description of the tasks is given here.

> Here you can see that Task B and F can be done at the same time.

> Each bar shows the amount of time allocated to each task.

▣ **Figure 1.27: What software could you use to create a Gantt chart?**

PERT charts

A **PERT** chart can be used to plan when project tasks will be completed. The diagram is made up of different nodes, which represent a different task that will be completed in the project. Arrows are then used to join the different **nodes** together to show the order in which the tasks will be completed, as seen in Figure 1.28.

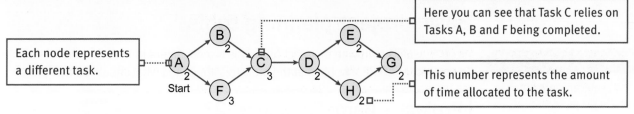

Each node represents a different task.

Here you can see that Task C relies on Tasks A, B and F being completed.

This number represents the amount of time allocated to the task.

◼ Figure 1.28: Identify how this PERT chart shows the same project information as the Gantt chart in Figure 1.27.

Critical path diagrams

A critical path analysis diagram is very similar to a PERT chart, because it also uses nodes for each task. However, in a critical path diagram, each node shows more information rather than just the task letter or number.

For each task, the node shows the earliest start time (EST), which indicates the earliest possible time that each task can start and the latest finish time (LFT), which indicates the latest possible time that each task can be completed. The ESTs and LFTs can show time in hours, days, weeks. These are labelled in Figure 1.29.

Here is an example critical path diagram.

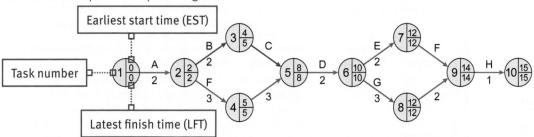

◼ Figure 1.29: Identify the similarities and differences between a critical path diagram and a PERT chart

Once the diagram has been completed, you can establish which tasks are critical.

If the EST and LFT are the *same* within a node, then that task will be critical. When the diagram is complete, you should see all the critical tasks and they will form a path from the beginning to the end of the diagram. (See the arrows in red in Figure 1.29.) If a task is on the critical path, then it is 'critical' to finishing the project on time. If a task on the critical path is delayed, then it will delay the whole project.

If the EST and LFT within a node are *different*, then that task will not be part of the critical path. These tasks have 'slack time', which means there is time within this task where there is no activity. If a task not on the critical path is delayed, it may not delay the whole project.

ACTIVITY

You are completing a project with the following timings given in the table.

1 In pairs, use the table to create a:
 • Gantt chart
 • PERT chart
 • critical path diagram.

2 In pairs, research the benefits and drawbacks of each diagram.

Task	Length (days)	Dependencies
A	1	-
B	3	A
C	60	B
D	1	A
E	10	A
F	2	C and E
G	15	F
H	40	E and G

CHECK MY LEARNING ◼◼

Give examples of three diagrams that can be used to plan time in a project. Explain how they are different. What information do they contain?

Basic project planning tools

GETTING STARTED

Read the requirements given in the project brief for GameExchange123. Where would you start in creating a user interface? How would you approach the project?

Projects usually start with a project brief. This is a document provided by the client. The project brief will set out what the project is about and what should be achieved.

Project – GameExchange123

GameExchange123

Project brief

GameExchange123 is an online company that operates in the UK. They buy used computer games and then sell them to make a profit. Users log in to the website, enter details of the games that they want to sell and are then offered a buying price. If they are happy with the price, they will post their games and the money will be transferred to their bank account.

The company has grown in recent years and now has approximately 500,000 users. 75% of their customers are aged 18–25. The company's annual revenue is £6.2 million. They want to set up a smartphone app to keep up with their competitors. The app should provide the same functionality as their website. They have asked you to design and develop the user interface of their new app. They want to view the design of the user interface at different stages and to have opportunities to provide feedback.

Requirements

Screen 1 – Homepage

The homepage should welcome the user to the app and display a list of games that are currently high in demand. There should be a search facility to allow the user to enter the name of a game they want to search for and the results will be displayed on the screen.

Screen 2 – Log-in/sign-up page

This page should allow users to enter their username and password. Once they have successfully done this, they will be shown their account information. They should be able to view and update their personal details.

If users do not already have an account, then there should be a link to a form allowing the user to sign up and create an account. The user should be able to enter their:

1 first name
2 surname
3 address
4 postcode
5 telephone number
6 email address
7 what type of games console they have.

Suitable outputs and prompts should be given to support the user when they are entering these details. The app should confirm when their account has been successfully set up.

Screen 3 – Buying page

This screen should allow users to enter details of the game they want to sell. They should be able to enter:

1 the barcode number
2 the condition of the box/packaging (i.e. poor, satisfactory, good, excellent)
3 if the user manual is still available (i.e. yes, no)
4 the condition of the disk (i.e. poor, satisfactory, good, excellent)

Suitable outputs and prompts should be given to support the user when they are entering these details. When all these details have been entered, the app should then display a buying price. The user can then accept or decline. If the user accepts the buying price, then a code should be generated and displayed on the screen for them to send with their game in the post.

Additional requirements

The user interface should:

1 be suitable for the hardware and software that is found on smartphones
2 be suitable for the age, skill level and past experiences of the user
3 have a range of suitable accessibility features
4 make effective use of design principles to allow users to navigate the user interface effectively and efficiently
5 use the most appropriate type of user interface to meet the requirements in this brief
6 promote the company house style by using the colours blue and black.

The project should be completed in six weeks.

After you have received a project brief, it is a good idea to break it down into different parts. You should also consider any information that is unclear and that you need more information about.

Task lists

A task list is a numbered list of tasks or actions that need to be completed. It can be used to list the different tasks within a project you need to complete or to list things you need to find out before the project starts.

LINK IT UP

To find out more about task lists, go to lesson 'Co-ordinating project tasks' in Learning aim B of this component.

Graphical descriptions

Graphical descriptions allow you to break down the different sections of a project visually. One way of doing this is to use a mind map with a central idea in the middle and branches representing different ideas for different sections of a project. The information on a mind map is usually brief and gives an overview of the whole project in a single diagram.

Written descriptions

A written description does the same thing as a mind map. However, it contains information about the different sections of a project using text rather than a visual diagram. It allows you to go into more depth about the different sections or parts of a project.

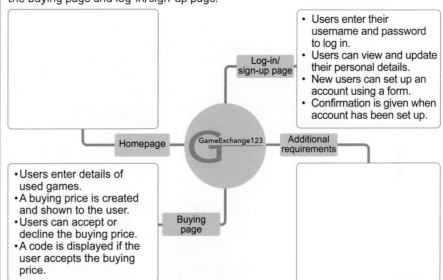

Project – GameExchange123
Example graphical description
The mind map in Figure 1.30 has been fully completed to show the requirements of the buying page and log-in/sign-up page.

- Users enter their username and password to log in.
- Users can view and update their personal details.
- New users can set up an account using a form.
- Confirmation is given when account has been set up.

Log-in/sign-up page

Homepage

GameExchange123

Additional requirements

Buying page

- Users enter details of used games.
- A buying price is created and shown to the user.
- Users can accept or decline the buying price.
- A code is displayed if the user accepts the buying price.

◻ **Figure 1.30: What are the benefits of using mind maps as opposed to task lists?**

ACTIVITY

1 In pairs, produce a written description of the buying page requirements given in the GameExchange123 project brief.
2 Discuss in pairs the benefits and drawbacks of using graphical and written descriptions for this project.

ACTIVITY

In pairs, copy and complete Figure 1.30 to give an overview of the homepage requirements and additional requirements given in the project brief. Remember, the information on a mind map should be brief and specific.

Mood boards

A mood board is another type of graphical description. It is usually a one-page document and can either be physical or digital depending on the type of project. Mood boards contain images, materials and pieces of text that are combined to show visually the overall 'mood,' 'look' and 'feel' of a product. Colour is also an important part of a mood board and can be used to add texture. You should be able to see the overall colour scheme that will run throughout a product, such as a user interface.

ACTIVITY

In pairs, research different examples of mood boards on the internet. What feeling do you think each mood board creates?

CHECK MY LEARNING

What tools are available to allow people to plan their projects? Give benefits and drawbacks of each method.

Planning the project basics

Before you start a project, you should clearly define what your aims and objectives are. Once these have been established, every task within the project should contribute to achieving them.

Aims and objectives

Aims are broad statements that will state what the overall goal of a project is. For example, one aim of the GameExchange123 project is 'To create a user interface that allows customers to interact with their online store efficiently and effectively.'

Objectives are the individual parts of the overall aim. It is important that aims and objectives are SMART. Objectives that are SMART are generally clearer, easier to understand and more likely to be achievable.

S

Specific
Aims and objectives must be clear and as precise as possible. You need to state exactly what you want to achieve (e.g. who, what, where, why).

M

Measurable
Aims and objectives must be measurable so that at the end of the project you will be able to see to what extent they have been met.

A

Achievable
Aims and objectives must be 'doable'. This means that they can be achieved by the person completing the project and within the time given.

R

Realistic
Aims and objectives must be feasible. It is important to set challenging aims and objectives, but they should not be too hard to complete.

T

Timely
Aims and objectives need to be given a time frame. You need to state a clear date and time as to when each task within the project will be completed.

◘ Figure 1.31: Why is it important that aims and objectives are SMART?

Project – GameExchange123

Example objectives

General objectives	SMART objectives
1 The user interface will have different screens.	1 The user interface will have a minimum of three screens.
2 I will spend several hours creating the user interface.	2 I will spend two hours creating each screen within the user interface.
3 The buying price of a game will be displayed immediately.	3 The buying price will be displayed within 10 seconds of the user pressing the submit button.
4 Users will be able to get a buying price for a range of different products.	4 Users will get a buying price for their used computer games.
5 The project will be completed sometime in the summer.	5 The project will be completed by 15 June 2018.

ACTIVITY

In pairs, write three SMART objectives for the GameExchange123 project brief.

Audience

The target audience is the people who will be using the system. It is important to consider the audience at the very start of a project to ensure that the system is suitable and will be accepted and used by the target audience.

If the target audience is not carefully considered at the start of a project, then the system may need to be changed, which takes more time and is likely to cost more money.

Project – GameExchange123

Target audience

When you are designing your user interface for GameExchange123, it is important to design one that is suitable for the users and matches their expectations. Remember the app is optional and therefore you want people to download it and use it. You should consider different accessibility needs, skill level needs and demographic needs.

Purpose

The purpose is the reason why something is created. Considering the purpose at the very start of a project ensures that the system does what the client wants and what they are paying money for.

ACTIVITY

1 In pairs, write down the purpose of the GameExchange123 system. Why is it being created?

75% of GameExchange123 customers are aged 18–25.

2 In pairs, discuss what you would need to consider about this age range when designing the user interface.

CHECK MY LEARNING

Explain what the acronym SMART means. Why is it so important to consider the audience and purpose of a project before starting?

Defining the project requirements

GETTING STARTED

Imagine you are using a website to book cinema tickets. In pairs, discuss the difference between the input and output requirements of this website. You should give examples of specific inputs you will need to enter and examples of outputs that will be displayed onscreen.

When you are defining the project requirements, it is a good idea to separate them into different groups. This makes it easier to see what hardware and software you are going to need to achieve them.

User requirements

User requirements are what the client wants the system to do or contain. For example:
- the styles they want to be used, including the colour choice, text styles or the text sizes
- the items they want on the screen and where they want them to be placed
- what tasks the user should be able to complete.

Project – GameExchange123
Example user requirements

1. The user interface should use the company house style colours blue and black.
2. The user interface should use methods of interaction found on smartphones.
3. The user interface for the homepage should list games that are currently high in demand.

Output requirements

Output requirements are what the system should give out for the user to see, hear or feel. What is outputted from a device will often determine what and how the user will respond.

 Table 1.12: Different methods of output

Method of output	Description
Visual	These are displayed on the screen for the user to see. For example, error messages that pop up on the screen to give a warning, or text that appears that shows something such as the result of a calculation.
Audio	These are sounded through speakers for the user to hear. For example, beeping noises to tell the user they are about to close a screen without saving, or a clicking noise to inform the user that they have successfully selected something on the screen.
Haptic	These allow the user to feel something. For example, a vibration to inform the user that there is new activity such as a new message, or it could be to grab their attention when the user interface has loaded.

KEY TERMS

Haptic relates to a sense of touch. Haptic outputs recreate the sense of touch by applying forces to the user.

Project – GameExchange123
Example output requirements

1. The user interface should display a list of games that meet the users' search criteria on the screen.
2. The user interface should display the user account information on the screen.
3. The user interface should confirm when a user has successfully set up an account on the screen.

Input requirements

Input requirements are what the system should allow the user to put into the system using their device.

⬛ Table 1.13: Different methods of user input

Method of input	Description
Mouse	This will be used to control the cursor and select items. For example, to click on the help menu option or to select an item from a menu.
Keyboard	This will be used to enter text into the computer. For example, to type in a username and password.
Voice	This will be used to say verbal commands to the computer. For example, you may want to search for something using your voice.
Touch	This is when you touch a device such as a touchscreen or touch pad to put commands into a computer. For example, you can swipe the screen up to move to another screen within the user interface.

Project – GameExchange123
Example input requirements

1 The user should use their onscreen keyboard to enter the name of a game they want to search.
2 The user should use their onscreen keyboard to enter their username and password.
3 The user should be able to use the touchscreen to either accept or decline a buying price.

User accessibility requirements

It is important to consider if any users have accessibility needs and the possibility of other users having accessibility needs in the future. It is not always possible to take every single accessibility need into account, so you should build generic options into the user interface.

Project – GameExchange123
Example user accessibility requirements

1 Include a zoom facility to allow the user to make parts of the screen bigger.
2 Allow the user as much time as they need to enter details of a used computer game.
3 Make the focus area of the buttons big so they can be easily selected.

LINK IT UP

To find out more about user accessibility requirements, go to lesson 'User accessibility needs' in Learning aim A of this component.

ACTIVITY

In pairs, complete the following tasks in the context of the GameExchange123 project brief.

1 Complete the list of user requirements to cover all requirements from the brief.
2 Complete the output and input requirements to cover all interactions between the user and the device from the brief.
3 Discuss with a partner three more accessibility features you think could be built into the user interface.

CHECK MY LEARNING

Identify which requirements from a project brief are user requirements, input requirements, output requirements and accessibility requirements. Explain the difference between them.

Project constraints and risks

GETTING STARTED

Think about the way you travel to school in the morning. Make a list of the possible things that could happen to influence the amount of time it takes you to travel there.

After you have established the project requirements, you need to look at all potential barriers that could prevent you from achieving them. This is important because you will be able to see if there are any project requirements that cannot be met, so that these can be discussed with the client before the project begins. This would then enable you to develop solutions to help overcome these barriers.

Constraints

KEY TERMS

Constraint is a limitation or restriction that you face while completing a project.

You should plan what **constraints** you face before you start a project. After you have assessed all the possible constraints, you may then recommend that the project:

1 can continue and *all* requirements can be met

2 can continue but *not all* requirements can be met

3 can continue but *some* requirements need to be adapted

4 *cannot* continue because not enough requirements can be met.

If any project requirements cannot be met or need to be adapted, the client should be informed and agree to these changes before the project continues.

There can be many different constraints within a project. The most common constraints are time, resources, dependencies and security.

Time

LINK IT UP

To find out more about iterative project methodology, go to lesson 'Project methodologies' in Learning aim B of this component.

The amount of time that you have available to complete a project is a big factor to consider. If you have a lot of time, you may be able to cover all the project requirements. If you are using an iterative project methodology, you may have lots of time to revisit parts of the system already completed to improve them further.

If you don't have a lot of time available, it could mean that you end up with a system that is good enough, rather than perfect. You need to prioritise each task that needs to be completed. For example, each task can be given a priority rating between 1 (not important) to 5 (extremely important). As you are working through a project, the tasks that are not as important can be dropped from the project if you are short of time.

Resources

You need to consider if you have all the resources you need at the start of a project, when you will need them, and how you will get them.

Technological resources These are the hardware and software resources. For example, you will need software to be able to create a user interface. You then need to ensure that the software has the tools available to be able to meet the project requirements.	**Human resources** These are the different people that will be involved in the project. For example, there may be a designer who will design the user interface and a programmer to create it. You therefore need to ensure you have the right people with the correct level of skills.
Premises resources These are the buildings that you have available to complete the project in. You will need to ensure you have a suitable room to be able to work on the project. You may also need other rooms such as a meeting room to be able to meet with the client.	**Equipment resources** These are other items that you may need. For example, you may need some sticky notes to jot down a task list or paper and pencils to sketch out some initial ideas.

◘ Figure 1.32: Think of some example resources that belong to each category

Task dependencies

The project methodology used will depend on how the tasks within a project depend on each other. For example, if you are using the waterfall methodology, then the tasks will follow on from each other. Each task or phase must be completed before another starts. This could delay the programmer, reducing the amount of time they have available to create the programming code.

Security

Projects may be constrained by codes of practice or by law. There are many computer related laws that must be followed when developing user interfaces.

- The overall look and feel of the user interface cannot copy another user interface that is already used by another organisation to comply with the Copyright, Designs and Patents Act 1988.
- If the user interface allows users to input personal information, then the developer must ensure these are stored safely to comply with the Data Protection Act 1998.
- Developers need to ensure that the user interface cannot be used by users to gain unauthorised access to areas of a computer they are not authorised to see. This is to comply with the Computer Misuse Act 1990.

Potential risks and contingency planning

A risk is something that could go wrong while completing the project. Different risks can have different impacts. If something goes wrong, this could mean:

- operational loss – the organisation cannot trade with its customers
- financial loss – the organisation will lose money from loss of sales
- damage to reputation – customers may lose their trust in the organisation.

For example, a new business is set up to sell Christmas decorations online. The planned launch date for the website is early November. However, a delay in developing the website means that it is not operational until the middle of December. As a result, the business sells fewer decorations and so it receives less income.

You should consider all possible risks, even if you think they are unlikely to happen. You then need to create a contingency plan. This is an outline that considers all possible risks, the estimated probability of them happening and a strategy of how the risk will be resolved.

Project – GameExchange123
Risks and contingency plan

▢ Table 1.14: Example risks and contingency plan

Potential risk	Probability	Possible impact	Contingency plan
The project may run behind schedule.	Possible	Other competitors may release an app first and gain some customers from GameExchange123.	Customers can continue to use GameExchange123's website instead of the app.
There could be a natural disaster.	Unlikely	User interface designs and communications with the customer may be lost.	Use cloud backup to create a copy of all designs and communications.

ACTIVITY

You will soon start to design a user interface that meets the requirements given in the GameExchange123 project brief. Remember, you have six weeks to design, create and refine your user interface and you only have the resources available in your school to use to complete this project.

In groups, discuss what project constraints there are in your school. You should include: time, resources, task dependencies and security.

CHECK MY LEARNING

What is a constraint? How can knowledge of constraints help to develop a contingency plan?

Planning project timescales

Some projects need more time than others. Thinking about the timescales involved can help you decide on the right length for a project and help decide whether an existing project plan is achievable.

Overall timescales

The overall timescale is the amount of time available to complete a project from the initial start date to the completion date. It is important to consider that a lot of projects start when the project brief is handed over from the client. This could mean you have less time than you may think to complete the project. Therefore, it is important to agree when the project will officially start before the project brief is handed out.

When tasks will be completed

When you know the overall timescale available, it is helpful to break down the whole project into different tasks and to decide when each task will be completed. It is also a good idea to break each task down further into smaller subtasks that can be completed separately.

◻ Table 1.15: Example tasks and subtasks

Main task	Subtask
Analyse the problem	• Meet client and discuss project brief • Define the project aims and objectives • Define the project audience and purpose • Define the user requirements • Define the input and output requirements • Assess the project constraints • Create a contingency plan
Design a solution to meet the problem	• Create a set of storyboards • Define the hardware and software requirements • Create a test strategy

Key milestones

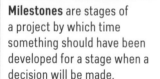
Milestones occur throughout the whole of a project and may include:

- dates by which each of the main tasks within a project will be completed
- dates when the client will be able to review the system and give feedback so that the system design can be updated. You may need to plan several client reviews into the project so that the client can review the system after each update
- dates of when the progress of the project is going to be reviewed. This may involve a date that includes a decision as to whether the project continues, or which tasks will be dropped from the project
- a date of when the whole project is going to be completed.

Resources

When you have assessed what resources you will need to complete the project, it is then important to consider when you will need them. This is because the resources may be in use by others and therefore may not be available when you need them, which could delay the project.

There is often a booking system where you can book resources in advance of you needing them. For example, you may want to book a meeting room to meet with the client or you may need to book a projector to show system details and designs to others.

Project – GameExchange123

Planning resources

GameExchange123 have stated that they want to review the user interface at different points to provide feedback, therefore the iterative methodology would be the most suitable.

Figure 1.33 shows a Gantt chart that has been put together for the homepage user interface. This is broken down into several subtasks and each subtask has been allocated a start date and end date. If resources are needed for each subtask, then these are also stated.

Task		Start Date	End Date	Resources	Week 1						Week 2				
					1	2	3	4	5		6	7	8	9	10
Task: Iteration 1 – Homepage															
Subtasks	Analyse and design homepage	5 November	7 November	Office, designer, graphics tablet											
	Develop prototype of homepage	8 November	9 November	Office, programmer and Visual Studio software											
	Customer reviews prototype	9 November	9 November	Meeting room											
	Update prototype based on customer feedback (review 1)	12 November	12 November	Office, programmer and Visual Studio software											
	Customer review 2	12 November	12 November	Meeting room											
	Update prototype based on customer feedback (review 2)	13 November	13 November	Office, programmer and Visual Studio software											
	Final customer review 3	13 November	13 November												
	Contingency time	14 November	14 November												
	Key milestone: homepage will be completed	15 November	15 November												
	Project review	16 November	16 November	Meeting room											

◘ Figure 1.33: If the tasks planned for Week 1 are delayed, what problems will this cause to the rest of the plan?

Complete the following task in the context of the GameExchange123 project brief.

In pairs, produce a suitable diagram such as a Gantt chart or PERT chart that shows how you would spend your time in this project. Remember, the project must be completed in six weeks. Make sure your diagram includes:
* the overall timescale of when you would start and end the project
* when tasks and subtasks will be completed
* key milestones, including when reviews with the client will be carried out
* when resources will be needed.

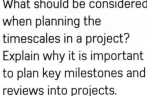

CHECK MY LEARNING

What should be considered when planning the timescales in a project? Explain why it is important to plan key milestones and reviews into projects.

What is a design specification?

LINK IT UP

To find out more about how to meet these requirements, go to lesson 'Defining the project requirements' in Learning aim B of this component.

As part of your project design you will need to produce a design specification. This will help you to explain to others what your new system will consist of and how it is going to work.

What requirements does a design specification need to meet?

When you are creating a design specification, you need to ensure that you meet the:
- user requirements
- input requirements
- output requirements
- accessibility requirements.

What should the design specification allow for?

Increased user confidence and familiarity

If there is no existing user interface, then you will need to ensure that the new interface is suitable for the user's skill level and demographics. For example, you will need to find out the age and past experiences of the target market and then ensure that the design meets their needs.

If you are designing a user interface that is going to replace an existing one, then you will need to consider what the previous user interface looked like. Where possible, you need to try and keep items in the same place as they were before. This is because if users can see that the layout is like something that they have used previously, then it will increase their confidence and they will be able to use the new user interface more intuitively. However, it is not always possible to keep the layout the same. Therefore, if you are changing where items are placed, it's important that these are communicated to the user.

LINK IT UP

To find out more about how to meet these requirements, go to lesson 'User skills and demographics' in Learning aim A of this component.

▣ Why is it important for mobile phone operating systems to leave the user interface unchanged?

Reduced learning time and time to complete tasks

It is important to design a user interface that will allow users to learn quickly its features to complete tasks.

You can reduce the amount of learning time and the time it takes users to complete tasks by:

- ensuring items are placed where users expect to see them so they can find them quickly, such as placing all navigation items in a menu bar
- having a help facility in case users are unsure what the new features do
- designing error messages to allow users to easily correct their mistakes
- providing help text for additional help to users if they need it.

Increased user attention

When people use something new, they will often use a 'trial and error' approach to work out how to use it. People can often feel disheartened if they are not able to make progress quickly and therefore lose their attention if they are not able to use something.

You can increase user attention by:

- using pop-up messages, flashing graphics, sound and animation to guide users when completing tasks
- ensuring the screen is uncluttered and only contains items or information that is needed to complete tasks
- making sure that all items and features are clearly labelled with their purpose
- making use of predetermined values and autofill to reduce the amount of work the user must do.

LINK IT UP

To find out more about how to increase user attention, go to lesson 'Design principles: keeping the user engaged' in Learning aim A of this component.

Reduced need for specialist knowledge

Specialist knowledge is often specific information that the user would need to know to complete a task. For example, users generally have an idea of how to close software such as where to click or what gestures to carry out. Therefore, if this does not follow the idea of the user, then this would be classed as an example of specialist knowledge as it is something specific for that one user interface.

A user interface that requires users to have specialist knowledge will be more difficult to use and learn. It will also increase the amount of time taken to complete tasks.

You can reduce the need for specialist knowledge by ensuring that the user interface requires general knowledge and skills that users already know or have. You should consider the likely devices that users will have experienced using and the skills they will have developed to use them, and ensure you make use of these in your user interface.

ACTIVITY

In the next lesson you will create a design specification for GameExchange123. Complete the following in pairs.

1 Discuss how the requirements of the project are going to impact your design specification.

2 Discuss how you will create a design that will reduce the need for users to have specialist knowledge.

GameExchange123 currently does not have a mobile phone app.

3 In your pairs, discuss how this is going to impact your design.

CHECK MY LEARNING

What is a design specification? What should you consider when creating the various elements of the specification? Why should these be considered at the design stage?

Creating sketches and storyboards

Before we create products, we often sketch out our initial ideas and plans on paper first. Creating an outline sketch has benefits and drawbacks and these will be explored in the lesson.

A visual user interface is something that the user will see. This part of the user interface can take a long time to develop as you need to ensure that the user understands how to use the device and can use it with ease.

Designing the look of the user interface first may save you time later in the project. The client can see what the user interface is going to look like so that they can provide feedback before it's developed.

Sketches

A sketch is a rough, often unfinished drawing that will help you generate ideas. You could skip this process and go straight to creating the product. However, our first idea is not always our best idea. We can sketch out our initial ideas in seconds to see if they are going to work or not.

A sketch allows you to see where items should be placed on the screen and what sizes they should be. You can quickly see if the screen design is going to meet the project requirements and design principles. You can then add more detail to your sketch or create a storyboard showing the design in more detail.

A sketch may be revisited and changed at many different points within an iterative methodology when feedback from the client is received.

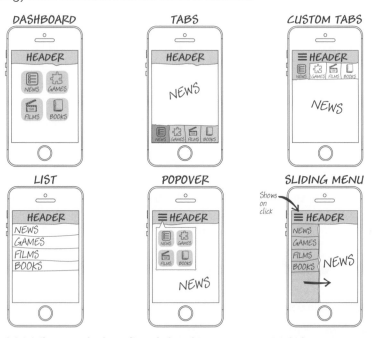

◘ Figure 1.34: What are the benefits of sketching out your initial ideas on paper first?

Storyboards

A storyboard is another tool that can be used to design the visual aspect of a user interface. Although a storyboard does include sketches, it will also give more information about the system that is being developed.

A storyboard illustrates the main events or sequence that will happen while a user views or interacts with a multimedia object such as a video or website. For example, it can show what the user interface will look like when it's first loaded on the screen and what it will look like after the user has input a command. Although a storyboard may take time to create, it will help you to share your vision for the user interface with others, including the client.

A storyboard should:

- show where items are going to be placed on the screen
- give an idea of how big the items are going to be in proportion to the size of the screen
- show what colours will be used
- demonstrate the methods that users will use to interact with the system
- present what the user interface will look like when the accessibility features are applied
- describe non-visual events such as sounds.

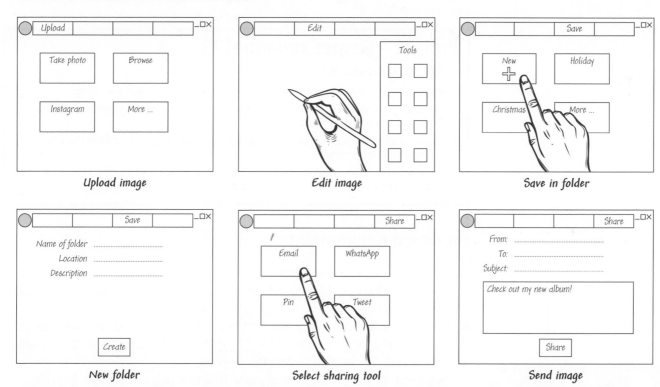

■ Figure 1.35: How can storyboards allow you to explore your ideas in more depth?

Defining the hardware, software and testing strategy

GETTING STARTED

Which software products are you familiar with? Which of them could be used to develop a user interface design? Are any other software products available in your school that would be better to use?

When you have defined the project requirements, the next step is to select the hardware and software that you will use to create your user interface.

Software requirements

The software requirements are a list of tools the software should contain to meet the project requirements and the user interface design.

The first key decision is to check that the software will be able to produce a user interface that will work on the device or devices that the user is going to use.

If it does, you then need to consider what tools you are going to need and then assess which piece of software has the best tools to be able to meet the project requirements most effectively.

Project – GameExchange123
Software requirements

Here are some software requirements to create the sign-up user interface.
1   Software should have tools to create a sign-up form containing text boxes, form fields, radio buttons and so on.
2   Software should have facilities to create pop-up messages to confirm the user account has been set up.
3   Software should have facilities to create a beeping sound and embed this within the final product so that it plays a beeping noise.

Hardware requirements

The hardware requirements will depend on what software you have chosen to use. Each piece of software will have a different set of hardware requirements. These can be split into the following.

- System hardware – hardware requirements to run the software on your computer. This might include the amount of RAM needed to run the software or storage space that needs to be available to store the program.
- **Peripheral** hardware – devices that you will use to access the software. This can be hardware such as a mouse and keyboard. Some projects may require more specialised hardware such as a graphics tablet to draw objects. For example, as the user interface for GameExchange123 needs to make a bleeping sound, speakers are therefore going to be needed. A microphone may also be needed to record the text that will be displayed on the screen so that it can be played to users with visual needs.

Test strategy

Testing is when you check that the system is working correctly and does not contain any errors or **bugs**.

A test strategy describes the testing that will be carried out. It does not specifically state what will be tested; instead it should describe the approach that will be taken to test the system.

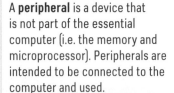

KEY TERMS

A **peripheral** is a device that is not part of the essential computer (i.e. the memory and microprocessor). Peripherals are intended to be connected to the computer and used.

Bugs are flaws in computer programs or systems.

A test strategy, once created, will not change and you can then create a test plan that will give more specific information on what will be tested and how it will be tested.

The test strategy will depend on which project methodology is used. For example, if the iterative methodology is used, then testing will be done more frequently during the project.

◻ Figure 1.36: What other features could be included in a test strategy?

Project – GameExchange123

Example of a test strategy

1 Testing must be carried out at the end of each **iteration**.
2 The user interface designer and the client should be able to test the product at the end of each iteration.
3 If any errors are found, they will be fixed before moving onto the next iteration in the project.

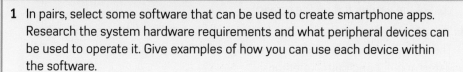

ACTIVITY

1 In pairs, select some software that can be used to create smartphone apps. Research the system hardware requirements and what peripheral devices can be used to operate it. Give examples of how you can use each device within the software.

Complete the following task in the context of the GameExchange123 project brief.

2 In pairs, discuss the software requirements for the homepage.
3 In pairs, discuss other features that could be included in the test strategy example.

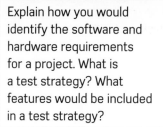

CHECK MY LEARNING

Explain how you would identify the software and hardware requirements for a project. What is a test strategy? What features would be included in a test strategy?

Learning aim B: assessment practice

How you will be assessed

Now that you have studied the topics in Learning aim B, you must show that you can use appropriate project planning techniques to plan and complete a project and design a user interface.

You need to show that you can select appropriate project planning tools that are suitable for the project brief that you will be given. This needs to include all major parts, including timescales, constraints and contingencies.

You also need to show that you can create a comprehensive design specification for the design of the user interface. This should be in sufficient detail to allow the designs to be used to create the user interface. You need to ensure that your design specification effectively uses design principles that you learned in Learning aim A.

CHECKPOINT

Strengthen
- Identify how different project methodologies can be used to structure projects.
- Identify how different tools can be used to create a project plan.
- Identify what elements should be included in a design specification.

Challenge
- Identify and explain different situations when each project methodology would be used.
- Analyse the suitability of different project planning techniques that can be used for a particular situation or project.
- Assess the effectiveness of a design specification and how effectively it incorporates standard design principles.

Mini project brief

TurfTurfABC is a company that sells garden turf. They want to set up a single webpage that will allow customers to calculate the total cost of the turf for the size of their garden.

80% of their customers are aged 30 and over. You have been asked to design the user interface for this webpage.

Requirements

1 The user should be able to enter the length and width of their garden in metres. Suitable prompts should be given if these have been left empty or if a mistake has been made.

2 There should be a calculate button and when clicked it should display the overall cost of the garden turf on the screen.

3 The webpage must be accessible from any device with an internet connection. Therefore, it should be suitable for a range of different devices with a range of different input and output methods.

4 The webpage should be suitable for the user's age and their past experiences.

5 The webpage should incorporate the company house style colours, which are black and green.

6 The company wants the webpage to be created within two weeks.

ASSESSMENT ACTIVITY 1 | LEARNING AIM | B

Creating a project plan

1 Use the most appropriate project planning tools such as mind maps and task lists to plan out the different parts of this project.

2 Create a project plan that could be followed to create this webpage. This should include the:

- aims and objectives
- audience and purpose
- project requirements, including user, input and output requirements
- timescales, including key milestones
- risks and constraints.

TIPS

The command word *create* means that you are required to use your own thoughts and ideas to come up with something, often a solution to a problem. This means that you are required to use your own ideas to come up with a project plan that can be used to manage this project effectively.

TIPS

Make sure you set SMART aims and objectives and provide comprehensive detail on the user requirements, input requirements, output requirements and user accessibility requirements.

ASSESSMENT ACTIVITY 2 | LEARNING AIM | B

Creating a design specification

Create an initial design specification for the webpage as described in the TurfTurfABC project brief. This should include:

- a visualisation of the webpage
- hardware requirements
- software requirements
- a test strategy.

TIPS

Make sure your design specification is in comprehensive detail to allow somebody to get enough information to understand how the user interface will look and work.

TAKE IT FURTHER

Identify which project methodology would be used to create this project. Justify why this is the most suitable methodology to complete the project for TurfTurfABC.

Make sure you give the benefits of your chosen methodology and the drawbacks of alternative methodologies.

Developing a functional user interface

GETTING STARTED

Think of a device that you use regularly. What do you think it would be like if the device only had a user interface and didn't process any data? What would it be able to do? What would it not be able to do?

For your assessment in Learning aim C, you are required to create a user interface. However, you are not required to show how the user interface processes data. In this lesson you will learn what your user interface should contain.

What is a system?

All digital devices work in the same way by input, process and output.

Input	Process	Output
The user inputs data such as a command into the system using the user interface	A user interface does not process data. This will collect data from the input stage, process them away from the user interface and then send the processed data back to the user interface.	The processed data is then displayed on the user interface for the user to see, hear or feel.

◻ Figure 1.37: How might a user respond to the output to give new input to the system?

Your user interface should show how it can be used to input data and then how the data will be outputted back to the user. You do not need to show how the inputs are processed in your assessment.

LINK IT UP

When you are developing your inputs and outputs, it is important to follow the ones that are stated on your design specification from Learning aim B.

Showing the outputs

It is useful to consider what outputs your user interface needs to give out. Once these are clearly defined, you can then work backwards and decide what inputs are required to make them happen.

You need to decide what output methods you will use, such as the following.
- Error messages – for example, at what points an error message will be displayed and what it will look like. You should also think about what the error message will contain. It should clearly tell the user what the error is and then give the user clear guidance as to how to overcome the error.
- Sounds – for example, at what points sounds will be played to the user and what they will sound like.
- Sense – for example, at what points the device will vibrate and what this will be used for.

Showing the inputs

Your user interface needs to show the different inputs. You will need to show which areas of your user interface require the use of the following.
- Key presses – for example, which areas of the user interface require the keyboard to select items or input typed data.
- Mouse clicks – for example, which areas of the user interface require the mouse to select items using the cursor.
- Touch – for example, which areas of the user interface require the use of the finger to carry out gestures.

Showing the navigation methods

Your user interface needs to show how the user is going to navigate around it. You need to carefully examine what methods of input are available on the device that will use the interface.

For example, will the user move around the user interface by:
- clicking or tapping on buttons or hyperlinks
- using the keyboard or onscreen key to enter keyboard shortcuts
- saying commands verbally using their natural voice?

Project – GameExchange123
Example user interface

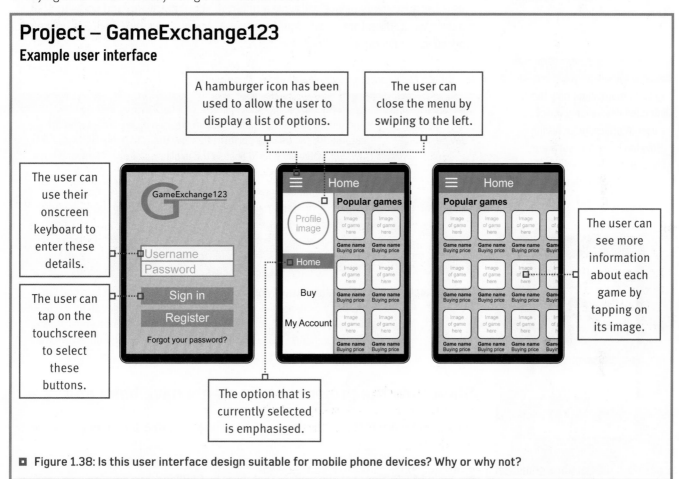

■ Figure 1.38: Is this user interface design suitable for mobile phone devices? Why or why not?

In pairs, complete the following task in the context of the GameExchange123 project brief.

1 Discuss the appropriateness of the inputs and outputs in the user interface in Figure 1.38.

2 Discuss the appropriateness of the navigation methods in the user interface in Figure 1.38.

3 Select a piece of software and create the user interface that shows the functionality for the buying page.

CHECK MY LEARNING ■ ■

What features must a user interface include to make it functional? Why are these essential if the user can use the user interface effectively and be able to provide feedback?

Showing the key aspects of a user interface

GETTING STARTED

Apart from showing the functionality, what else should you consider when creating your user interface? What else might the user want to see before providing their feedback?

In the previous lesson you learned what a user interface must include to make it functional. In this lesson you are going to learn what the user interface must show to make it more effective and easier to use.

Show awareness of intended device

Your user interface needs to show full awareness of the device that will be using it. This is because every device will have a different set of hardware and software that makes it work. Therefore, a user interface that is designed for one device is unlikely to work successfully on another device.

LINK IT UP

To learn more about how the intended device can impact a user interface, go to lesson 'How hardware and software affect user interfaces' in Learning aim A of this component.

◨ Table 1.16: Example devices and areas to consider

Example device	What should you consider?
Touchscreen device	If the device has a touchscreen, then you can incorporate different gestures for the user to perform to allow them to use the device. However, you will need to assess the likelihood of users knowing what the different gestures are and how users will learn them.
Laptop computer	Laptop computers generally have smaller screens in comparison to desktop computers. You therefore need to show how the user interface is suitable for smaller screens. Some laptops make use of touchscreen technology while others don't. Some laptops make use of touch pads; however, some people still prefer to use a mouse. Therefore, you need to consider how the user interface is suitable for all these different areas.
Smartwatches	Smartwatches usually have very small screens. You therefore need to consider which features are the most essential that need to be displayed, and how the user will access the features that are less essential. These watches generally make use of touchscreen technology, but may have other input methods such as sliders and buttons that can be used.

◨ What changes would you make if this user interface was on a smartwatch?

Show how the project requirements have been met

The user interface that you develop must show how the project requirements have been met.

◨ Table 1.17: Different requirements that must be fulfilled when developing a user interface

Requirement	What should you consider?
User requirements	Your user interface needs to show how the user requirements have been met. Most users will have very specific needs and it is important to ensure that the user interface does exactly what the user wants.
Input and output requirements	Your user interface needs to show how the input and output requirements on your design specification have been achieved. For example, if the user wanted a message to appear to confirm an action, then your user interface needs to show what this will look like.
Accessibility requirements	Your user interface needs to be accessible for its users. You therefore need to show what accessibility features you have included, where they are located, and what the user interface will look like once they have been applied.

LINK IT UP

To find out more about how to meet these requirements, go to lesson 'Defining the project requirements' in Learning aim B of this component.

Show the overall look

Your user interface must show the overall look. Though it is likely to have several different screens, each screen should look like it is part of the same user interface. This can be achieved by:

- using the same colours on every screen within the user interface
- using the same font styles and font sizes on every screen within the user interface
- using language that is friendly and inviting to make people use the user interface
- keeping the items in the same place on each screen so the user does not need to keep guessing where the items have been moved to when they go to a different screen.

Show the overall feel

Your user interface must show the overall feel. This means it must show how the user interface behaves when a user interacts with it. For example, it should show what happens when the user:

- clicks on the buttons
- hovers over items on the screen
- carries out certain gestures
- makes a mistake while carrying out a task.

Show the ease of use

Your user interface must be easy to use. As you are developing it, you will know exactly how it works and therefore will be able to use it easily. However, new users may not find it easy to use.

Ask potential users to trial the design and observe them carrying out tasks. You can then see how easily the users are able to use it and gain feedback to make improvements to the design.

To make your user interface easy to use, you should ensure:

- the type of interface – text-based, menu-based, graphical-based – is suitable
- the design matches user's expectations (such as colours, sounds, pictures)
- the different parts of the screen are clearly labelled
- tip text is used to guide the user if they need additional help.

ACTIVITY

Complete the following task in the context of the user interface shown in Figure 1.38 from the previous lesson. In pairs discuss the following.

1 How the user interface shows awareness of the hardware and software found on mobile phones.
2 Which requirements from the GameExchange123 project brief have been fully and partially achieved.
3 Which groups of people GameExchange123 could ask to test the user interface for its ease of use.

CHECK MY LEARNING

Give two examples of how different devices can impact the design of a user interface. What techniques can you use to show the overall look and feel of a user interface?

Refining the user interface

When you have completed your user interface, you need to allow potential users to test it and provide feedback.

Refining your user interface

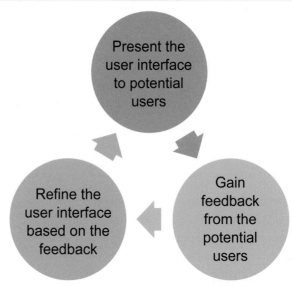

■ Figure 1.39: When do you think you would stop repeating this cycle?

Stage 1: Present user interface to potential users

When you have completed your user interface, you then need potential users to test it. You may choose to do this in stages or in one go. The users who are involved could include:
- the client who is paying for the user interface
- the users that will be using the user interface
- other similar users with similar demographics (for example, age, experiences) to those who will be using the user interface.

When you give your user interface to the potential market you may want to:
- allow the target audience to trial the user interface freely and allow them to provide feedback
- ask the user to focus on areas of the design and allow them to provide feedback
- ask the user to complete specific tasks and then ask them specific questions.

It is important to listen to the feedback given and ask follow-up questions to understand the issues that are raised. Sometimes users may provide vague statements such as those in Figure 1.40.

However, vague statements like these can make it more difficult to improve the user interface. Therefore, it's important to ask follow-up questions, for example:
- Can you give me an example?
- Which area of the user interface are you referring to?
- Why do you think that?

'I think it could be better.'

'The user interface is difficult to use.'

'The user interface is slow.'

'The button didn't work when I clicked on it.'

■ Figure 1.40: Why are these statements vague?

You also need to consider how you are going to store the feedback given. For example, you could write down a summary of what a person says. This will help you keep a record of the important information given. It is important that you note the essential parts to make sure that you don't forget or miss anything. You may want to:

- ask the user to complete a questionnaire
- observe the user interface in use and make notes during your observations
- interview the user and record their feedback.

Stage 2: Refine the user interface

Once you have gathered the user feedback, you need to refine the user interface by making improvements to it. It is important that any changes made are based on user feedback and not your own personal feelings. Sometimes, you may only need to make minor changes. However, other times you may need to completely redesign one section or even the whole user interface.

Stage 3: Repeat the iterative process

Once the user interface has been refined, the potential users should then be able to use the updated version and be given further opportunities to provide feedback. At this stage:

1 the user may be happy with the changes
2 the user may have new ideas of things they want to be changed
3 the changes that have been made may cause other issues that need to be refined.

Depending on the outcome, Stages 1 and 2 may need to be repeated several times until the user is completely happy with its design.

Documenting the changes

When refining a user interface, save different versions of each iteration. If you make changes that the client is not happy with, then you can go back to the previous iteration. You should also note what has been changed within the user interface during each iteration. The client can then sign this document to confirm that they are happy with the changes made.

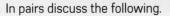
ACTIVITY

In pairs discuss the following.

1 Why is it important to gain feedback from potential users?
2 What are the benefits to the client and the project team of user feedback?
3 What are the possible drawbacks of involving the client and the impacts that too much user feedback can have on the project?

Look at the user interface design given in Figure 1.38. Imagine you are the creator of this user interface.

4 Write down four specific questions you could ask potential users to gain feedback on its design.

CHECK MY LEARNING

Why is it important to gain user feedback? Why is it important to gain specific feedback?

Reviewing the user interface

In this lesson you will learn how to review your user interface effectively. Next lesson you
will learn how to review the project planning techniques used to manage its creation.

Reviewing the user interface checklists

How well have you met the project requirements?

During a review, you should check how well the project requirements have been met
as the client is paying for the user interface and therefore it should do what they want.

Item	Item to check	Achieved?
1	Have you met all the user requirements?	
2	Have you met all the input and output requirements?	
3	Have you met all the accessibility requirements?	

How suitable is the user interface for the audience and purpose?

You should check how suitable the user interface is for the users who will be using it. If it
is not appropriate, then it could slow down the speed at which users can complete tasks.

Item	Item to check	Achieved?
1	Is the user interface suitable for users with accessibility needs, such as: • visual needs • motor needs • hearing needs • cognitive needs? • speech needs	
2	Is the user interface suitable for the user skill level, such as: • expert skills • occasional skills • regular skills • novice skills?	
3	Is the user interface suitable for the user demographics, such as: • age • beliefs, values and culture? • past experiences	
4	Does the user interface allow the user to complete the tasks they need to?	

Is the user interface easy to use?

You should check that your user interface is easy to use by the target market. This is
because if it is difficult to use, then it may deter people from using it.

Item	Item to check	Achieved?
1	Does the user interface match user perceptions, such as: • colour and sound • symbols and pictures?	
2	Does the user interface sustain the user's attention, such as: • ensuring the screen is uncluttered • using labels • using predetermined/default values and autofill • using tip text?	
3	Is the design of the user interface intuitive? • Do the button/icon graphics match what the button does? • Are the pop-up messages helpful and informative? • Is there a help feature for the user to access? • Does the user interface have a consistent design? • Can the user easily reverse an action?	

How effectively have design principles been met?

You should ensure your user interface implements design principles to ensure it's more effective.

Item	Item to check	Achieved?
1	Have you used appropriate colour choices, such as: • made limited use of colours • used the correct organisational house style colours • used colours that contrast with each other?	
2	Have you used appropriate font sizes/styles, such as: • used a font style/size that is readable • used a sans-serif font?	
3	Have you used appropriate language that is: • age-appropriate • appropriate for the user skill level?	
4	Have you provided the right amount of information, such as: • to allow users to complete a task • linked the amount of information to the amount of white space available?	
5	Have you used appropriate use of layout, such as: • ensured that each screen is consistent with each other • kept layout as close as possible to what the user is expecting • placed important items in prominent/obvious positions • made use of navigation components?	

What areas could be developed further?

When you have completed the checklists in this lesson, note that any ticks in the 'achieved' column are the key strengths of your user interface. You will easily see if there are areas that you have not ticked and will be able to set these as targets for improvements.

If there is enough time left in the project, then you may want to go back and make these changes. Sometimes due to time constraints, it may not be possible to make these changes. However, your areas for development can still inform your design work on other user interfaces that you may create in the future.

ACTIVITY

You are going to practise reviewing a user interface. You should review the user interface that you created in the lesson 'Developing a functional user interface' in this Learning aim. You should:

1 use the checklists in this section to determine if each item has been achieved, partly achieved or not achieved at all

2 use the information from Question 1 to make a list of areas that could be improved further

3 explain how these changes will make the user interface more effective.

CHECK MY LEARNING

Why is it important to review a user interface? What should you consider when you are reviewing a user interface?

Reviewing the project planning techniques

In this lesson, you will learn how to review the project planning techniques used within the project effectively.

Reviewing the project planning techniques

How did the project planning tools meet the needs of the task?

You should consider how the project planning tools met the needs of the task.

Item	Item to check	Yes?
1	Were the use of textual project planning tools effective in meeting the needs of the project, such as: • task lists • written descriptions?	
2	Were the use of graphical project planning tools effective in meeting the needs of the project, such as: • mood boards • mind maps • graphical descriptions?	
3	Were the use of time management diagrams useful in meeting the needs of the project, such as: • Gantt charts • PERT charts • critical path diagrams?	
4	Did you set SMART aims/objectives? Did the use of SMART aims and objectives allow you to easily determine how successfully the user interface met the project requirements? Did your aims/objectives help you to know how well your project was progressing?	
5	Did you accurately consider all potential risks to the project before starting?	
6	Did the use of your contingency plan allow you to still meet the project deadline following unplanned events?	

How did the project methodology meet the needs of the task?

You should consider if your chosen project methodology was suitable for the project. This is important as you may consider using the same project methodology in the future and therefore you will be able to better consider if this methodology is the most suitable.

Item	Item to check	Yes?
1	Was the iterative project methodology suitable for the task? For example: • was your method suitable for the tasks you did • were there any occasions when you could have used a different methodology?	
2	Did the project methodology allow enough opportunities to gather user feedback?	
3	Was the project methodology suitable for the stated user requirements?	
4	Were the task dependencies created by this project methodology suitable for the project?	

What was the impact of using the iterative design approach?

You should consider how the iterative design approach impacted the project. You may consider using this approach in the future and therefore you will be able to better analyse the benefits and drawbacks of this methodology.

Item	Item to check	Yes?
1	Did this methodology reduce the number of task dependencies, giving you more flexibility to complete project tasks as you wished?	
2	The iterative methodology gives more contact with a client than the waterfall methodology. Did this help both the design of the user interface and the overall project?	
3	Did this project methodology allow you to keep revising different tasks or parts of the user interface to perfect them further?	

How did you overcome project constraints?

It's important to consider if the project constraints were overcome. This is because you may need to carry out a project in the future with similar constraints. You will therefore be able to better plan the project constraints and create a better contingency plan before starting a project.

Item	Item to check	Yes?
1	Did you manage to complete the project within the allocated amount of time?	
2	Did you have all the resources available to you when you needed them?	
3	Did you manage to overcome all security implications?	

What have you learned?

Although this project has finished, a project manager will continue to work on many different projects. Project planning techniques are generic and can be used across all assignments and tasks. Therefore, the outcome from this review could impact how you choose techniques in the future.

A tick in any of the tables in this lesson indicates that this part of the project was a success. You should then focus on the areas that were not successful – for example by considering the following issues.

- The project planning techniques were not appropriate for the task.
- You may not have fully considered everything before starting the project.
- The project may have been too ambitious and unachievable (and in the amount of time available).
- You may not have organised your time effectively.

ACTIVITY

In Learning aim B you should have completed some or all the following tasks.
- A set of SMART objectives
- A task list
- A graphical/textual description
- A time plan

In pairs, you are going to practise reviewing these project planning techniques.

1 Use the checklists in this section to determine if each technique was suitable or not for the tasks undertaken in Learning aim B.

2 Consider the areas that you did not tick. Discuss possible reasons why this was the case.

3 Discuss whether you would use the same project planning techniques if you had to carry out a similar project in the future. If not, what would you do differently and why?

CHECK MY LEARNING

Why is it important to review the project planning techniques used? What factors would you consider when determining whether the techniques used were suitable?

Learning aim C: assessment practice

How you will be assessed

Now that you have studied all the topics in Learning aim C, you must now show that you can follow your project plan and design specification to develop a user interface. You need to show that you can manage your time effectively and follow your plan independently. You also need to show that you have created a comprehensive user interface that shows all features.

You need to show that you have used opportunities to gather feedback from potential users to refine the user interface and document all changes made. You must show how the iterations improve the effectiveness and efficiency of the user interface.

You must then show that you are able to consider the strengths and weaknesses of your user interface and project plan.

CHECKPOINT

Strengthen

- State what a user interface should show and include.
- Describe the benefits of using the iterative process involving potential users.
- State what you should include when determining the strengths and weaknesses of a user interface.
- State what you should include when determining the strengths and weaknesses of the project planning techniques.

Challenge

- Assess the usefulness of reviewing the user interface and how this can influence the design of other user interfaces in the future.
- Assess the usefulness of reviewing the project planning techniques and how this can influence the planning of other projects in the future.
- Assess the usefulness of involving the client and the benefits and drawbacks this can have on the project.

Develop and refine a user interface

1 At the end of Learning aim B you created a design specification for a new webpage for TurfTurfABC. Using suitable software tools, you now need to develop the user interface, using your design specification, to help ensure that the interface meets the project requirements. This should include:

- the overall look and feel
- how the user inputs data
- how the interface responds and will output to the user
- how the user navigates around the user interface
- how the user interactions match user expectations.

2 When you have completed your user interface, you then need to gather feedback by:

- presenting the user interface to potential users
- allowing potential users to use the user interface and then obtain and record feedback
- refining the user interface to account for potential user feedback
- repeating this process until the user interface is complete.

TIPS

The command word *develop* means that you are required to create an initial starting point and then continue to extend it to cover all the given requirements eventually. This means that you need to choose appropriate software and then create an initial area of your user interface and then build on it until it is complete.

Review the user interface and project planning techniques

When you have completed your user interface, you need to review the strengths and weaknesses of your user interface and project planning techniques.

User interface

1 Describe how your user interface makes use of different design principles. To what extent has it made good use of these principles? How do you know?

2 Describe how users interact with your design. To what extent is it easy for users to use? How do you know?

3 Describe how your user interface is suitable for its audience and purpose.

4 State how the user interface can be developed further and analyse how these changes would better meet both user requirements and design principles.

Project planning techniques

1 Evaluate the effectiveness of your chosen methodology.

2 Assess the extent to which your choices helped to make the project a success.

3 Explain how you overcame project constraints.

TIPS

The command word *analyse* means that you are required to break the question down into different parts and then give an in-depth account which shows your understanding about each separate part.

TIPS

The command word *explain* means that you are required to give reasons how or why something is what it is. This means that you need to give reasons why the decisions you made were either suitable or not suitable.

TAKE IT FURTHER

Technology is constantly changing. For example, the development of touchscreen technology and voice control are changing the way that we interact with our devices. Think of possible developments in both hardware and software in the future. For each development, discuss the following.

- How this could impact the user interface that you have created.
- How the way we apply different design principles may change.
- What new design principles it could create.

02 Collecting, Presenting and Interpreting Data

Introduction

Data is part of modern life. The systems that we interact with daily – mobile phones, contactless payments, websites and many others – collect large amounts of data. This data can provide useful information to organisations. They can analyse it to identify trends and opportunities for improving their customers' experience or to sell more of their goods and services.

In this component you will discover how data is collected and used to support decision-making and how it can be presented in ways that help make it easy to understand.

Large quantities of data can be very difficult to understand. You will also learn how to manipulate data and use it to create dashboards that summarise and present data clearly.

LEARNING AIMS

In this component you will:

A	Investigate the role and impact of using data on individuals and organisations
B	Create a dashboard using data manipulation tools
C	Draw conclusions and review data presentation methods.

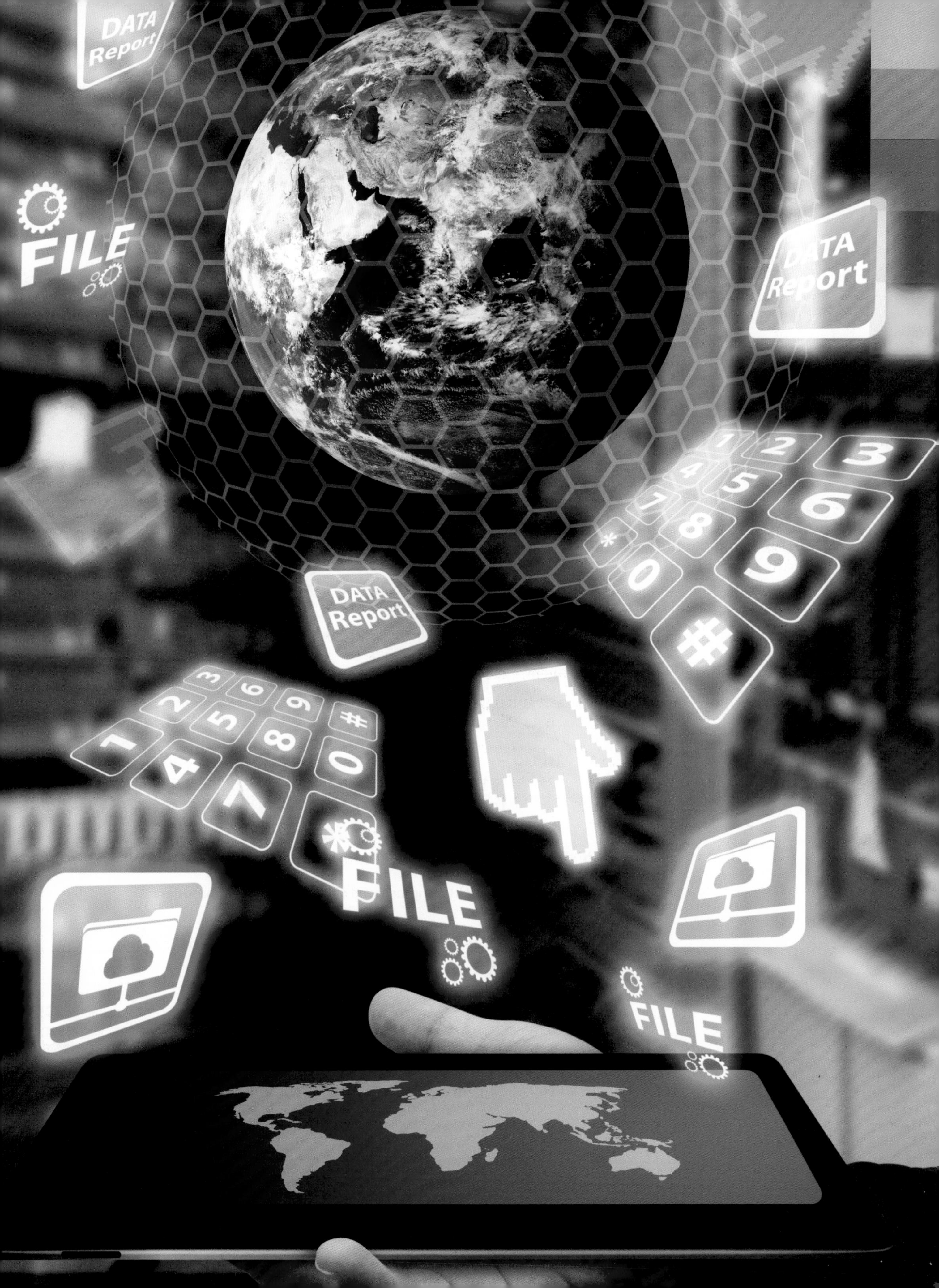

DATA
Report
FILE
DATA
Report
DATA
Report
FILE
FILE

Data and information

You have probably heard the terms 'data' and 'information' used a lot, but what do they mean and what is the difference between them? This is a key question as you learn about changing data into information.

What is data?

Data is a series of numbers or letters that has no structure or context and which by itself has no meaning and has not been processed. To provide structure or meaning to the data it needs to be processed in some way. Here is an example of some unprocessed data.

101, Ashford, 101217, 122, 3, 29, 203.55

102, Liverpool, 141217, 324, 4, 10, 245.29

103, Watford, 161217, 93, 2, 10, 123.55

105, Norwich, 201217, 183, 2, 50, 185.20

No context is provided for this data; for example, we don't know where it has come from, or what it is to be used for. It has no structure and its meaning is unclear.

What is information?

Information is data that has been processed. The processing may involve doing several different things to the data, such as adding structure. Figure 2.1 shows the above data in a structured format.

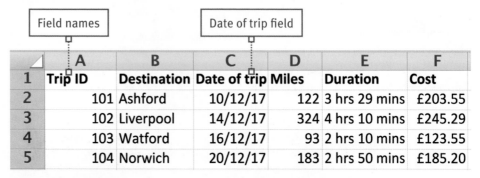

Field names

Date of trip field

	A	B	C	D	E	F
1	Trip ID	Destination	Date of trip	Miles	Duration	Cost
2	101	Ashford	10/12/17	122	3 hrs 29 mins	£203.55
3	102	Liverpool	14/12/17	324	4 hrs 10 mins	£245.29
4	103	Watford	16/12/17	93	2 hrs 10 mins	£123.55
5	104	Norwich	20/12/17	183	2 hrs 50 mins	£185.20

■ Figure 2.1: Compare the unprocessed data with this structured data

Figure 2.2 shows what information is made from.

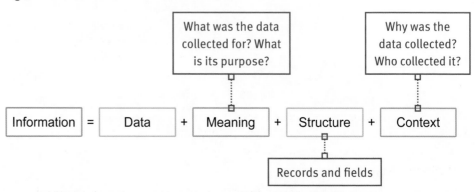

What was the data collected for? What is its purpose?

Why was the data collected? Who collected it?

Information = Data + Meaning + Structure + Context

Records and fields

■ Figure 2.2: Why might someone have collected the data in Figure 2.1?

Giving structure and meaning to data

Data is often structured by splitting it into **fields** and **records** in a table format.

Each field has a name or title, which is usually shown in the top row of the table. Figure 2.1 shows the same data listed as the unprocessed data but with field names added.

Spreadsheet and database software is used to create and maintain structured data. Spreadsheets allow text and numeric data to be stored in a table format of rows and columns. Databases are a more sophisticated way to create structured tables of fields and records and link different tables together. This can also be done by linking data in one spreadsheet to an external data source or linking different spreadsheets together within a workbook.

Not all information can be structured into fields and records. The information in this book, for example, could not be represented that way. Instead, structure is provided by dividing the book into chapters, with headings and sub-headings providing further structure.

Structure isn't the only requirement to change data into information. To make information useful, we need to understand its context, how it has been collected and how it is to be used. The way data is collected can have an impact on its accuracy and therefore how useful it is.

The most important characteristic of information is that it is meaningful. It tells you something you need to know or that would be useful to know. Historical weather data provides an example of this. Lists of rainfall and sunshine amounts for each month for a particular location by themselves are not very useful. But when planning a holiday to that location, charts showing the average sunshine hours and rainfall amounts for each month can help you plan when to go and what clothes to take with you (and if you might need an umbrella!).

How can an athlete's training data be turned into meaningful information?

ACTIVITY

At the start of this lesson you were asked to think about the different data you use. Make a list of the data you regularly use and identify how it is structured – for example, by using records and fields. Also consider for each type of data you use, what the raw unprocessed data consists of and how that data can become information. You could use a table like this (an example has been completed).

Raw data	Structure (Fields)	Content	Information
Football scores	Team Match date Score Points	Liverpool 3/3/2018 1, 0 3	• Position of each team in the league table and recent changes (move up or down a place) • Likelihood of winning the league or relegation • Eligibility for European competitions • Comparison of performance with other teams and over the season (getting better or worse)

CHECK MY LEARNING

Give the four main characteristics of data and the four main characteristics of information.

How can data be turned into information? Give two examples of how a hospital might take data and turn it into information.

How to present information

In this lesson you will look at the different ways that information can be represented and the situations in which it might be used.

Text

This book contains examples of information represented as text. Text is widely used to present information in books, on websites, in reports and in many other types of documents. Text can provide large or small amounts of information, which can be very detailed. However, it can take a long time to write detailed text. Text also provides a permanent record (whereas spoken – unrecorded – information does not) and can be used in noisy environments where it may be hard to hear someone speaking. However, text by itself can be difficult to understand unless it is supported by pictures or diagrams, as in an instruction book or manual. You also need to understand the language the text is written in.

Text is often used where **qualitative information** needs to be presented. Qualitative information is about the qualities that can be described but cannot easily be measured or represented by numbers. For example, if you asked everyone in your class to cook a meal and then had a tasting session to decide which was the best, the information collected about how good the meal tastes would be qualitative. This might be collected in the form of a list of people's comments about the meal.

Qualitative information is descriptive and is usually collected in a documentary format using word-processed documents, notes or audio or video recordings. A review of a new computer game in a magazine, blog or podcast is an example of qualitative information in the form of a word-processed document (printed in the magazine or uploaded on to the blog) or an audio recording (for the podcast).

Numbers

Numbers are commonly used to represent information. This is sometimes called **quantitative information**. This is information that can be measured and is best represented by numbers, rather than by text. For example, if you measured the height of everyone in your class then this would be quantitative data.

Quantitative data can have statistical methods applied to it. For example, you can calculate the average height of people in your class by totalling all the heights and dividing the total by the number of people you measured.

Large quantities of either text or numbers are not easy to understand and identify the key information so several other methods can be used to represent information that makes it easier to understand.

Tables

Tables are a useful way to represent both text and numbers where they can be divided into different groups or categories. Tables provide a grid with rows and columns and the information can be split into different categories using either the rows or the columns or both. Figure 2.3 shows an example of a table.

Sales figures by region

Region	South	Midlands	North
Quarter 1	£2,896	£3,865	£4,084
Quarter 2	£2,956	£3,685	£4,218
Quarter 3	£3,019	£3,482	£4,188
Quarter 4	£2,986	£3,384	£4,295

◘ Figure 2.3: Which region has increasing sales, and which has decreasing?

Graphs and charts

Graphs and charts are commonly used to summarise numerical information. Trying to understand what large amounts of numerical data are telling you can be hard. For example, if you look at a company's sales data in numerical form it can be difficult to see if, over a period of time, sales are increasing or decreasing. However, when the data is displayed using a chart it can be much easier to spot trends and changes in sales amounts. Figure 2.4 shows an example graph.

Sales figures by region

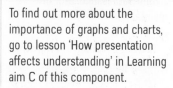

■ Figure 2.4: Why is the increase or decrease in sales easier to see in the graph than in the table?

Infographics

In some situations we may need to present information that cannot easily be represented with a single table or graph by using an **infographic**.

An infographic will usually only consist of a single page (either of printed paper or a web page).

Infographics provide a useful and quick summary of important information; however, infographics may not be suitable to present data that is complex or needs a lot of explanation.

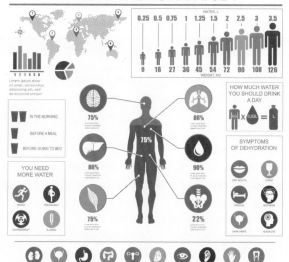

■ Which methods have been used to present information in this infographic?

LINK IT UP

To find out more about the importance of graphs and charts, go to lesson 'How presentation affects understanding' in Learning aim C of this component.

KEY TERMS

Infographics combine several methods of presenting complex information, such as graphs, diagrams, images and tables, in a brief, clear and visual way.

ACTIVITY

Sanjay is in Year 10. He has been at Greenwood Academy since he was 11 years old. He has been studying maths, English and IT since Year 7 but he only started taking German in Year 9. On average, he has missed four school days a year through sickness. There are progress assessments in every subject twice per term.

1   What would be the best way to represent data about Sanjay's progress in maths since year 7 and in German over the past three months?

2   What would be the best way to represent the data about his absence? As numbers, tables, charts or an infographic?

3   Explain why your chosen method of representation is the best one.

CHECK MY LEARNING

Give the benefits and drawbacks of presenting data in a variety of different ways, including text, tables, graphs and infographics.

Making data suitable for processing

GETTING STARTED

Have you created a new password when registering on a website recently? Were you asked to enter the password twice? Why was this done? What problem might occur if this was not done?

KEY TERMS

Verification involves entering data more than once to ensure the entries are the same.

Validation involves testing that the input data conforms to certain rules.

Valid data is correct or suitable.

Invalid data is incorrect or unsuitable.

There is a concept in computing called GIGO, which stands for 'garbage in, garbage out'. If the data you input into a system for processing is incorrect then the output from the system will also be incorrect. It is very important that every precaution is taken to ensure that the data being input into a system is as accurate and error free as possible.

The two main methods for checking that data being input into a system is sensible are **verification** and **validation**. Data can be input into a system for processing either by a human operator for example, by someone completing an online customer registration on an e-commerce website, or electronically from an existing electronic data file. Either way, validation can be used to ensure the data input is **valid** and any **invalid** data is rejected.

Validation methods

Validation involves testing that the input data conforms to certain rules. Testing can be used with some types of data input where it is possible to identify invalid inputs using rules. Dates are good examples; if you enter your date of birth as 32/8/2004 it is clearly a mistake since the rules for dates state that 32 is not a valid number for the day. If the month is 8 (August) then the day must be in the range 1–31. Of course, passing a validation test does not guarantee the data is correct; a date of birth may be a valid date, but it can still be the wrong date of birth for the person.

Table 2.1 shows several different validation methods.

◼ Table 2.1: Validation medthods

Validation method	Description
Range check	This can be used for numerical entries that must fall within a certain range. The date example given above is a range check since the day part of the date must fall in the range 1–31 and the month part must be in the range 1–12. It can also be used with text entries, such as between A and F.
Type check	This is used to ensure data is of the right data type. The most common data types are text, numeric and date. The text data type will typically accept any kind of data, including numbers, and so might be used for names, postcodes, phone numbers, etc. It might seem odd that phone numbers should be text, but since they are never used in calculations and commonly start with a zero, phone numbers should use a text data type. Numeric data types will only accept numbers, and date data types will only accept valid dates.
Lookup check	In some cases the input data must be from a list of valid inputs that is provided. A postcode is an example of this. The Post Office provides a list of valid postcodes so any postcode input to a system should be on the list. Many online services validate registering customers' postcodes against this list to simplify address entry and ensure a valid address is used.
Presence check	Some data entry fields cannot be left empty (for example, when registering for an online service, you must enter your family name). A presence check will make sure the field contains an entry, although it cannot check that whatever is entered in the fields is correct (for example, if you spell your family name incorrectly a presence check will not detect this as it is only checking that something has been entered in the field).
Length check	If the input data must be of a certain length, then any input that is shorter or longer than the required length should be rejected. An example of this would be mobile telephone numbers. Currently UK mobile numbers are 11 digits long; if a number is input that is longer or shorter than this then it must be an invalid number.

Register new account

Name* Last Name

Address*

City*

Phone Number

Email*

* - required fields

Create Account Cancel

◼ A required field is usually denoted by an asterisk

Verification methods

Unlike validation, which checks the input against certain rules, verification ensures that the input is checked more than once. A common example of this is when entering a new password. You are usually asked to enter the new password twice. The two entries you make are compared to ensure that they are the same. This helps prevent typing errors that would create a password that could not be used (remember when typing passwords they are usually starred out so you can't see any errors).

Another example of double entry verification is a stock take in a warehouse where stock amounts are entered twice, perhaps by two different people. However, this method does not guarantee all mistakes are avoided.

Another form of verification is proofreading. This is normally used in a slightly different situation in that it is used to check documents, such as reports, for spelling and grammar errors, rather than for checking input data before processing. Nevertheless, it is an important technique for reducing errors in documentary information. It is easy to make mistakes when typing text, so proofreading involves reading what you have written again to check for any errors. However, proofreading is no guarantee that errors are removed; often we read what the text *should* say, not what it *actually* says. Also, proofreading your own work is hard because you tend to read what you meant to say and miss subtle errors (such as typing 'form' rather than 'from').

◘ **Would you find it useful to print out the document you were proofreading?**

Collecting data

Organisations need to make many decisions about how they run their business and how changes might affect them. For example, they might want to know if the business should increase or reduce prices, or what effect changes in wages, interest rates or currency exchange rates might have. Collecting and analysing data can help an organisation make these decisions and predict the impact changes can have on the business.

Data collection and data collection features

There are two main categories of data collection methods, which are based on how the data is sourced.

- Primary data – data that is collected directly from the original source is referred to as primary data. You can easily collect primary data yourself by creating a survey and asking people to complete it.
- Secondary data – data that is collected by organisations other than the people using the data is known as secondary data. For example, if you wanted to research population growth in certain areas of the UK you could use data collected by the government in the national census. Since you have not directly collected this data it is considered secondary data.

Using primary data means you have direct control over the data collected and its accuracy. However, it also means you need to have the resources available to collect, verify, store and process the data. In some cases, secondary sources must be used because it is not economically viable to collect primary data. When using either primary or secondary data, several features of the data collection need to be considered.

◻ Table 2.2: Features of data collection

What methods were used?	Primary data can be collected using surveys with set questions, either:
	• in person by a researcher (on the phone or face to face) • using a website form for respondents to complete.
	Primary data can also be collected by interviews, observations or by analysing documents. The data can be collected automatically, for example:
	• temperature, rain and wind sensors to collect weather data • barcode scanning at the supermarket checkout • data about visitors to websites (including location of visitor, the browser software they are using, which site they came from) • more detailed personal data (e.g. address, age, gender) can be collected if the website asks visitors to register.
How large was the sample?	This is how much data is collected.
	• For a survey (primary data) the sample size is the number of people who respond. • For secondary data the sample size will be set by whoever originally collected the data.
	The benefit of a small sample size is that it is relatively quick and easy to collect. However, a small sample may not be representative of the real situation. The larger the size of the sample the more likely it is that the results will be accurate.
Who was in the sample?	When collecting data from people (as opposed to automatic data collection) you need to think about who you will ask to complete the questionnaire. If you want your results to reflect the general population, you need to make sure your sample is representative of the general population; for example:
	• a mix of gender types • a mix of people from different age groups • a range of educational backgrounds • a range of ethnic backgrounds.
Where the data was collected?	The geographical location that the data is collected from may affect the results.
	• People who live in the countryside are likely to have quite different views about plans for new buildings than those who live in the city. • A survey collecting data about people's eating habits would get different results from people living in the UK than from people living in China.
When the data was collected?	Primary data collection is likely to be current, unless you decide to use a survey you completed some time ago.
	Secondary data may not be up to date. You need to check when the data was first collected. Unless you specifically want to use historical data, you would need to make sure the data is current.

Big data

'Big data' refers to the way in which many organisations collect large quantities of data. Much of this is collected automatically via the organisation's transaction processing systems, such as e-commerce websites or supermarket checkout systems. Big data typically:

- involves systems that contain very large volumes of data (multiple terabytes)
- includes many different varieties of data (text, images, audio/video)
- requires data to be processed very quickly.

Large volumes of data are collected by many systems that people interact with daily.

- Social media websites – collect data about their users, including the material they post on the site, groups or pages they interact with (liking pages, retweeting etc.) and the time and geographical location of their activity.
- Supermarkets – loyalty schemes collect data about the items users purchase.
- Mobile networks – they are legally required to store data about calls their users make and texts sent. Mobile phone networks can also collect data about your location.
- Digital television – can monitor your viewing habits, downloads and subscriptions.
- E-commerce websites – collect data about the products you browse for and the items you purchase.
- Search engines – collect data about the things you search for.
- ATM/cash machines – banks collect data about the date, time and location cash is withdrawn.
- Wi-Fi access points – when you register to use a public Wi-Fi access point data is collected about you, your email address, location etc.

The data collected by these systems is often used to analyse customer habits and interests. This information can be used to build detailed customer profiles, which can be used for targeted adverts.

You may have noticed that if you search for an item or browse for it on an e-commerce website, adverts for that or similar items will start to appear on other websites. This data can also be used to identify purchasing trends, such as items that are often purchased together, which can be used by retailers in store layout and advertising.

LINK IT UP

For more about the reliability and quality of collected information, go to lesson 'Why quality is important' in Learning aim A of this component.

DID YOU KNOW?

Credit and debit card transactions in the UK take place at a rate of around 1 billion a month, with each transaction requiring authorisation by a bank within a few seconds.

ACTIVITY

In small groups, discuss the data that is collected about you by, for example, social media sites, such as Facebook® or Twitter® , and devices, such as your mobile phone and fitness trackers.

1 What does this data tell the collecting organisations about you? Are you happy for this data to be collected?

2 What ways could this data be used? Are there ways that it could be misused?

3 Working in small groups, consider how you might collect data in the following scenarios. You need to decide on:
- the type of data collection (primary or secondary)
- the method of data collection
- the size of the sample
- who is in the sample (if relevant)
- when and where the data will be collected.

Scenarios

A You want to investigate the effects of global warming in the area where you live.

B A business website owner has asked you to find out where people who visit the website are located and what kind of device (e.g. mobile or desktop) they use to access the site.

C You are planning to develop a computer game and you want to know what type of games people play the most and what are the most popular devices for game playing.

CHECK MY LEARNING

Give three ways that primary data can be collected. Give a benefit and drawback of each.

Each week 5,000 people use a shopping centre. How would you collect information from a sample of these shoppers? What issues would you need to consider?

Give three ways you can try to ensure the results of data collection represent the views of the public.

Why quality is important

To make good decisions, both in business and in life, people need quality information.

The quality of information

How we define the quality of information is determined by a number of factors, such as how and when it was collected and who collected it.

Source/collection method

There are several ways a survey can be presented. For example, in person, over the telephone or via an online form.

- If secondary data collection methods are used, there needs to be confidence that the data that has been collected by the third party is correct and accurate.
- If primary data collection is to be used, then methods need to be chosen that ensure the results are correct.

Whichever method is used to complete the survey, it should be noted that people may not always give honest answers. This is especially the case if the survey is completed in person rather than by completing a form, or if the person completing the survey is required to give their name. The type of questions may also influence the honesty of answers. For example, people generally under-report calorie and alcohol intake and over-report the amount of exercise taken.

Accuracy

The accuracy of data will often depend on the methods of collection. Primary methods that use electronic techniques can often be very accurate. For example, when your shopping is scanned at the supermarket, the scanner reads the barcode on each product and looks up the item on a database of products; therefore the list of items that are purchased is usually 100 per cent accurate. Another example is the accelerometer in fitness watches and smartphones that counts steps with a reasonable degree of accuracy and allows activities such as walking and running to be recorded, trends identified and comparisons made with other fitness enthusiasts.

When people enter data the opportunity for error increases. This is one reason why validation and verification methods are used, but they cannot prevent all input errors.

Age

It is important to know the age of the data; in other words, how long ago it was originally collected.

Many aspects of business and life can change very quickly and so data collected several years ago might not accurately reflect a current situation. For example, if you research rapidly changing areas, such as the internet or mobile phone usage, you need to use the very latest data as data collected just a few years ago will no longer be accurate.

Completeness

Completeness is about having all the data needed to make a decision. For example, if you have a job interview on a particular date and time, but you don't know how long it takes to get to the location, then you don't have all the information you need to decide what time to leave home.

GETTING STARTED

In small groups, discuss what might happen if inaccurate information was used to make decisions. For example, suppose an inaccurate report came out that suggested that cycling was damaging to your health. What kind of decisions might be made by governments, local councils and individuals based on that inaccurate information?

■ What are the benefits and drawbacks of carrying out a survey through an online form?

■ Some insurance policies require a small GPS black box to be installed in the car to measure driver performance. What data do you think a black box can collect?

LINK IT UP

To find out more about validation and verification, go to lesson 'Making data suitable for processing' in Learning aim A of this component.

When using secondary sources, you may find a data source that relates to the area you are interested in but has aspects of the data missing, so for the application you have in mind, it is incomplete.

Another possibility is that you design a survey to collect data from people but when you analyse the results you realise there are questions that you failed to include in the design of the survey.

Amount of detail

Detailed data provides individual facts about something. For example, detailed sales data would have figures for individual sales rather than just totals by region, salesperson or day. The amount of detail in the data needs to be appropriate for the application that uses it.

If the data is too detailed it will be difficult to spot trends. The data may need to be summarised or presented in a different format (e.g. a graph) to make its meaning clearer.

Alternatively, if the data lacks detail you may not be able to use it for its intended purpose. For example, if a large retailer was considering which of its many stores throughout the UK needed further development and which might be closed, then data about the sales made in recent years for each region of the UK would not have sufficient detail as the retailer would need sales figures for the individual stores.

Format/presentation

The data can be formatted in various ways, such as in a table or graph. If the data is poorly formatted or presented, then it may make it hard to interpret and to make decisions using the data. For example, lots of numbers presented in a table can be hard to make sense of but may be much clearer as a chart.

Volume

The amount of data collected can have a major impact on the results. If you just ask four people what their favourite computer game is, you are not likely to get an accurate idea of the most popular computer games across the UK. However, if you ask 400 people you might get a more accurate picture. The more people you ask, the more accurate the results are likely to be.

This also applies to secondary data collection. For example, if you wanted to look at the effect of global warming on the UK climate and you took temperature data from the Met Office (the government organisation that collects weather data and makes forecasts) for two locations in the UK over three months, you would not get a very accurate idea of the overall UK climate. You would need to sample many more locations, over many years to get a reasonably accurate picture.

Who uses data modelling?

Organisations need to make many different decisions about how they run their business. Data modelling can help organisations understand the impact these decisions might have on their business.

Creating a **data model** involves setting up relationships between data; for example, there is a relationship between spending money and savings. The more money you spend the less savings you will have. Data models can be used by organisations or individuals to help them plan by allowing them to investigate how changes can affect them, such as increases in prices, reductions in expenditure, consumer spending, changes to taxes, etc.

Sectors and uses

A wide range of different business sectors use data models to help them plan and run their business. Table 2.3 includes some examples.

KEY TERMS

Data models are a way of showing the relationships between data and investigating the possible outcomes of change.

☐ Table 2.3: How business sectors use data models

Sector	Examples of companies and data collected	How data modelling can be used in decision-making
Transport	Virgin Trains, Ryanair Passenger numbers by route, day and time	Where and when to adapt transport schedules to meet changing demands. For example, where a new housing estate has been built the frequency and capacity of buses serving the area may need to be adjusted.
Education	Schools and colleges Student progress, grades, attendance	When students need additional support or other interventions. For example, where learners' grades are falling, catch-up classes may be needed.
Retail	Tesco, John Lewis Sales of individual items by store, items currently in stock	Predicting when item stock will fall to the level when it needs to be reordered from the supplier. By using supplier lead-time data, items can be ordered in time to prevent stock running out (called 'just-in-time' ordering). Data from loyalty schemes can be used to target customers for an offer or adverts they might be interested in based on their purchasing history.
Banking	Barclays, Nationwide Customer financial history	Financial management involving estimating the risk of loaning a customer money based on their financial history.
Entertainment	Sony Music Number of music tracks or films downloaded	Can show the types of bands/music that record companies should sign up and promote and the types of films that companies should invest in making.
Government	Population growth/decline in different parts of the country	Can be used to analyse changes in the population to plan for public services. For example, where new schools, hospitals and other public services might be needed because of population growth.
Health care	NHS Patient numbers arriving at Accident and Emergency (A&E) department by hour, day, week and month	Where to deploy staff during busy periods. Training appropriate numbers of staff to meet the future demand.
Construction	Progress on a building project against plan	When to order materials so they are available when required (another example of just-in-time ordering). Ensuring workmen with relevant skills are scheduled to be on site when required.

Communication	BT, Vodafone Data traffic in different parts of the country	Where to increase capacity by upgrading the network to meet increasing demand. For example, if data from network equipment shows very high loading or that customers are getting low individual download speeds, then installing additional networking equipment or cabling can be justified.
Health and safety	Local councils Accident data, including location, time/date and cause of accident	Where to implement accident reduction measures. For example, if accident statistics show that a road junction has had a lot of accidents, then changes to the road layout, such as using traffic lights, a mini roundabout or other traffic calming measures, might be considered.

Case study – airline seat pricing

The prices airlines charge for seats on a flight are set using a complex data model. Most airlines do not have fixed pricing for a route but use dynamic pricing – where prices change over time using a data model. The model considers all sorts of different factors. The cost of flying an aeroplane to a destination includes several things, from the cost of fuel (which can vary a lot over time) and the cost of the wages of the crew to the charges airports make for the aircraft to land and the cost of buying and maintaining the aeroplane itself.

There are other factors as well. One is the type of route – for example, flights from London to Majorca are mostly taken by holidaymakers. Typically, people on holiday will tend to book their flight some time before the holiday starts, so the fares will start off quite high to take advantage of that, then if the flight still has space closer to the departure date, the price will be dropped to try to fill the plane. However, on a route that is mostly used by business people – for example, London to Frankfurt – prices may start off low to try to fill up the plane, then close to the departure date prices rise quite sharply as business travellers will be willing to pay a premium for a last-minute booking. The overall aim of the pricing model is to maximise the income an airline can make from each flight. However, airlines operate in a highly competitive market, so it is also important that the model keeps the prices competitive.

■ Can you think of any other real-life scenarios where a complex data model is used?

ACTIVITY

Select one of the sectors from Table 2.3 and imagine it needs to make a decision of some kind. For example, the government might want to know if it should build a bypass to divert traffic around your town, or a local bicycle shop might be wondering if it should start to sell electric bikes.

Make a list of the types of data the organisation might want to collect to help it decide; for example, the bicycle shop might want to know how many electric bikes have been sold recently, what kind of people might be interested in an electric bike, how much they would be willing to pay, etc.

For each item of information you need to list:
- where it will be collected from
- the data collection methods and features that are relevant.

CHECK MY LEARNING

What is a data model?

Data security for individuals

Modern life involves the recording of large quantities of data about many aspects of people's lives: where they are, what they spend money on and who they communicate with. In this lesson we look at possible security threats that individuals face.

In this lesson we look at threats related to the data collected by organisations about individuals, which can be annoying or unpleasant and might cause distress or damage. There are many different threats, and their impact can range from minor to major.

Invasion of privacy

With so much data about people's private lives stored on computer systems there is a potential threat to their privacy. Mobile phone service providers, for example, keep records about what numbers you called, for how long and when. This information could be used to build up a picture of your private life and who you communicate with.

Information collected by banks about our credit and debit card purchases and other transactions, as well as data collected by retailers about our purchases, mean that a comprehensive record of our lives exists across a variety of computer systems. This can lead to concerns about privacy, how the information might be used and the problems that might be caused if it fell into the wrong hands.

◘ What could a retailer do with the data it has collected about you?

While in most situations this data is collected and used for legitimate reasons, the potential exists for this data to be misused. This can sometimes just be annoying, such as promotional emails or letters. However, there are also possibilities that data collection may cause distress or damage – for example, by encouraging people who are already in debt to take on additional financial commitments such as loans.

Many people willingly contribute to the amount of data held about them by using social media sites, such as Facebook or Instagram®, to post personal information about themselves, such as their date of birth, where they live and work and when they are away on holiday. Those with malicious intentions, such as stalkers, burglars or cyberbullies, could potentially use this information.

Fraud

Data held by organisations could potentially be used for fraudulent purposes, such as obtaining money illegally, which would cause severe distress.

ACTIVITY

What is ID theft? How does it occur and what can you do to avoid it? Research this topic and produce a poster or infographic reminding people of the dangers of ID theft and the precautions they need to take.

Targeting vulnerable groups

With so much data available about individuals, some of which may be publicly accessible on social media sites, people with malicious intentions can target vulnerable groups, such as young people, elderly people and people with disabilities. Elderly people, for example, are often unfamiliar with technology and can be vulnerable to scams, such as unsuitable financial investments. Young people may share information on social media, which could result in data about them being collected and shared with third parties. People with disabilities may share information that may lead to them being targeted by specific adverts.

 What information do you and your friends share on social media?

Inaccurate information

With so much data about us and our lives held on computer systems, the consequences of inaccurate information can be quite serious. For example, when moving to a new house you need to change the address that your bank has for you. The easiest way to do this is via your online banking site when you log in. However, if you accidently enter the address incorrectly and letters your bank send to you are returned to the bank, the bank will block your account and you will need to contact them to correct the error.

Errors in computerised billing systems are not uncommon, with customers occasionally receiving bills that are clearly incorrect.

ACTIVITY

Working in small groups, research the requirements of the current data protection laws and create a poster reminding individuals and organisations about its main requirements.

CHECK MY LEARNING

In pairs, take turns to think of data which is collected about you or your family and then have your partner think of a way in which that data could be misused that is annoying or potentially harmful.

DID YOU KNOW?

A woman in the US received a household electricity bill for $284bn (over £200 billion)!

In 2017, some 'smart' energy meters installed in UK homes were reported to be showing energy usage worth many thousands of pounds in a single day. Concerns have also been raised about privacy issues and smart meters. Search for 'smart meters' to find out more about the issues related to smart energy usage meters.

Learning aim A: assessment practice

How you will be assessed

Now that you have studied all the topics in Learning aim A, you need to show that you understand the different data collection methods and features that are used and how these have an impact on the quality of the data and the decisions made using that data. You need to investigate the methods and features of data collection in relation to two sectors.

Your teacher will give you an assignment to complete and will explain the evidence you need to provide and the submission date.

Try the following tasks to help you build the skills and knowledge you will need to complete your assignment.

CHECKPOINT

Strengthen
- Identify four different types of data collection methods.
- Describe five features of each data collection method.
- Describe the ways different sectors use data collection.
- Explain how collected data can be used in decision-making.

Challenge
- Explain how the choice of data collection methods can impact on the quality of data collected.
- Give four different types of decisions that are made using data.
- Evaluate the suitability of different types of data collection methods to the requirements of particular sectors.
- Explain the importance of the quality of data collected in two different sectors.

TIPS

Your teacher may suggest the two sectors to use or you may select them yourself. Do some research into the sector, what it collects data for and how it uses it to make decisions.

If you are selecting the two sectors yourself, try to choose sectors that are quite different in the way they collect and use data; for example, if one of the sectors mostly collects data by primary methods, it would be useful if the other used mainly secondary data so you have a range of information.

TIPS

In both assessment activities it is important to relate what you say about the two sectors to examples.

ASSESSMENT ACTIVITY 1 | LEARNING AIM | A

Assessment of data collection methods

Assess the data collection methods and features used in two different sectors.

The two different sectors you could use are:
- retail – some supermarkets use loyalty cards that collect a lot of information about their customers and what they buy
- education – most schools and colleges collect data on the performance (targets, grades, attendance, etc.) of their students.

For each of the chosen sectors you need to assess the following.
- Use of primary or secondary data collection methods.
- Data collection features, including:
  □ size of sample
  □ who was in the sample
  □ where the data was collected
  □ when the data was collected
  □ data collection methods (in other words, how the data was collected).

Working in small groups, make a list of the data that is likely to be collected in the two chosen sectors. For each data item or group of items:

- say how the data is collected
- list the features, such as the amount of data, when it is collected and who collects it.

For each data item or group of items think of at least one way the data could be used to help the organisation make decisions. For example, when a supermarket loyalty card is registered the customer enters their gender. Knowing the gender split of its customers could help the supermarket decide how to target and market its products and the promotions it offers to customers.

ASSESSMENT ACTIVITY 2　LEARNING AIM　A

Discuss how data is used in decision-making in two different sectors.

Using the same two sectors that you have used for Activity 1, you need to discuss how the data they collect can be used to help them make decisions.

You also need to discuss the following.

- How the choice of data collection method and features can have an impact on the accuracy of the data.
- How the data collection methods and the accuracy of the data can have an impact on the decision-making process.

TIPS

When you answer questions, you need to make sure that you respond in the right way. You will find it helpful if you become familiar with the words examiners use to indicate the type of answer you should give. For example, 'assess' and 'discuss'.

Assess – when you assess something you are required to cover the different factors that answer the question and then choose which are the most important or relevant. You are also required to give a conclusion by providing reasons why these are the most important or relevant.

Discuss – when you discuss something you need to look at all aspects – for example, if you discuss people working from home you might look at some of the benefits and drawbacks. You might even say what you think about it.

TAKE IT FURTHER

Consider the possible privacy, legal and security issues for the collection of data in your chosen sectors. What do the data collecting organisations need to do to comply with the legal requirements when collecting the data? What are the privacy and security issues for the people about whom the data is collected?

TIPS

When discussing how the accuracy and quality of data might have an impact on decision-making, consider how the data is collected and how errors or inaccuracies may occur.

Think about what decisions might be based on that data and, using specific examples, suggest ways in which those errors or inaccuracies may affect the decisions that are made based on that data.

When looking at data collection methods, accuracy, and how these impact on the decision-making process, you need to provide detailed, justified conclusions to access the higher grades.

What is a dashboard?

The focus of Learning aim B is the creation of a **dashboard**. First, we need to understand what a dashboard is and how dashboards are used.

Dashboards

When dealing with large quantities of data it can be very difficult to pick out the most important information. A variety of techniques can be used to filter out unimportant data, as well as summarise and display relevant information. This can include using tables, graphs and formatting for emphasis. A dashboard can be a webpage, database or spreadsheet. It provides an 'at a glance' view of the key information presented using visual representations.

The data used in a dashboard is refined, manipulated and presented to make it easier to understand. Dashboards often allow the user to customise the display so, for example, they can select the data that is particularly relevant to them.

Health tracking dashboard

Many people who are keen to keep fit use phone and smartwatch apps to track their daily step count and other physical activities such as cycling or fitness classes. These apps often summarise the data they collect using a dashboard.

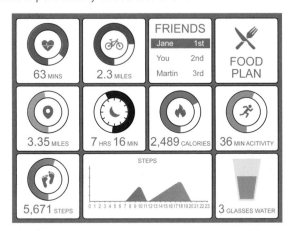

What information can you gather about the user from this dashboard?

Student dashboard

Most schools track student performance, targets, grades, attendance, etc. Over a whole term this is a lot of data, which can be summarised in various ways using graphs, percentages or averages. There are a number of database systems designed specifically for tracking student data. They can provide a dashboard view showing a summary of the key information for each student. This can be particularly useful when reviewing individual students' progress, and, for example, at parents' evenings.

Example dashboard

Figure 2.5 shows a simple dashboard that will be referred to throughout this Learning aim to demonstrate some of the techniques that can be used to create a dashboard. It uses data from the Met Office website, collected from one of many weather stations in the UK. (This example uses data from the Heathrow Airport weather station.)

The dashboard allows you to select any month and it will display the average maximum and minimum temperature, rainfall and sunshine hours from the ten years of data that has been collected. The dashboard also displays charts showing temperature, rainfall and sunshine data for each of the ten years for the chosen month.

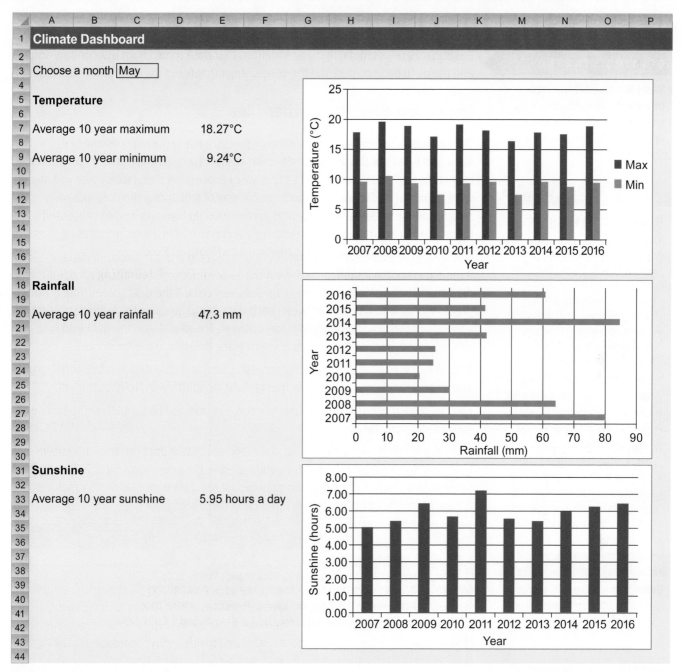

■ Figure 2.5: What could this dashboard be used for?

In small groups, develop an outline design for a dashboard of your own displaying data on a subject of your choice. For example, you could create a dashboard for a sports team you follow. This could show the score from the last game they played, plus a few recent games presented in a table, their position in the league table along with the points they have and details of the next game they will play. You could use a graph to show how their points have increased over the last month or so, perhaps shown along with their main rivals.

As well as the design and layout of the dashboard, research where your dashboard could source its data.

Refer to one of the dashboards you found at the start of the lesson. Where does the data for the dashboard come from and how is it collected? Does the dashboard allow the user to customise it in some way (for example, to change the data that is displayed)? If so, how?

Importing data

Dashboards rely on data; in many situations that data comes from a secondary source and needs to be imported into the spreadsheet that feeds the data to the dashboard.

Importing data from other files

Data can usually be imported from the original source into a spreadsheet like Microsoft Excel® or Google Sheets™ quite easily. However, there are a variety of text formats (such as plain unformatted text, word-processing files, tables) that you might want to import and there needs to be some way of structuring the data into rows and columns in the spreadsheet. A typical example would be using a word-processed table. This kind of data is very easy to copy and paste from a word-processing program like Microsoft Word into a spreadsheet such as Microsoft Excel.

If the data is not in a table then there must be some way of **delimiting** (dividing) the data so it can be placed in different spreadsheet cells. If the data comes from a word-processed file and has tabs between each data item, then, like the table data, it can easily be copied and pasted into a spreadsheet. The tabs divide the data into fields, so the spreadsheet software uses these to place the data into different cells.

Data in text files (rather than word-processed files) is a little different but both Google Sheets and Excel provide facilities that make it straightforward to import them.

You can search online to find details of how to import text files into the spreadsheet software you are using.

Comma delimited files are the most common type of text data file; they are known as CSV (Comma Separated Values) files and have the file extension .CSV. CSV files are the same as any other text file, but commas delimit the data items. Using CSV files in Excel is easy as its one of the file formats that Excel can directly open.

GETTING STARTED

What are the differences between a text file, a word-processing file and a spreadsheet file?

DID YOU KNOW?

Text files come in a variety of different formats.
- Plain text files contain text and nothing else; these files often end with the file extension .txt and can be created by programs such as Notepad.
- Word-processing files are much more complex and contain lots of formatting information, such as font type and size, bold, italics and page formatting information, such as margins and page breaks. You can't create or edit word-processed files in text editors such as Notepad; you must use a word-processing program like Microsoft Word.

KEY TERMS

Delimiting is the use of one or more characters to separate one data item from another.

DID YOU KNOW?

You can easily create text files using the Notepad program that is provided with Windows. Just type 'Notepad' in the Windows search box to find the program.

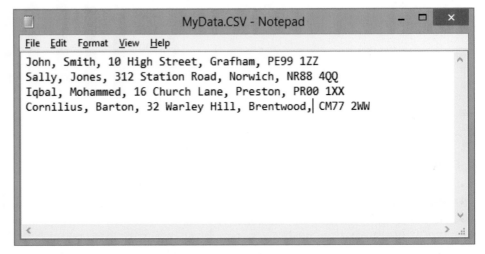

◼ Importing a comma separated text file

Importing data from the internet

Webpage tables can also be imported into spreadsheets. First, you need to use your internet browser to find the webpage that has the table you want to import. Then use the data import features in the spreadsheet software you are using to import the data. Excel has several options for importing data under the *Data* menu. Google Sheets has a function called *ImportHTML*. If you search online for ImportHTML then you can find detailed instructions on how to use it.

Text to columns

The *Text to Columns* feature found on the *Data* menu of Excel and Google Sheets is useful where you have copied and pasted text from another source (such as a webpage or document) but the data remains in a single column and is not split into separate fields. By selecting the single column of data and using the *Text to Columns* option, the data should be split into separate columns. However, there needs to be some way of separating the data into different fields or columns. As mentioned previously, this is often done using a comma, but the text to columns feature allows you to select other separators such as a dash, full stop or colon.

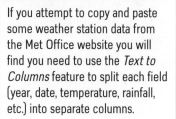

DID YOU KNOW?

If you attempt to copy and paste some weather station data from the Met Office website you will find you need to use the *Text to Columns* feature to split each field (year, date, temperature, rainfall, etc.) into separate columns.

Data sources

To practise importing data you need data sources you can use. There are a number of large data sets available on the internet.

- data.world (https://data.world/) is a site where you can access data created by other people about a wide variety of topics.
- The World Bank (http://www.worldbank.org/) has economic data about every country in the world. You can download a file containing details of a wide variety of development indicators. Search 'World Bank development indicators'.
- UK government (https://data.gov.uk/). You can access a wide range of data collected by the UK government. The site contains data about a wide range of topics, including education, transport, health, government spending, etc.

ACTIVITY

Select data sources from the list provided then try the following.
- Download the files, using different formats where possible (for example, CSV and TXT).
- Open the files using different programs (for example, Word, Excel).
- Make a note of whether it successfully opens or not.
- Make a note of how it looks once opened.

CHECK MY LEARNING

What are the steps required to import a text file into the spreadsheet software you use? Make a step-by-step list.

Spreadsheet formulae

You may already be familiar with spreadsheets but in this Learning aim we will use spreadsheet software to create a dashboard. Spreadsheets use formulae to do a wide range of calculations, including simple arithmetic through to complex statistical and engineering functions.

Structure and format of a spreadsheet

A spreadsheet file is split into a number of **worksheets**. Each worksheet has a table format with columns identified by letters and rows identified by numbers as shown in Figure 2.6. The box at each intersection of a row and column is called a **cell**.

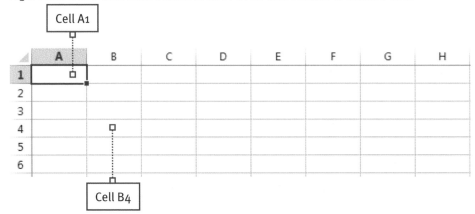

■ Figure 2.6: Have you used a spreadsheet before? What did you use it for?

Common formulae

Within each cell you can enter text or numbers, but formulae provide the real power of a spreadsheet as they allow calculations to be carried out automatically. Formulae must start with an equals sign and can contain numbers and/or references to cells that contain numbers. The arithmetic operators used are as follows.

Add   +   Subtract   –   Multiply   *   Divide   /

An example of a simple formula is shown in Figure 2.7.

Formulae, like the one in Figure 2.7, use actual numbers or cell references (such as B4) and arithmetic operators to do a calculation. Where a cell reference is used, it's the value in that cell that is used in the calculation.

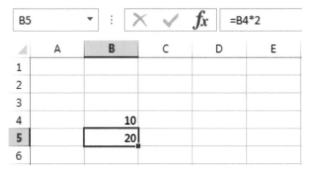

■ Figure 2.7: Which operator is being used?

Creating a formula

When you enter a formula into a spreadsheet cell you will see the result of the calculation shown in the cell, not the formula. (If you see the formula in the cell you may have forgotten to start it with an equals sign or have formula view activated.) If you want to edit a formula, you can do so in the formula bar at the top of the screen, or by double clicking on the cell that contains the formula.

Note that if your formula refers to a cell that contains text, rather than a number, you will get a '#VALUE!' error message in the cell. If this occurs, make sure the formula refers to cells that contain numbers rather than text.

Operator precedence

When using multiple arithmetic operators in the same formula you need to be aware of the order in which the operators are applied (called operator precedence). For example, what is the result of the formula =2+3*4?

You might imagine the operators are applied left to right, so 2+3 is 5 and then 5*4 is 20, but this would be wrong. The multiplication takes precedence over the addition and so it is done first. So 3*4 is 12 then 12+2 is 14. The order of precedence is as follows.

1 Brackets – anything in brackets is calculated first, so =(2+3)*4 would give a result of 20

2 Exponents (powers of) or roots (for example, 42^2 or $\sqrt{8}$)

3 Multiplication and division

4 Addition and subtraction

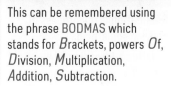

DID YOU KNOW?

This can be remembered using the phrase BODMAS which stands for *B*rackets, powers *O*f, *D*ivision, *M*ultiplication, *A*ddition, *S*ubtraction.

ACTIVITY

Create a simple spreadsheet as shown or use the given spreadsheet at www.pearsonschools.co.uk/techawardDITsupport

	A	B	C	D
1	10			
2	15			
3	20			
4				

1 Write a formula in cell B1 that adds together the values in A1, A2 and A3.

2 Write a formula in cell B2 that subtracts the value in A1 from the value in A3.

3 Write a formula in cell B3 that multiples the value in A2 by 2.5.

4 Write a formula in cell B4 that divides the value in A3 by 3.

5 Write a formula in cell C1 that subtracts 5 from the value in A2 then multiplies it by 4. (Make sure it is done in this order with the subtraction first.)

6 Write a formula in D1 that adds A1 and A2 then multiples the result by A3. What result do you get? Work out the result using a calculator, does it agree with the one in the spreadsheet? If not, why not?

CHECK MY LEARNING

What result would the formula =5*4*(3+8) display?

You enter a formula into a cell, but it displays the result: #VALUE!. What is likely to be the problem? How would you address the problem?

Cell referencing

When creating a formula in a spreadsheet you often reference a cell that contains a value used in the formula. The way spreadsheets copy formulae and automatically change the cell references is known as **replication**. It's a very useful feature but it is important you have a proper understanding of how it works so you can make full use of it.

Relative addressing

There are several ways you can copy a formula from one cell to another. If the cells are next to each other, you can use the cell 'handle', which can be found on the bottom right-hand corner of the currently selected cell. Dragging this will copy the formula across into other cells that you drag over, as shown in Figure 2.8. You can also use the traditional copy and paste options in the *Edit* menu.

When you copy formulae, the spreadsheet modifies the cell references in the formula to reflect the changes in the row and/or column. This is called **relative addressing** as the cell addresses change relative to where the formula is copied.

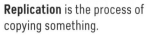

Copying the formula one cell to the right will change the references from column B to C.

	A	B	C	D
1				
2		10	15	35
3		20	25	40
4		=B2+B3		
5				

◘ **Figure 2.8: What would the formulae be if you copied it to D4?**

In most situations, relative addressing is what you need. However, there are some situations where you don't want this. Figure 2.9 shows a spreadsheet with a fixed discount percentage in cell G1 that is to be applied to all the prices in cells D3:D8.

E3 | =D3*G1

	A	B	C	D	E	F	G
1						Discount %	10%
2	Stock No	Price	Quantity	Total	Discount		
3	1223	£13.50	2	£27.00	£2.70		
4	1345	£19.00	5	£95.00			
5	9685	£8.50	3	£25.50			
6	3665	£3.99	6	£23.94			
7	4286	£12.45	8	£99.60			
8	7334	£22.50	3	£67.50			

◘ **Figure 2.9: What do you expect the value in E4 to be when the formula is applied?**

The formula in E3 (=D3*G1) calculates the amount of discount for the first item.

1. If this formula is copied to the row below, relative addressing will change it to =D4*G2.

2. The D4 part of the formula is fine, that is the total price of the next item, but G2 is empty as the discount percentage is in G1.

This is a situation where we want to switch off relative addressing and fix the address to G1, so it does not change.

3. This is done by including dollar signs ($) in front of the column letter and row number we want to fix.

4. The formula becomes =D4*$G$1.

5 When this formula is copied the D$ part of the address changes (since it is a relative address) but the G1 part of the formula stays the same. This is called **absolute addressing**.

Named ranges

As well as using the cell references to identify cells or ranges of cells (such as G1 or D3:D8), you can give cells or ranges a name.

1 Select the cell or range you want to name and from the *Formulas* menu in Excel choose *Define Name*, or in Google Sheets, from the *Data* menu choose *Named ranges*.

2 Use the name you've given the range in your formulae. For example, if you named D3:D8 in the spreadsheet shown in Figure 2.9 'Totals', you could enter the formula =sum(Totals).

3 One advantage of using named ranges is that they are absolute references. If you named the cell G1 in Figure 2.9 'Discount' and then entered the formula =D3*Discount, you can then copy this formula down and it will work as the reference to Discount is absolute.

KEY TERMS

Absolute addresses do not change when the formula is copied. They are created by including a $ sign in front of the column letter and/or row number.

LINK IT UP

To find out more about data, go to lesson 'Data and information' in Learning aim A of this component.

ACTIVITY

Create a spreadsheet as shown, or use the given spreadsheet at www.pearsonschools.co.uk/techawardDITsupport, that calculates how much members of staff at a cafe are paid. There are three waiters at the cafe: Wendy, Sunita and Abdul.

	A	B	C	D	E	F	G
1	**Cafe wages**						
2	Hourly rate of pay						
3	Waiter	Wendy		Suunita		Abdul	
4		Week 1 hours	Week 2 hours	Week 1 hours	Week 2 hours	Week 1 hours	Week 2 hours
5	Hours	36	25	38	40	29	31
6	Pay due						
7							

1 Create a formula in B6 which will multiply the hours worked by the rate of pay (in C2) and which you can copy across the other columns in row 6. Copy the formula and check it correctly calculates everyone's wages.

2 Each employee makes a £5 contribution every week for health insurance which will pay them if they are off sick. Add a title for this in E2, such as 'Insurance' and enter the amount in F2.

3 Add a formula in B7 that will subtract the insurance payment (in F2 – remember to use absolute addressing) from Wendy's week 1 hours (in B6). Copy this formula across to G7 and check that the calculations are done correctly.

4 Give two other examples where relative and absolute addressing are required.

CHECK MY LEARNING

Explain the difference between relative and absolute cell addressing.

What is the difference between the formula =E8+$B2 and =E8+B$2?

Decision-making functions

KEY TERMS

Function is a type of formula that carries out a calculation. Spreadsheets have many different functions than can be used.

Being able to use formulae in a spreadsheet is very useful but an even more powerful tool is the ability to make choices about how the formula works and, for example, to choose different calculations using the IF **function**.

Like formulae, functions start with an equals sign. This is followed by the function name and a set of brackets containing the function's input data. The input data required depends on the function you are using and contains the values or cell references that the function needs to work.

The IF function

IF functions can be used to make a choice based on a test. The test can simply be seeing if a cell contains a particular value. *If* the cell does contain that value, then the function carries out one action; *if* it doesn't, then the function does something different. This is why it is called the 'IF' function.

In the climate dashboard in lesson 'What is a dashboard?', it should only pick out the weather data that applies to the month the user has selected. Figure 2.10 shows just part of the weather data, with the user's selected month shown in G1 (represented as a number, i.e. 2 for February). An IF function is used to pick out only the data that matches the user's selection.

	H5			f_x	=IF(B5=$G$1,C5,0)			
	A	B	C	D	E	F	G	H
1	**Weather Data**					Month	2	
2			Temperature					
3	Year	Month	max	min	af	rainfall	Sunshine	
4	2007	1	10.5	5.1	2	56	56.6#	0
5	2007	2	9.9	3.9	5	92.9	59.3#	9.9
6	2007	3	12.5	4.4	2	43.8	164.7#	0
7	2007	4	18.9	7.7	0	3.6	224.6#	0

◻ Figure 2.10: What do the $ signs in $G$1 do?

The IF function used in the example is explained in Figure 2.11.

The IF function tests the month number (in B5).	If not, then zero is placed in the cell.

$$=IF(B5=\$G\$1,C5,0)$$

To see if it is the same as the month entered by the user (in G1 – absolute referencing is used here so the formula will work when it is copied down the column).	If it is then the maximum temperature (in C5) is placed in the cell.

◻ Figure 2.11: Do you understand how each part of this IF function works?

IF functions can use several different comparison operators in the 'test' argument. The one used in Figure 2.11 is equals (=) but there are several others.

>   Greater than: C6>10 would test the value in C6 to see if it was greater than 10.
<   Less than: F5<G4 would test the value in F5 to see if it was less than the value in G4.

The following comparison operators can also be used.

>= Greater than or equal to   <> Not equal to
<= Less than or equal to   (less than or greater than)

The SUMIF function

SUMIF is a combination of the SUM function and the IF function. The SUM function adds up a range of cells, while the SUMIF function only includes a value from the range if it meets a particular criterion.

The criteria can be a fixed value or a reference to a cell that contains a value. This gives us a better way to pick out the temperatures that match the selected month. Rather than having an IF function for every row in the table of data, we can just use a single SUMIF function at the bottom of the column of data. This is shown in Figure 2.12.

C124				fx	=SUMIF(B4:B123,G1,C4:C123)		
	A	B	C	D	E	F	G	H
1	Weather Data					Month	2	
2			Temperature					
3	Year	Month	max	min	af	rainfall	Sunshine	
118	2016	7	24	14.5	0	16	182.8#	0
119	2016	8	24.7	14.6	0	21.6	201.4#	0
120	2016	9	22.4	13.7	0	42.2	122.1#	0
121	2016	10	15.9	8.7	0	21.6	105.6#	0
122	2016	11	10.5	3.8	3	86.4	77.4#	0
123	2016	12	10.2	3.4	7	10.4	55.1#	0
124			88.5					88.5
125								

■ Figure 2.12: Using the SUMIF function

Here the function only adds up the data (in C4:C123) if the month numbers (in B4:B123) match the criterion, which is the selected month (in G1).

ACTIVITY

1 Create a spreadsheet as shown or use the given spreadsheet at www.pearsonschools.co.uk/techawardDITsupport.

	A	B	C	D	E	F
1	Grade record				Pass mark	45
2	Student names		Paper 1 mark		Passed?	
3	Sumita	Shah	50			
4	Lucy	Burrows	43			
5	Javan	Okeke	62			
6	Oliver	Adams	39			
7	Alice	Spring	46			
8	Alfie	Jenkins	44			

2 Enter an IF formula in E3, which will display the word 'Yes' if the student has achieved the pass mark (in F1) or higher, and 'No' if they have not. Copy the formula down the column.

3 Create a spreadsheet as shown or use the given spreadsheet at www.pearsonschools.co.uk/techawardDITsupport.

	A	B	C	D	E	F
1	Invoice record					
2	Invoice number	Customer	Value	Paid?	VAT due	VAT amount
3	1201	ABC Company	£50.45	No	Yes	
4	1202	Star Corporation	£250.00	Yes	Yes	
5	1203	International Group	£125.25	No	No	
6	1204	Central Trading	£63.80	No	No	
7	1205	Atlantic Co	£167.25	Yes	Yes	
8	1206	East and West	£205.50	No	No	
9		Total owing				
10						

4 Enter a formula in C9 that adds up the values in C3:C8 only if they have not been paid.

5 Some of the invoices need to have VAT added to them. If the invoice has 'Yes' in column E, then use an IF function to calculate the VAT amount in column F (VAT is the value*20%); otherwise just place a zero in that column.

CHECK MY LEARNING

Make a list of the comparison operator symbols and explain what each one does.

Write a brief guide to the IF and SUMIF function, explaining how they work and how they can be used.

Lookup functions

Dashboards often need to extract specific information from a lot of data; therefore, the ability to look up individual data items from a large data table is a very useful feature.

The VLOOKUP function

In the climate dashboard, as well as the averages for temperature, rain and sunshine, a graph is also drawn showing the data for the same month across ten years.

To draw the graph, the data for each weather measurement needs to be extracted from the main table of data and imported into a table showing only the values for the selected month. This can then quite easily be used to draw a chart.

To extract the data from the main table, a VLOOKUP function is used. It is called this because it 'looks up' the data vertically down the columns of the spreadsheet. The way the function can be used is shown in Figure 2.13.

	K6		f_x	=VLOOKUP($G$1,B4:D15,2,FALSE)									
	A	B	C	D	E	F	G	H	I	J	K	L	M
1	Weather Data					Month	2						
2			Temperature										
3	Year	Month	max	min	af	rainfall	Sunshine						
4	2007	1	10.5	5.1	2	56	56.6#	0					
5	2007	2	9.9	3.9	5	92.9	59.3#	9.9		Year	Max	Min	Rainfall
6	2007	3	12.5	4.4	2	43.8	164.7#	0		2007	9.9	3.9	92.9
7	2007	4	18.9	7.7	0	3.6	224.6#	0		2008	11	2	15.4
8	2007	5	17.9	9.7	0	80	149.6#	0		2009	7.8	2.1	69.6
9	2007	6	21.2	12.6	0	63.8	139.7#	0		2010	6.9	1.7	100.4
10	2007	7	21.4	13.1	0	115.2	159.9#	0		2011	10.2	4.8	42.8
11	2007	8	21.5	12.9	0	41	192.6#	0		2012	8	1.3	16.8
12	2007	9	19.9	11.4	0	17.4	141.1#	0		2013	6.7	1.2	32.8
13	2007	10	15.4	8.5	0	37.8	98.4#	0		2014	4.4	10.6	89.8
14	2007	11	11.4	4.6	3	84.8	81.3#	0		2015	8	1.8	38.6
15	2007	12	8.9	3.1	9	44.6	61.4#	0		2016	9.4	2.9	43.8
16	2008	1	10.4	4.7	0	69	60.2#	0		Average	8.23	3.23	54.29
17	2008	2	11	2	7	15.4	130.0#	11					
18	2008	3	10.6	3.7	2	69.8	85.7#	0					

◘ Figure 2.13: Using the VLOOKUP function

The VLOOKUP function needs four different pieces of information to work. Figure 2.14 explains how the function works, with reference to the example in Figure 2.13.

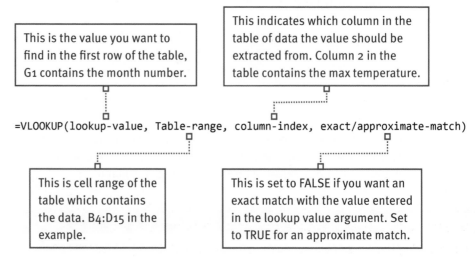

This is the value you want to find in the first row of the table, G1 contains the month number.

This indicates which column in the table of data the value should be extracted from. Column 2 in the table contains the max temperature.

=VLOOKUP(lookup-value, Table-range, column-index, exact/approximate-match)

This is cell range of the table which contains the data. B4:D15 in the example.

This is set to FALSE if you want an exact match with the value entered in the lookup value argument. Set to TRUE for an approximate match.

◘ Figure 2.14: Do you understand how each part of this VLOOKUP function works?

As well as the VLOOKUP function there is an HLOOKUP function. This works in the same way but rather than searching vertically down the rows of a table to find a lookup value and then returning a corresponding value from that row, the HLOOKUP searches horizontally across the columns in a table.

Create a spreadsheet as shown or use the given spreadsheet at www.pearsonschools.co.uk/techawardDITsupport.

	A	B	C	D	E
1	Supermarket stock				
2	Enter code		Quantity in stock		
3					
4	Item code	Description	Price	Quantity	
5	A012	Baked beans	£0.45	308	
6	A015	Coffee	£1.49	250	
7	A023	Dog biscuit	£2.25	175	
8	B145	Orange juice	£0.85	66	
9	B148	Tea bags	£2.49	103	
10	B198	Sausages	£1.95	94	
11	C699	Rice	£0.99	235	
12	C845	Tomato sauce	£1.35	123	
13	C967	Milk	£0.99	56	

In this supermarket stock spreadsheet there is a list of items and the quantity in stock in the table A5:D13 (although the table of stock would be much larger than this). To make checking of stock quick and easy, the user of the spreadsheet would like to enter a stock number in B2 and see the quantity in stock (from the fourth column in the table A5:D13).

1 Create a VLOOKUP formula in E2 that will show the quantity in stock of the item code entered in B2.

2 Look at this HLOOKUP formula and label what each part does.
=HLOOKUP("Tuesday",B2:F6,2,FALSE)

3 If used with the following table of data, what would the result of this HLOOKUP formula be?

	A	B	C	D	E	F
1						
2		Monday	Tuesday	Wednesday	Thursday	Friday
3	Room 1	Science	Maths	Maths	French	English
4	Room 2	English	IT		IT	
5	Room 3	Maths	Business	Science	Maths	Business
6	Room 4	History	French	IT		Science
7						

Give the four pieces of information needed in a VLOOKUP function.

Write a step-by-step guide showing how to use both VLOOKUP and HLOOKUP functions, using examples.

Count functions

GETTING STARTED

Make a list of all the functions you have previously learned about and what they do.

Research three new functions you are unfamiliar with and find out what they do and how to use them.

When dealing with large amounts of data, being able to count items is very useful. Fortunately, there are several functions that can do this for you.

The COUNT function

The COUNT function will count the number of cells in a range that have numbers in them. It won't count them if they have text in them or if they are blank. An example of the COUNT function is shown in Figure 2.15.

B10 fx =COUNT(B3:B9)

	A	B	C	D
1	**Sales**			
2	**Date**	**Value**		
3	16/01/17	£450		
4	17/01/17	£550		
5	18/01/17	£1,250		
6	20/01/17	£125		
7	20/01/17	£2,400		
8	21/01/17	£650		
9	21/01/17	£1,150		
10		7		

Figure 2.15: What result would =COUNT(B3:B6) produce?

In this example, the COUNT function simply counts the number of values contained in the cell range B3:B9.

The COUNTIF function

A very useful variation on the COUNT function is the COUNTIF function. This function allows you to set a criterion for those cells you want to count; for example, you can tell the function only to count those cells that contain values over a certain amount. Figure 2.16 shows how the COUNTIF function has been used to count only those cells that contain values over 1000.

D3 fx =COUNTIF(B3:B9,">1000")

	A	B	C	D	E
1	**Sales**				
2	**Date**	**Value**	**Number of high value sales**		
3	16/01/17	£450		3	
4	17/01/17	£550			
5	18/01/17	£1,250			
6	20/01/17	£125			
7	20/01/17	£2,400			
8	21/01/17	£650			
9	21/01/17	£1,150			
10		7			

Figure 2.16: What result would =COUNTIF(B3:B9, ">500") produce?

The COUNT function will only count numbers; however you can use the COUNTIF to count text values. If you had a list of invoices, each of which was shown as 'paid' or 'unpaid', you could count how many unpaid invoices there are in the list. The COUNTIF function will do that for you and an example is shown in Figure 2.17.

The COUNTBLANK function

In some situations, you might want to know how many cells within a range contain no values. The COUNTBLANK function will do that for you. Like the COUNT function, you only need the range of cells that you want to count the blanks in.

| D11 | | ▾ | : | ✕ | ✓ | fx | =COUNTIF(D3:D9, "Unpaid") |

	A	B	C	D	E
1	Invoices				
2	Invoice No	Sent to	Amount	Status	
3	1263	Smith and Co	£120.00	Paid	
4	1264	ABC Ltd	£75.00	Paid	
5	1265	NorthWest	£235.00	Unpaid	
6	1266	Alpha Systems	£95.00	Paid	
7	1267	Super Services	£329.00	Unpaid	
8	1268	Winston and Jones	£210.00	Unpaid	
9	1269	Z to A corporation	£85.00	Paid	
10					
11			Number unpaid	3	

◾ Figure 2.17: How many unpaid invoices are there?

ACTIVITY

Create a spreadsheet as shown or use the given spreadsheet at www.pearsonschools.co.uk/techawardDITsupport.

	A	B	C	D	E	F	G	H	I
1	Attendance records								
2	Student	ID number	Monday	Tuesday	Wednesday	Thursday	Friday	Number absent	Letter?
3	Allan	1014	1	1		1	1		
4	Patel	1015		1	1	1	1		
5	Jones	1088	1		1		1		
6	Green	1265		1	1	1			
7	Carter	1095	1	1	1	1	1		
8	Elphick	1203		1			1		
9	Lee	1109	1		1	1	1		
10	McCullough	1175	1	1	1	1			
11	Attending								
12	Absent								
13	No of students								

In this attendance spreadsheet there is a '1' in the cell corresponding to the student and day when the student attended; if the student does not attend on a particular date then the cell is left blank.

1 Enter a formula in B13 using the COUNT function to count the number of students on the register.

2 Enter a formula in C11 to count the number of students attending on Monday. Copy it across D11:G11.

3 Enter a formula in C12 using the COUNTBLANK function to count the number of absences. Copy it across D12:G12.

4 Enter a formula using the COUNT function in H3 to work out how many days the student was absent. Copy the formula down through H4:H10.

5 If students are absent for more than two days in a week a letter is sent to their parents/guardians. Enter a formula using the IF function in I3 to display the word 'Letter' in the cell if a letter is required or leave it blank if one is not required. Copy the formula down through I4:I10.

6 How many letters are needed? Enter a formula using the COUNTIF function in I11 showing how many are required.

CHECK MY LEARNING

Write a brief description explaining how the COUNT, COUNTIF and COUNTBLANK functions work.

Give an example for each function.

Logical operators

In some situations, you need to combine several tests. For example, you have previously used an IF function to test if a student has achieved the pass mark. But if a student needed to take two exams, how could you test if the student had passed both? Logical operators allow you to do this.

Logical operators

There are a number of logical operators you can use within your spreadsheets to combine tests within functions; the most common are shown in Table 2.4.

◻ Table 2.4: Logical operators

Operator	Example	Description
AND	=AND(B3>10, B4<5)	Will display TRUE if *both* B3 is greater than 10 *and* B4 is less than 5
OR	=OR(B3>10, B4<5)	Will display TRUE if *either* B3 is greater than 10 *or* B4 is less than 5
NOT	=NOT(B2>10)	Will display FALSE if B2 is greater than 10

By themselves the logical operators are not very useful, but when combined with other functions, such as the IF function, they can be put to good use.

Using logical operators with the IF function

Using the logical operators, it is possible to use the IF function to create formulae that have two tests (two different criteria).

Figure 2.18 shows a spreadsheet where an employee's targets are only achieved when both the sales target and the customer satisfaction target are met. It uses the AND operator to test the two criteria.

fx =if(AND(B6>$B$3,B7>$B$4),"Yes","No")

	A	B	C	D	E
1	IF example				
2	**Targets:**				
3	Sales Target	£5,000			
4	Customer rating	8			
5		Jan	Feb	March	April
6	Sales achieved	£5,600	£4,800	£5,100	£4,950
7	Average customer rating	7.5	8	8.5	7
8					
9	All targets acheived?	No	No	Yes	No

◻ Figure 2.18: How would the results differ if OR was used instead of AND?

In this example there are two targets, one for total sales value and the other for average customer satisfaction rating.

ACTIVITY

1 Modify the spreadsheets you created in lesson 'Decision-making functions'.

	A	B	C	D	E	F
1	**Grade record**				**Pass mark**	45
2	**Student names**		**Paper 1 mark**		**Passed?**	
3	Sumita	Shah	50			
4	Lucy	Burrows	43			
5	Javan	Okeke	62			
6	Oliver	Adams	39			
7	Alice	Spring	46			
8	Alfie	Jenkins	44			

2 Add marks for Paper 2 in D3:D8. Modify the formula in E3 so it only displays 'Yes' if they have achieved the pass mark or above in BOTH papers.

	A	B	C	D	E	F
1	Invoice record					
2	Invoice number	Customer	Value	Paid?	VAT due	VAT amount
3	1201	ABC Company	£50.45	No	Yes	
4	1202	Star Corporation	£250.00	Yes	Yes	
5	1203	International Group	£125.25	No	No	
6	1204	Central Trading	£63.80	No	No	
7	1205	Atlantic Co	£167.25	Yes	Yes	
8	1206	East and West	£205.50	No	No	
9		**Total owing**				
10						

3 Enter the information shown in E2:E8 indicating if the invoices are overdue for payment. Add a formula using the IF function in F3 that will display the words 'Send letter' only if the invoice is not paid AND it is overdue. Copy the formula down the column.

CHECK MY LEARNING

Work with a partner and swap the work you have done on the two spreadsheets in the activity and check that you have both got the formulas correct.

Discuss the results, and if you have different formulas check with your teacher.

Sorting

Large data sets can sometimes make more sense if they are sorted in a particular order and, fortunately, spreadsheet software allows us to sort data in a number of different ways.

Sorting lists

Spreadsheet software can sort lists of data into ascending or descending order using any of the columns within the data. There are two ways you can do this.

1 The simplest way is to first click anywhere in the column you wish to sort the data by. Then click on the *Data* menu and then click the *A–Z* or *Z–A* icons in the *Sort & Filter* section of the toolbar (or choose the sort options in the *Data* menu in Google Sheets).

- A–Z will sort the data in alphabetical order or in ascending order if the column contains numbers.
- The Z–A option will sort by reverse alphabetical order or descending order for numbers.
- The sort recognises the first row of the data and titles and does not sort these in with rest of the data.

2 Alternatively, in Excel you can click the *Sort* icon in the *Data* menu, which allows you to sort on several fields (columns) at the same time and indicate if your data has a title row or not.

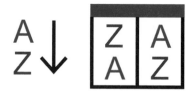

□ Why might these functions be useful when sorting data?

□ Sorting things is usually done to make it easier to find an item

Don't forget that once you have sorted some data it may not be possible to return it to its original order unless you save a version of the spreadsheet file in the unsorted order. You can use the undo option to unsort the data, but this won't work if you have saved the sorted spreadsheet file.

DID YOU KNOW?

Some people use a database rather than a spreadsheet for storing lists of data. Spreadsheets provide a simple and easy method of storing small amounts of data in a single table. Databases provide more sophisticated features and can store very large amounts of data; however, they are generally more complex to set up than spreadsheets. The key feature of database software such as Microsoft Access® is the ability to store data in multiple related tables of data, something that you can't do in spreadsheet software.

ACTIVITY

Create a spreadsheet as shown or use the given spreadsheet at
www.pearsonschools.co.uk/techawardDITsupport.

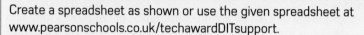

	A	B	C	D	E
1	**Dogs available for adoption**				
2	**Name**	**Breed**	**Age**	**Gender**	**Weight (kg)**
3	Shep	Border Collie	6	M	15
4	Lilly	Jack Russell	4	F	10
5	Winston	Pug	5	M	7
6	Spot	Dalmation	3	M	20
7	Boss	Doberman	5	M	30
8	Jackie	Jack Russell	7	F	8
9	Bernard	French Bulldog	5	F	10
10	Ollie	Jack Russell	6	M	7

1 Try sorting the data by any column and see what happens. Use the undo button to return the data to it is original order.

2 Create a filter to show only Jack Russell dogs. Remove the filter when you are finished.

3 Sort the list by age.

4 Sort the list by weight.

5 Sort the list by breed.

CHECK MY LEARNING

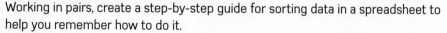

Working in pairs, create a step-by-step guide for sorting data in a spreadsheet to help you remember how to do it.

One person talks as the other follows the instructions directly on a spreadsheet. Work together to refine the instructions to limit the number of steps the person must follow.

Filtering data

GETTING STARTED

Working in a small group, discuss how you might create a dashboard that displays the units, assignments and grades you have to achieve on this qualification and what kind of data you might want to filter and extract to create the dashboard.

Sorting data in a list is useful, but once a filter has been applied to a data list it is also possible to display only those rows within the list that match certain criteria.

Selecting data using a filter

Before you can use a filter, you need to turn the filter feature on by clicking in the list of data you want to use, then going to the *Data* menu and choosing *Filter* (in Excel) or *Create a filter* (in Google Sheets). Check you have the little drop-down arrows next to each title in the top row. Clicking on the drop-down arrows displays the filter menu.

You can filter the data displayed in a list by an individual value either by ensuring only those values you want displayed are checked in the list shown on the filter menu, or by typing the single value you want displayed in the text box. For example, Figure 2.19 shows how you see only those customers who live in London.

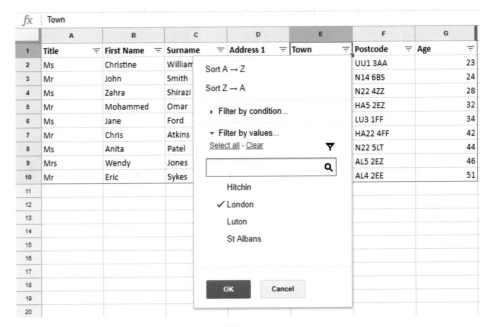

■ **Figure 2.19: When might you want to filter data?**

Once you click *OK* on the *Filter* menu, only the rows with records that match the filter you have applied are shown. The drop-down box arrow changes to a filter icon in the title of the column where you have applied the filter. This is to remind you that this column is filtering the records. You can apply additional filters for other columns if you want. To turn off the filter just click on the filter icon to drop the box down again and click on the *Select all* link, then click *OK*.

You can also use filters to create more complex conditions to control which rows to display. For example, you want only to display those customers who are aged 40 or over.

You can do this in both Excel and Google Sheets.

- On the filter menu in Google Sheets you use the *Filter by condition* option to create a 'Greater than or equal to 40' filter.
- In Excel, also in the filter menu, you use the *Number filters* link to create the same type of filter.

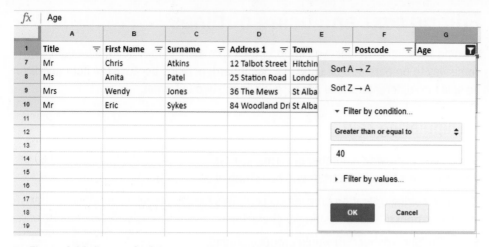

■ Figure 2.20: Do you find Excel or Google sheets easier to use?

As well as filters for 'Greater than or equal to', you can also create filters in the same way for 'Less than' and 'Less than or equal to' and simply 'equals'.

With text values you can also create filters that will select text that begins with a certain character, ends with a certain character or does or doesn't contain certain characters. All of these are listed under the *Filter by condition* link in Google Sheets, or in Excel they are listed under the *Text filters* link (which replaces the *Numbers filter* link when the cells contain text).

ACTIVITY

1   Create a spreadsheet as shown or use the given spreadsheet at www.pearsonschools.co.uk/techawardDITsupport.

	A	B	C	D	E	F	G
1	Used cars for sale						
2	Make	Model	Year	Mileage	Fuel	No of doors	Price
3	Ford	Fiesta	2013	29,500	Petrol	3	£3,495
4	VW	Golf	2015	36,500	Diesel	5	£4,995
5	Vauxhall	Astra	2014	28,000	Diesel	3	£3,800
6	Renault	Clio	2012	45,600	Petrol	3	£2,995
7	Mini	Cooper	2014	32,200	Petrol	3	£3,500
8	Ford	Sierra	2013	52,000	Diesel	5	£4,200
9	Nissan	Note	2014	45,500	Petrol	5	£4,500
10	Fiat	500	2015	27,800	Petrol	3	£3,900

2   Create a filter for the data so only petrol cars are shown.

3   Remove the petrol filter. You want to buy a Ford car with three doors. Apply filters to find which cars match your requirements.

4   Remove the filters previously applied. You are looking for a car that has done less than 40,000 miles, uses diesel fuel and has five doors. Use filters to find which car matches your requirements.

CHECK MY LEARNING

Create a simple guide for using filters in the spreadsheet software you use.

Editing text and using outlines

KEY TERMS

String operation is editing (manipulation) that is carried out on a **text string**.

Text string is a sequence of characters; for example, the password 46*IKpQE is a text string of eight characters.

In some situations, the data you import into a spreadsheet may need to be edited in some way to prepare it to be used in a dashboard, perhaps because the data needs to be split into different parts or because it is in the wrong format.

Manipulating text

Spreadsheets provide a number of **string operation** functions that can be used to trim characters from the start or end of a string of text.

One of the string operation functions is LEFT. This function trims a specified number of characters from the left of a string of characters.

So =LEFT("Spreadsheet",6) would produce Spread.

There is also a RIGHT function, which trims a number of characters from the right of a string.

So =RIGHT("Spreadsheet",5) would produce sheet.

A good example of where the string operation functions could be used is in the weather data downloaded from the Met Office website and used in the climate dashboard.

The sunshine hours include a character at the end of the numbers that indicates which type of instrument was used to collect the data. In the case of the Heathrow weather station, this means a '#' character is added. Spreadsheets therefore treat this as text rather than numbers and the '#' character must be trimmed off before the data can be treated as numbers and used in the dashboard.

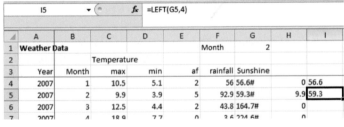

	I5		fx	=LEFT(G5,4)				
	A	B	C	D	E	F	G	H	I
1	Weather Data					Month	2		
2			Temperature						
3	Year	Month	max	min	af	rainfall	Sunshine		
4	2007	1	10.5	5.1	2	56	56.6#	0	56.6
5	2007	2	9.9	3.9	5	92.9	59.3#	9.9	59.3
6	2007	3	12.5	4.4	2	43.8	164.7#	0	
7	2007	4	18.9	7.7	0	3.6	224.6#	0	

□ Figure 2.21: What would =LEFT(G5,2) produce?

One way this might be accomplished is by using the LEFT function. Figure 2.21 shows how this function has been used to pick up the leftmost four characters from 59.3# in G5 to produce 59.3 in I5.

However, although this works fine in cell G5, this would not work in G6. The sunshine hours vary between 3- and 4-digit numbers (with 1 decimal place). G6 has a 4-digit number so it would not work as trimming four characters cuts off the last digit.

1 To trim only the final '#' of a string that is between five and six characters long, we need another function, =LEN.

2 This provides the length of a string (so =LEN(G6) would give you six characters).

3 The LEN function can be combined with the LEFT function to find out how many characters there are in the string, then trim off one less character than the length.

4 This will ensure that the last character (the '#') will always be cut off no matter how long the string is.

	I5		fx	=LEFT(G5,LEN(G5)-1)				
	A	B	C	D	E	F	G	H	I
1	Weather Data					Month	2		
2			Temperature						
3	Year	Month	max	min	af	rainfall	Sunshine		
4	2007	1	10.5	5.1	2	56	56.6#	0	56.6
5	2007	2	9.9	3.9	5	92.9	59.3#	9.9	59.3
6	2007	3	12.5	4.4	2	43.8	164.7#	0	164.7
7	2007	4	18.9	7.7	0	3.6	224.6#	0	224.6
8	2007	5	17.9	9.7	0	80	149.6#	0	149.6
9	2007	6	21.2	12.6	0	63.8	139.7#	0	139.7

□ Figure 2.22: What would =LEN(G5) produce?

Once the '#' character has been removed, the sunshine hours values can be treated as numbers and included in calculations, graphs etc.

Another useful text manipulation function is =FIND. This will tell you the position of a particular character within a string. It is used like this: =FIND(character to be found, string to look in).

For example, cell A2 contained the string "John Smith" and, if you wanted to find the space between the first and second name, using =Find(" ", A2) would return the value 5.

Column B uses the FIND function to find the space in the names in column A as described above. The formulae in column C then uses that value to trim the surname from the first name.

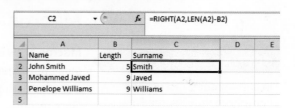

◪ Figure 2.23: What formula would be needed to extract the first name rather than the surname?

Outlines

One technique you can use to help summarise large amounts of data is using outlines, which allow you to collapse the detail in a large amount of data showing just subtotals and totals.

Figure 2.24 shows some of the weather data used in the dashboard we have been looking at. The data has been summarised by applying a subtotal outline and selecting the option to calculate an average for the values at each change of year.

Clicking the minus signs on the left of the outlined data allows you to collapse the data so just the yearly and total average appear, as shown in Figure 2.25.

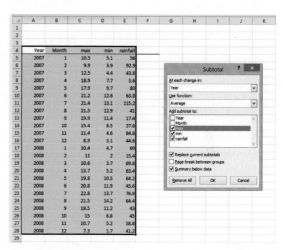

◪ Figure 2.24: Why might it be useful to see the average amount of rainfall across a number of years?

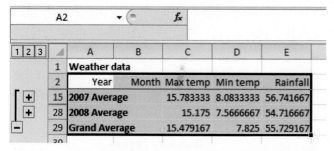

◪ Figure 2.25: How could you reduce the number of digits after the decimal point?

Once the data is collapsed, you can click the plus buttons to expand it again.

ACTIVITY

Create a spreadsheet as shown or use the given spreadsheet at www.pearsonschools.co.uk/ techawardDITsupport.

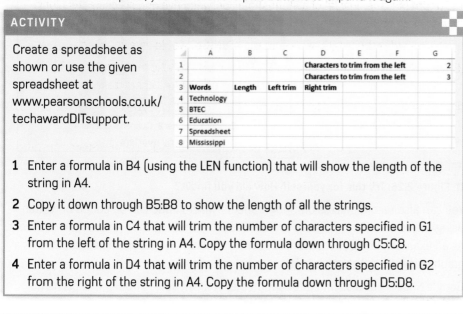

1 Enter a formula in B4 (using the LEN function) that will show the length of the string in A4.

2 Copy it down through B5:B8 to show the length of all the strings.

3 Enter a formula in C4 that will trim the number of characters specified in G1 from the left of the string in A4. Copy the formula down through C5:C8.

4 Enter a formula in D4 that will trim the number of characters specified in G2 from the right of the string in A4. Copy the formula down through D5:D8.

CHECK MY LEARNING

What would =Right("check my learning", 6) produce?

What would =Left("Information Technology", 9) produce?

Macros

Macros allow the automation of various actions in a spreadsheet. They let you build a mini application that other people can use without becoming involved in the internal workings of the spreadsheet application. A macro records you completing a task. Once recorded, it can then carry out the task automatically for you.

Microsoft Excel has a built-in macro recorder, so you can record the actions you want in the macro and run them at any time. You can also attach the macro to a button, so you can click the button to run the macro.

The *Record Macro* option is in the *View* menu. You must remember that once you have turned the *Record Macro* on, everything you do will be recorded in the macro. For example, if you wanted a button on your spreadsheet that would change the graph on the sheet from one type to another, first, you would turn the *Macro Recorder* on and give the macro a name, then click on the chart and from the chart menu click the *Change Chart* type icon and choose a different chart type. Then you must remember to return to the *View* menu and turn off the *Record Macro*.

To attach your macro to a button you need to display the *Developer* tab, which can be found in the *Customize Ribbon* in the *Options* dialog (*File* menu, *Options*).

1 Once you have added the *Developer* tab to the ribbon, you can use the *Insert* menu on that tab and select a button from the form controls.

2 When you drag out a button on the sheet a dialog will pop up asking which macro you want to attach to the button.

3 Select the one you just recorded for changing the graph type and then change the caption on the button from Button 1 to 'Change Chart' or something similar.

The result is shown in Figure 2.26.

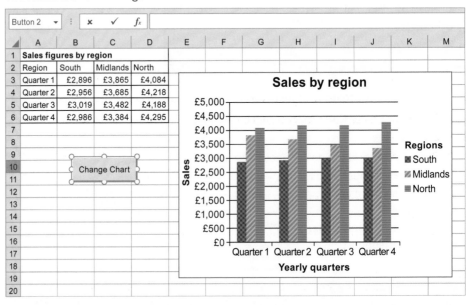

◘ Figure 2.26: Try this for yourself. How did you find it?

You can also record macros on Google sheets. Macro Code can be edited or written using the script editor. You have to write the programming code for the macro to work. As an example, let's say you wanted to write a macro on a Google Sheet that draws a graph using the data shown in Figure 2.27.

Google Sheets has a script editor option that you can access from the *Tools* menu.

	A	B	C	D	E	F
1	Temperature					
2		Monday	Tuesday	Wednesday	Thursday	Friday
3	London	10	12	13	11	9
4	Bristol	10	9	9	10	12
5	Birmingham	7	9	8	8	7
6	Manchester	8	6	6	5	5
7	Glasgow	8	8	6	5	4

◘ Figure 2.27: Do you prefer creating macros in Excel or Google Sheets?

The macros script to draw a graph from this data is shown in Figure 2.28.

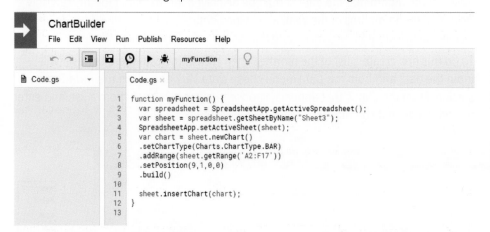

```
function myFunction() {
  var spreadsheet = SpreadsheetApp.getActiveSpreadsheet();
  var sheet = spreadsheet.getSheetByName("Sheet3");
  SpreadsheetApp.setActiveSheet(sheet);
  var chart = sheet.newChart()
  .setChartType(Charts.ChartType.BAR)
  .addRange(sheet.getRange('A2:F17'))
  .setPosition(9,1,0,0)
  .build()

  sheet.insertChart(chart);
}
```

◘ Figure 2.28: Do you understand how this macro script code creates a graph?

As with Excel, you can create a button on the sheet and attach the macro script to it so the macros run when you click the button. You can do this using *Insert* menu, *Drawing* option.

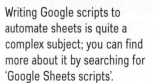

DID YOU KNOW?

Writing Google scripts to automate sheets is quite a complex subject; you can find more about it by searching for 'Google Sheets scripts'.

Creating macros for Excel can also be quite complex; you can see some simple examples of how by searching for 'Excel macros'.

ACTIVITY

1 Create a spreadsheet with four worksheets. The first will be the menu sheet.

2 Record or create three macros, which will swap from the menu sheet to Sheet 2, 3 and 4.

3 Create three buttons on the menu sheet labelled 'Go to Sheet 2', 'Go to Sheet 3' and 'Go to Sheet 4' and assign the correct macro to each.

4 Test the menu works correctly by clicking each button in turn and check that it takes you to the correct sheet. Add a button to each of the sheets 2, 3 and 4, which will return you to the menu sheet (Sheet 1).

CHECK MY LEARNING

How can macros be used to make a spreadsheet or dashboard more efficient?

Data validation

In many situations the user will need to input at least some of the data into a spreadsheet. Making sure that the data is correct is important, and using data validation can help to do that, although it can't guarantee it is correct.

Using a list to validate input

Where the user input can be selected from a relatively small number of valid entries, a fixed list of correct entries can be used to restrict the possible user input. For example, in the climate dashboard, we have been looking at how the user needs to select the month that the data should be displayed for. The input for this can only be one of the 12 months of the year, and by presenting the user with a drop-down box listing the months, we can ensure that only a valid input can be made.

To do this first create a list of the months. Then click in the cell where the user will input the data and from the *Data* menu chose *Data Validation* from the *Data Tools* section. From the dialog that appears, choose to allow items only from a list, and enter the cell range that contains the list, see Figure 2.29.

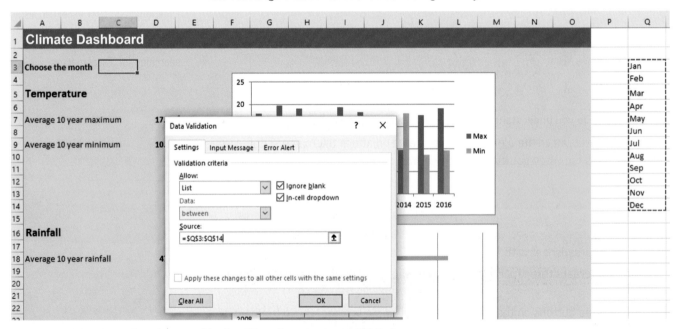

■ Figure 2.29: What other data would a fixed list of entries be useful for?

When you click *OK*, the cell where the user enters the month has a drop-down arrow that allows the user to choose only from the listed months.

Type check

You can also use data validation for other types of data entry. For example, you can use it to make sure only inputs of a particular data type, such as **integer**, decimal or date can be entered. These options can also be found on the *Data Validation* dialog box, under the *Allow* drop-down box.

Length check

The drop-down box also has an option to allow you to restrict the length of text that can be input, as shown in Figure 2.30.

LINK IT UP

To find out more about meaningful information and error messages to guide users go to lesson 'Design principles: layout' in Component 1, Learning aim A.

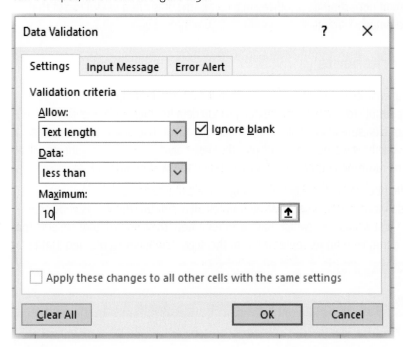

■ Figure 2.30: What are the Input Message and Error Alert tabs on the dialog box used for?

It is worth noting that if you are setting validation rules like this you should really set up input messages and error alerts, so a user knows what they are supposed to enter in the cell and why their input has been rejected.

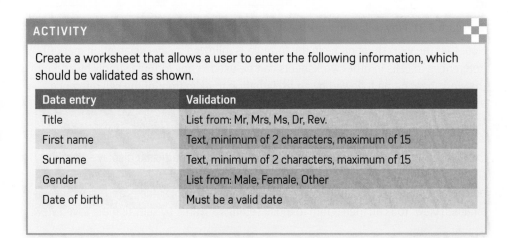

ACTIVITY

Create a worksheet that allows a user to enter the following information, which should be validated as shown.

Data entry	Validation
Title	List from: Mr, Mrs, Ms, Dr, Rev.
First name	Text, minimum of 2 characters, maximum of 15
Surname	Text, minimum of 2 characters, maximum of 15
Gender	List from: Male, Female, Other
Date of birth	Must be a valid date

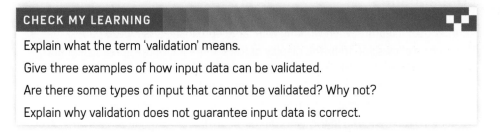

CHECK MY LEARNING

Explain what the term 'validation' means.

Give three examples of how input data can be validated.

Are there some types of input that cannot be validated? Why not?

Explain why validation does not guarantee input data is correct.

Linking spreadsheets and views

When dealing with a large amount of data, or data that is split into clear divisions (such as different departments or offices in a company), it is often useful to put that data into different worksheets.

Linking worksheets

The formulae used in cells so far have only referenced other cells in the same worksheet; however, it is possible to create formulae that pick up data in other worksheets and even different workbooks (spreadsheet files). This technique is very useful in a dashboard as typically one worksheet will be used to display the dashboard, but other worksheets will be used to hold the raw (unprocessed) data, which makes the dashboard work.

The climate dashboard we have been looking at uses this technique. One sheet displays the dashboard and a second sheet holds all the data. Figure 2.31 shows the formula in the first worksheet (which has been renamed 'Dashboard') that collects the average ten-year maximum temperature from the second worksheet (named 'Data').

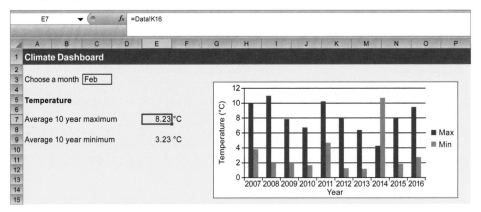

■ Figure 2.31: Why is linking worksheets a useful tool?

Note that the worksheet name in the formula is followed by an exclamation mark (!). References to cells in other worksheets can be used in any formula simply by adding the worksheet name followed by an exclamation mark in front of the cell reference.

Views

Excel allows you to create custom views so you can save a particular display and print settings. You can then easily reapply them at any time. For example, you can set a zoom percentage, hide columns or rows and select a variety of print settings and save these as a named view. You can then return to those settings anytime by selecting the saved view.

Freeze panes

Another useful feature when working with large spreadsheet is *Freeze panes*. This feature allows you to fix the display of rows at the left of the spreadsheet and columns at the top, so they remain where they are when you scroll across to the right or down the spreadsheet. This means you can keep titles in view and makes it easier to understand what you are seeing as you can still see the row or column titles. The feature can be found in the *View* tab or *Menu*, in both Google Sheets and Excel.

ACTIVITY

You need to create a grading dashboard that will display students' overall grade for this Tech Award'.

A student has a Level 1 Merit for Component 1 and a Level 2 Pass for Component 2. In the exam (Component 3) they were awarded 25 points.

The grading on the qualification is quite complex (you can find it described in the qualification specification). Your dashboard will need a worksheet to display the results and another linked worksheet where all the calculations are done.

For the components marked by your teacher (Components 1 and 2), the teacher awards an overall grade for each component, and the grade you get is converted into a number of points.

Figure 2.32 shows an example of how this calculation might be done on the calculations worksheet. It uses a VLOOKUP formula to pick the correct number of points for the grade awarded by your teacher. Data validation can be used to display only the list of grades from F3:F7 in cells C3 and C4.

	D3		fx	=VLOOKUP(C3,$F$3:$G$7,2,FALSE)					
	A	B		C	D	E	F	G	H
1							Internal		
2	Component			Grade awarded			Grade	Points	
3	1	Exploring User Interface Design Principles and Project Planning Techniques		L1 Merit	15		L1 Pass	9	
4	2	Collecting, Presenting and Interpreting Data		L2 Pass	22		L1 Merit	15	
5							L2 Pass	22	
6							L2 Merit	29	
7							L2 Distinction	36	
8									

■ Figure 2.32: Check you understand what the VLOOKUP formula means

Component 3 is externally assessed, and a number of points are awarded when the exam is marked. The points awarded for Component 3 are added together with the points from Components 1 and 2 to produce a total number of points. Your overall qualification grade is calculated using your total points and the table of grade thresholds. For example, if the grade threshold for a Level 2 Pass is between 69 and 81 points and you have a total of 70 points, you will achieve that grade.

Figure 2.33 shows an example of how your correct final grade could be displayed using a series of IF functions combined with AND operators to correctly identify which grade threshold a points total fits in.

	C15		fx	=IF(AND(D10<G15,D10>=G14),"Level 1 Merit","")					
	A	B		C	D	E	F	G	H
1							Internal		
2	Component			Grade awarded			Grade	Points	
3	1	Exploring User Interface Design Principles and Project Planning Techniques		L1 Merit	15		L1 Pass	9	
4	2	Collecting, Presenting and Interpreting Data		L2 Pass	22		L1 Merit	15	
5							L2 Pass	22	
6							L2 Merit	29	
7							L2 Distinction	36	
8	3	Effective Digital Working Practices		Points awarded	15				
9									
10				Total points	52				
11									
12				Overall grade achieved			Points thresholds		
13							Level 1 Pass	30	
14							Level 1 Merit	43	
15				Level 1 Merit			Level 1 Distinction	56	
16							Level 2 Pass	69	
17							Level 2 Merit	82	
18							Level 2 Distinction	95	
19							Level 2 Distinction*	108	
20									

■ Figure 2.33: Do you think this is a useful tool?

Create a spreadsheet as shown or use the given spreadsheet at www.pearsonschools.co.uk/techawardDITsupport. Complete all the required formulae. (Remember the IF statement for the top and bottom grades won't need an AND since an unclassified grade is anything less than 30 and a Distinction* is greater than or equal to 108.) Create a dashboard sheet that displays the final results along with the grades for the internal components and the points for the external component. The dashboard sheet will need to pick up the grading information from the data sheet.

Once you have completed the dashboard you can try it out with different grades and check it works. You can also use it to keep track of your own grades.

There is a rule that you must achieve at least a Level 1 Pass in all three components to pass the qualification overall. How can you include this requirement in the dashboard?

CHECK MY LEARNING

Your teacher might find a dashboard like this very useful but would want it to be able to display the results for all students in your class. They would also like to be able to select a particular student's results on the dashboard. How might this be achieved?

Conditional formatting

The ability to have formatting that changes automatically depending on the contents of a cell is a useful feature. It can be used to highlight important information, such as values falling above or below certain limits. This is called conditional formatting.

Conditional formatting

For conditional formatting to work, you need to decide on the following.

- What cell or range of cells you will apply the conditional formatting to. You should apply conditional formatting to cells that contain text or numbers that will change, usually because of user input.
- What change to the value in the cell will cause the formatting to change. There are lots of options here; for example, you can change the formatting on the cells if they are empty or if they contain values that are greater or less than a threshold value.
- How you want the formatting to change. For example, you might have the text colour change, become bold or the background colour change.

You have created a profit and loss statement spreadsheet and you want important totals to change colour depending on whether the total is a positive value (a profit) or a negative value (a loss). You would need to do the following.

1 Make sure you select cells you want to change.

2 In Excel, choose the *Home* menu and click the *Conditional formatting* icon.

3 In the menu, create a rule that can change the formatting of the cell depending on the values in it. In Google Sheets, conditional formatting can be set up from the *Format* menu.

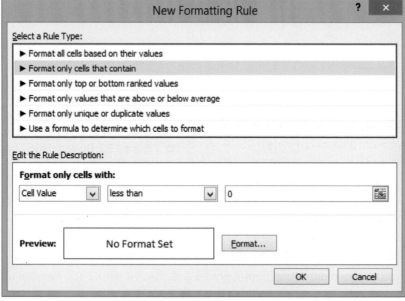

■ Figure 2.34: Setting a conditional formatting rule

■ Figure 2.35: Setting a conditional formatting colour scale

Figure 2.34 shows an example of setting up a conditional formatting rule in Excel.

As well as applying a single colour, you can also apply colour scales across a range of cells. Figure 2.35 shows an example of this in Google Sheets, but you can do the same in Excel.

In Excel you can also use data bars. These are similar to a bar chart in that the cell is filled with a coloured bar that represents the size of the value in the cell. Another option in Excel is *Icon Sets* with which you can use to add icons, such as arrows, that indicate the values are increasing or decreasing. Figure 2.36 shows both data bars and icon sets added across B13:D13.

	A	B	C	D
1		Vikings Youth Football Membership Numbers 2016-2018		
2				
3		2016	2017	2018
4	Under 6	15	15	18
5	Under 7	14	10	12
6	Under 8	12	12	12
7	Under 9	27	28	28
8	Under 10	28	28	28
9	Under 11	14	13	12
10	Under 12	12	12	11
11	Under 13	18	16	18
12	Under 14	11	14	18
13	Under 15	11	12	12

◘ Figure 2.36: Data bars and icon sets

ACTIVITY

Create a spreadsheet as shown or use the given spreadsheet at www.pearsonschools.co.uk/techawardDITsupport.

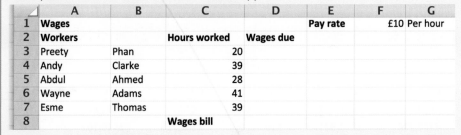

	A	B	C	D	E	F	G
1	Wages				Pay rate	£10	Per hour
2	Workers		Hours worked	Wages due			
3	Preety	Phan	20				
4	Andy	Clarke	39				
5	Abdul	Ahmed	28				
6	Wayne	Adams	41				
7	Esme	Thomas	39				
8			Wages bill				

1 Enter a formula in D3 that will calculate the wages due using the hourly rate in F1.

2 Add conditional formatting to the cell so the hours worked in cells C3:C7 are shown with a green background if the worker has worked 37 hours or less and with an orange background if they worked over 37 hours. Copy the formula down from cell D4 to D7.

3 Enter a formula in D8 that will add up all the workers' wages.

4 Apply conditional formatting to D8 that will show a yellow background if the wages bill is below £1,800 and changes to red if the wages bill is £1,800 or higher.

5 Increase the pay rate in F1 and see at what point it changes the background in D8 to red.

CHECK MY LEARNING

Explain why it would not be a good idea to apply conditional formatting to a cell that just contains a number rather than a formula?

Showing data summaries

The main purpose of a dashboard is to provide a useful summary of important information. There are several different ways that data can be summarised; here we look at the use of totals, percentages and counts.

Totals

Using totals within a dashboard is one of the common methods of summarising numeric data. Figure 2.37 shows an example of sales data from a company that has a number of shops in different parts of the country. The totals from the detailed data worksheet are used in the dashboard.

fx | =Data!C8

	A	B	C	D	E	F	G
1	**Super stores sales data**						
2			**Q1**	**Q2**	**Q3**	**Q4**	
3	**South region**		£318,809	£324,809	£327,643	£332,361	
4							
5	**Midlands region**		£193,858	£192,691	£189,634	£188,287	
6							
7	**North region**		£389,510	£387,267	£390,467	£390,579	

◘ Figure 2.37: What formula has been used to transfer the data from the data sheet to the Dashboard sheet?

While totals can be useful, they do not make it easy to make comparisons within the data. For example, if you want to know which region had the best sales across all the quarters, it still requires a careful look at the data in the dashboard to answer the question.

Percentages

fx | =G8/G19

	A	B	C	D	E	F	G	H
1	Shop Sales							
2								
3	**Region**	**Store**	**Q1**	**Q2**	**Q3**	**Q4**	**Totals**	**% contribution**
4	South	Watford	£42,268	£46,961	£45,562	£48,105	£182,896	
5		Milton Keynes	£102,228	£101,941	£103,228	£102,765	£410,162	
6		Luton	£98,332	£96,955	£100,102	£101,853	£394,812	
7		Cambridge	£75,981	£78,952	£78,751	£79,638	£309,322	
8		**Region total**	£318,809	£324,809	£327,643	£332,361	£1,297,192	35.77%
9	Midlands	Northampton	£39,529	£39,250	£38,145	£38,100	£160,215	
10		Coventry	£68,108	£67,618	£67,157	£66,675	£269,425	
11		Stoke	£86,221	£85,823	£84,332	£83,512	£341,888	
12		**Region total**	£193,858	£192,691	£189,634	£188,287	£771,528	21.27%
13	North	Sheffield	£98,652	£99,109	£100,942	£99,517	£398,220	
14		Hull	£82,648	£82,962	£83,154	£83,025	£331,789	
15		Manchester	£112,056	£109,523	£110,348	£111,843	£443,770	
16		York	£96,154	£95,673	£96,023	£96,194	£384,044	
17		**Region total**	£389,510	£387,267	£390,467	£390,579	£1,557,823	42.96%

◘ Figure 2.38: What is the overall total of sales?

Percentages are a useful way to compare numerical values. A percentage is a part of a whole and is out of 100. It is a fraction of 100. If 10 out 20 students in your class are female, that is half the class. Half as a fraction of 100 is 50 or 50%.

We can use percentages with the super stores dashboard to show how much each region contributed to the total sales of the whole company. To do this across all quarters, we need to total up the sales for each region. These totals are shown in Figure 2.38 in cells G8, G12 and G17.

Once you have the overall total of sales, these totals can then be used to calculate a percentage contribution that each region makes to the overall total sales. This is done by dividing the regional total by the overall total and multiplying the result by 100 (or simply applying percentage formatting to the cell). This can be seen in cell H8 of Figure 2.38. The percentage data can be added to the dashboard.

Counts

Counting items using one of the count functions (such as COUNT or COUNTIF) can provide useful information for a dashboard, especially where there is a large quantity of data driving the dashboard. This isn't the case with the super stores dashboard we have been looking at. Examples of the sort of dashboards that might use counts include ones used to keep track of items in stock in a shop or warehouse and ones used to track student attendance.

LINK IT UP

To find out more about COUNT and COUNTIF functions, go to lesson 'Count functions' in Learning aim B of this component.

ACTIVITY

Carry out a simple survey among a small group of your classmates. For example, you could create a simple course evaluation survey with four or five questions.

Each question can use a scale of 1 to 5 (with 5 being 'strongly agree' and 1 being 'strongly disagree'), for example:

Q1 I feel I have learned a lot on this course.

Strongly disagree (1)

Disagree (2)

Neither agree nor disagree (3)

Agree (4)

Strongly agree (5)

Other questions could be:

Q2 I have really enjoyed this course.

Q3 I believe this course will help me in the future.

Q4 I understand how to complete the course assignments.

If you make all the questions positive (as shown above), then the higher the overall score, the happier you can assume people are with the course.

Once you have collected the responses, create a spreadsheet to summarise the data.

The spreadsheet should use SUM functions to add up the scores and use COUNTIF functions. Percentages should then be calculated for each response.

CHECK MY LEARNING

Explain how percentages are calculated.

Describe how you can summarise data using percentages and other measures.

Explain the difference between a total, an average and a percentage.

Showing information summaries

There are several different situations where presenting summaries of information on a dashboard can be useful. You might want to break down data by dividing it into various categories, such as class or year.

Different people working within an organisation often require different data.

- Senior managers will often want a summary that gives an overview of the whole performance of the business.
- Department managers will want summaries of the data relating just to the department they are responsible for.
- Employees responsible for a particular task or project may want detailed data (not necessarily summarised) about their area of responsibility.

Sales breakdowns

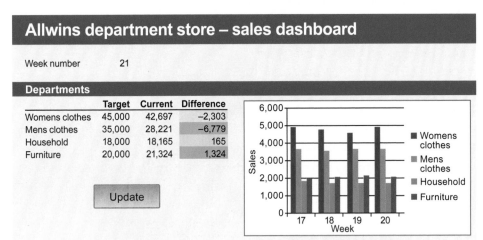

Figure 2.39: What can you say about how each department is performing?

Organisations that sell things, such as supermarkets, car dealerships and banks (banks sell financial products like loans, mortgages, insurance, etc.), need to keep track of the sales they make. Sales organisations commonly have targets for the amount or value of sales they hope to make each week, month and year. Dashboards can be very useful to sales managers to view breakdowns of sales by department or individual salesperson and track progress towards targets.

Department breakdowns

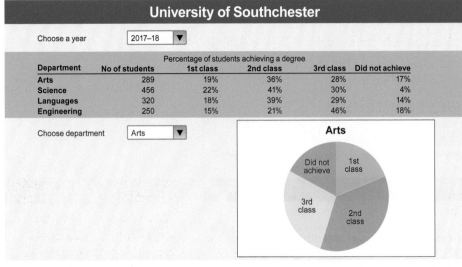

Figure 2.40: What comparisons can you make between the different departments?

Within many organisations, senior managers need to track and compare the performance of the different departments in the organisation. For example, in a university, senior managers will want to see performance data broken down by different departments that deliver courses on particular subjects. This would allow managers to investigate why some departments perform better than others and to provide the information they need to put support in place for the less well-performing departments.

Time allocations

As well as presenting financial information, such as sales and budgets, a dashboard can be used to present information about dates and times. A calendar or diary is just a type of dashboard that pre-dates electronic versions. You can use a spreadsheet to create a diary or timetable dashboard, but with so many other dedicated applications (such as Google Calendar™ and Microsoft Outlook®) including features such as reminders and mobile/desktop integration, it is far easier to use one of them.

Another type of time allocation is that used in a project plan. Project plans divide projects into individual tasks and plan the amount of time and resources (including people and equipment) to allocate to each task. The project plan can also be used to track actual time spent on a project and so monitor its performance against targets. Spreadsheets are commonly used for project planning and a dashboard could be added to present the key project information.

LINK IT UP

For more about project planning and creating project plans, go to lesson 'Planning project timescales' in Component 1, Learning aim B.

Budget allocations

Organisations commonly use budgets to allocate money to projects or departments. Not only does each department or project need to know how much money it will have available to spend, it also needs to keep track of how its money has been spent. While it is of course necessary to keep detailed records and documents detailing how money is spent, a dashboard can provide a useful way of viewing the overall situation with a budget.

For example, a builder building a house or other construction project will be working to a budget (probably based on the original estimate for the cost of the project the builder gave to the client) and will want to know how much money has been spent compared to the money available.

Figure 2.41 shows an example of a dashboard that could be used for that purpose.

Building projects

Project number		103		

Expenditure

Task	Progress	Budget	Actual	
Groundwork	100%	£1,500	£1,800	Over
Foundations	100%	£800	£750	Under
Brickworks	75%	£2,000	£1,200	Under
Roofing	10%	£1,800	£500	Under
Fit out	0%	£3,000	£0	Under
Finish	0%	£2,500	£0	Under
Totals		**£11,600**	**£4,250**	

■ Figure 2.41: How has colour been used to show spending?

ACTIVITY

1 Create a project plan spreadsheet for completing one of your assignments.

2 Your teacher should be able to give start dates and deadline dates for completion.

3 Break the project down into as many tasks that you can think of and give each a start and end date.

4 Using spreadsheet date functions, such as NOW, in combination with decision-making IF functions, you can identify which tasks should have been completed by the current date.

5 You can add conditional formatting to colour code those tasks that should have been completed by now and those that are not yet due.

CHECK MY LEARNING

Make a list of the different ways in which a dashboard could be used to summarise different kinds of information.

Presentation methods 1

Presenting the data on the dashboard clearly and effectively is important so users can understand and interpret the data. You also need to ensure your dashboard is appropriate for its intended users.

Form controls

Allowing the user to have some control over how the data is used or how it is displayed is a useful feature for any dashboard. Form controls, such as drop-down menus, spinners, tick boxes and radio buttons, can be used to provide convenient ways for users to select various options.

◘　Table 2.5: Types of form controls

Form control	Description	Example
Drop-down menu	User can select one from a list that drops down when the arrow is clicked (also called a combo box).	Option 1 / Option 2 / Option 3 / Option 4
Spinner	Allows the user to scroll through a number of different options.	▲ ▼
Tick box	Any combination can be selected to switch different options on.	☐ Option 1 / ✓ Option 2 / ☐ Option 3 / ☐ Option 4
Radio button	Only one button can be selected; selecting another button automatically deselects the previously selected button.	Gender: ◉ Male ○ Female

The climate dashboard we have been looking at provides an example of the use of a drop-down menu to select the month for which the climate data is to be displayed. See Figure 2.42.

The drop-down menu is created using the *Data validation* feature and picks up the list of months from the data sheet.

Form controls, such as tick boxes or radio buttons, would need a macro to make them work. Using the climate dashboard for example, you could record a couple of simple macros that swap the chart types (such as a line chart to a bar chart) and attach the macros to radio buttons to provide a simple method for the user to change the chart type.

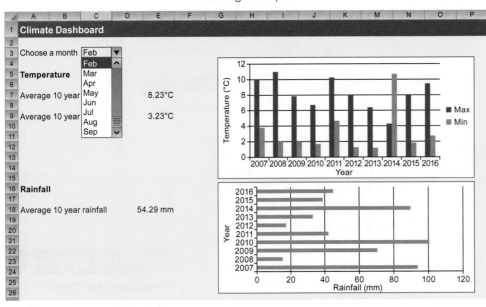

◘　Figure 2.42: Where does the list of months in the drop-down box come from?

Graphs and charts

Visual presentation methods, such as graphs and charts, provide an effective way to present numerical data and allow trends (such as values that increase or decrease over time) to be more easily spotted. Graphs and charts created within a spreadsheet are dynamic, so if the data changes, the chart automatically changes to reflect the new data.

Looking at the numbers displayed on the super stores sales data dashboard it isn't immediately obvious if the sales for each region are increasing or decreasing. However, if you add a simple bar chart to the dashboard it becomes clear that the South region sales are increasing while the Midland region sales are falling. The chart shown in Figure 2.43 is based on the data in A2:F7; the percentage data is of course left out of the bar chart.

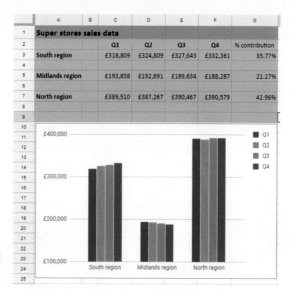

■ Figure 2.43: Which region is showing an increase in sales?

With percentage data, a pie chart is a good type of chart to use since the whole circle represents 100% and you can easily see the size of the different segments that make up the whole. Figure 2.44 shows the percentage contribution data on the super stores dashboard used to create a pie chart.

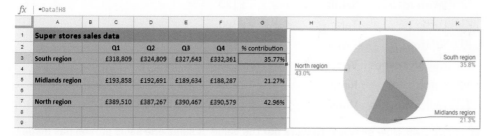

■ Figure 2.44: Which region has the largest percentage of sales?

LINK IT UP

To find out more on the effectiveness of graphs and charts, go to lesson 'How presentation affects understanding' in Learning aim C of this component.

ACTIVITY

Create a dashboard with a data sheet like the super stores one. Add the following features to the dashboard.

1 Use data validation to create a drop-down menu on the dashboard that allows the user to select the shop for which they want to see the quarterly sales totals. This will require the use of a VLOOKUP formula to select the sales figures to display based on the choice the user makes in the drop-down list of stores.

2 Add a bar chart showing the sales data in the form of a graph.

3 Create a line graph showing the sales data. Which do you think makes the data clearer: the bar chart or the line graph? Give reasons for your answer.

4 Using the survey spreadsheet you created in lesson 'Showing data summaries', add bar charts showing how many responses of each type there where to each question.

CHECK MY LEARNING

Explain what is meant by form controls.

Give the different types of form controls and examples of how they could be used in a dashboard.

Presentation methods 2

Spreadsheets have many features that help present data in ways that make it more meaningful. Here we will look at pivot tables, conditional formatting and selecting data ranges, all of which can be useful when creating dashboards.

Pivot table

A pivot table is a powerful, but quite a complex tool, that allows you to rearrange a data list in a way that makes the data easier to understand. A pivot table works best with data that is divided up using several criteria, such as by office and by sales person.

The best way to understand how a pivot table can be used to format and summarise data is to look at an example. Looking at three super store shops, each store has several sales people and a spreadsheet is kept in the head office, which records each sale made by each sales person. An example is shown in Figure 2.45.

	A	B	C
1	**Store**	**Sales person**	**Sale value**
2	Watford	Javier	£125
3	Watford	Samia	£75
4	Milton Keynes	Abi	£200
5	Luton	Samia	£175
6	Milton Keynes	Abi	£90
7	Watford	Samia	£120
8	Luton	Tara	£300
9	Watford	Javier	£65
10	Milton Keynes	Winston	£55
11	Luton	Riley	£250
12	Milton Keynes	Winston	£85

◪ **Figure 2.45: How easy is it to work out the value of sales one sales person has made?**

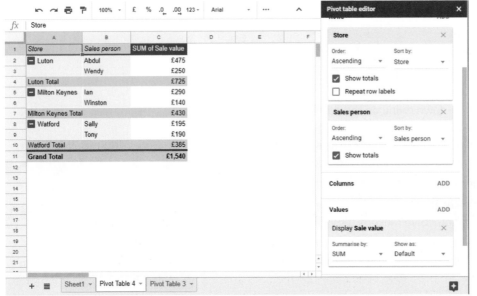

The way this data is currently listed doesn't really show the total value of sales either by store or by sales person. You could manually reformat the data and use some formulae to show this information, but the pivot table does it all for you. Figure 2.46 shows the same data with the features available in a pivot table applied.

The pivot table automatically adds up the sales for each sales person and provides a subtotal for each store. It also adds up all the sales to reach a grand total.

◪ **Figure 2.46: What are the total sales made in the Watford branch?**

Conditional formatting

Conditional formatting can be used very effectively on a dashboard to highlight important changes. For example, where targets for sales or expenditure have been set, conditional formatting can be used to highlight figures that are above or below targets.

Conditional formatting can also be used as a form of alert; for example, on a school dashboard by putting a red background behind the attendance figures of any student who falls below the school target.

Select data/range

Depending on the type of dashboard you are creating, you might want to give users the ability to select different ranges of data. For example, you might want to give users the option of showing the data relating to a specific department, month or region. There are several methods you can use to select different ranges of data; for example, the climate dashboard we have looked at uses a drop-down box listing the months linked to a VLOOKUP function to select data for a given month. The data displayed and the charts then relate only to the range of data for the selected month.

LINK IT UP

To find out more about conditional formatting go to lesson 'Conditional formatting' in Learning aim B of this component.

ACTIVITY

Create a spreadsheet as shown or use the given spreadsheet at www.pearsonschools.co.uk/techawardDITsupport.

	A	B	C	D	E
1	**Westgate Airport - departures**				
2	**Flight No**	**Day**	**Destination**	**Airline**	**No of passengers**
3	SJ125	Monday	Rome	Super-Jet	123
4	ES234	Monday	Paris	Europe-Air	98
5	AL987	Monday	Rome	Atlantic	150
6	GF332	Monday	Berlin	Go Fly	154
7	EA856	Tuesday	Madrid	Europe-Air	87
8	SJ948	Tuesday	Dublin	Super-Jet	69
9	GF486	Tuesday	Paris	Go Fly	102
10	AL190	Wednesday	Madrid	Atlantic	142
11	GF220	Wednesday	Rome	Go Fly	98
12	SJ748	Wednesday	Madrid	Super-Jet	84
13	EA381	Wednesday	Berlin	Europe-Air	116
14	GF603	Wednesday	Dublin	Go Fly	96

Use a pivot table to adjust the data that is displayed, to find answers to the following questions.

1 How many passengers travelled to each different destination? Which destination had the most passengers fly there?

2 How many passengers travelled with each airline? Which airline flew the most passengers?

3 How many passengers flew on each day? Which day was most popular?

4 Use conditional formatting to change the background colours in the cells that display the number of passengers (E3:E14). For example, up to 90 passengers, colour blue, 91 to 120, green and over 120, red.

CHECK MY LEARNING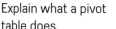

Explain what a pivot table does.

Describe what kind of data it works best with, and what sort of data it doesn't work with.

Presentation features

Dashboards are the 'front window' of the system. They need to look professional and clear and emphasise the most important information in a way that can be understood easily.

Font size, style and colour

To make the dashboard accessible, font sizes should be used to make text readable. There should be a hierarchy of text sizes, with main headings and titles larger than subheadings. For example, you might choose to have all main headings size 16, subheadings size 14 and the rest of the text size 11.

There should be consistency within the dashboard with all the text of the same level (for example, all the titles, all the subtitles etc.) using the same font and size. In terms of colour, you should just use a small number of colours or shades and use them consistently. Too many different colours can make the dashboard look messy.

Cell borders and shading

	A	B	C	D
1	*Budget*			
2	Expenditure	Jan	Feb	Mar
3	Rent	£900	£900	£900
4	Wages	£1,200	£1,250	£1,300
5	Electricity	£150	£150	£150
6	Stock purchase	£1,300	£1,350	£1,425
7	Marketing	£250	£300	£350
8	Other	£200	£200	£200
9	Total	£4,000	£4,150	£4,325

Adding borders to cells and/or shading them is another way you can make the dashboard look professional. It can also make viewing the dashboard easier, separating related information and emphasising important information. However, avoid overusing it and ensure it is consistent and the colours do not clash or make reading text difficult. An example is shown in Figure 2.47.

▣ Figure 2.47: Does the use of colours and borders make important information stand out?

Graphics

Adding graphics, such as a company logo, to a dashboard will help to reinforce a brand and link it to the organisation that creates or uses it.

You might also add graphics, which represent the data being shown, to a dashboard. For example, many schools use dashboards to display the current performance of individual students and along with the data for the student their photograph is also displayed.

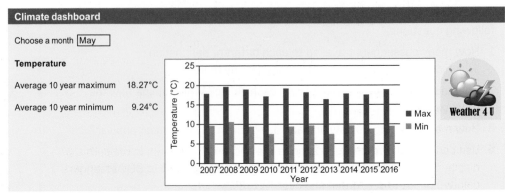

▣ Figure 2.48: What do you think the graphic adds to this climate dashboard?

Formatting charts and graphs

Although the chart-drawing tools in spreadsheets do a good job of creating charts, there are several ways you can enhance the charts and make their meaning clearer for the user of the dashboard.

Axis labels

Graphs have axes which run up the side and along the bottom of the graph, called the *x*-axis and the *y*-axis. To make the meaning of the graph clear, these axes need labels which show what they represent.

Titles

Adding a title to a graph or chart also makes it clear what the chart or graph shows. Like the axis labels, titles may not be added by the chart-creation tools and need to be input manually. Figure 2.49 shows a chart with appropriate axis labels and a title.

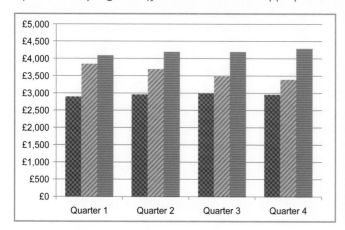
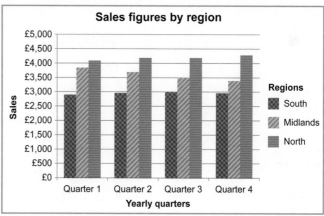

■ Figure 2.49: Which chart makes it easier to understand the information being shown? Why?

ACTIVITY

1 Using the Westgate Airport spreadsheet you created in the previous lesson, collapse the pivot table so just the days and total passengers are displayed and create a pie chart with this data.

2 Create a suitable title for the pie chart.

3 With the data in the pivot table expanded, create a bar chart showing how many passengers travelled to each destination on each day. Make sure the chart has clear and meaningful axis labels and a title.

4 Improve the appearance of the original data sheet you created for the Westgate Airport spreadsheet by applying appropriate font, colour shading and border formatting. Add an appropriate graph or image to the spreadsheet. When choosing the type of graph to use, bear in mind that a pie chart can only show one variable whereas bar and line charts can plot multiple variables on the same graph.

5 Extend the airport spreadsheet by adding departure times to the data and gate numbers. Then create a dashboard sheet that displays departures for a given day (which the user can select) or for a particular airline.

CHECK MY LEARNING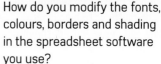

How do you modify the fonts, colours, borders and shading in the spreadsheet software you use?

Working in small groups, discuss how to make spreadsheets and dashboards both user friendly and effective in communicating their meaning (some internet research can help with this).

Learning aim B: assessment practice

How you will be assessed

Now that you have studied all of the topics in Learning aim B, you will need to show that you can apply all of the things you have learned to create a dashboard of your own.

Your teacher will give you an assignment to complete and will explain the evidence you need to provide and the submission date.

To complete the assignment, you will be given a large data set that you will need to:
- import into spreadsheet software
- use a variety of data manipulation methods to produce summaries of the data
- display the data summaries in a dashboard using a variety of suitable presentation methods.

Try the following tasks to help you build the skills and knowledge you'll need to complete your assignment.

CHECKPOINT

Strengthen
- Look carefully at any data you are going to use to create a dashboard and make sure you understand what it is telling you. Identify clearly which information you want to include in your dashboard and which is less important.
- Describe the different data manipulation tools that can be used to create effective dashboards.

Challenge
- Describe how you will use formatting to make the dashboard clear and professional.
- Assess the suitability of different presentation methods to make your dashboard clear and useful.

ASSESSMENT ACTIVITY 1   LEARNING AIM   B

Manipulate data using a variety of methods

Note: For this activity your teacher may give you a data set to use, or you could use the data set referred to in this activity from the Department of Transport.

Your school would like to encourage its students to use healthy and pollution reducing methods to get to school (such as walking and cycling) rather than being dropped by a parent in their car or taking the bus (although taking the bus is preferable to using a car). In order to support this, the school has asked you to create a 'Travel to school' dashboard.

- The data for this dashboard may come from your teacher, or you could refer to a survey carried out by the government on the methods children used to travel to school in 2014 (The Department of Transport National Travel Survey). You can find the results of the survey in the 'Travel to school factsheet: 2014' found here: https://www.gov.uk/government/publications/nts-factsheets

---

TIPS

To meet the criteria for this learning aim you need to carry out practical tasks, selecting and using methods to manipulate data and producing a dashboard. You need to provide evidence of these tasks, such as annotated screenshots showing the main development steps you went through, as well as the final completed dashboard.

- Using a variety of methods, manipulate the data you have identified. For example, you could create totals showing how many people travel by each method of transport and also calculate percentages that show what proportion of the children use each method. You could also calculate averages for data such as the distance travelled using each method.
- The following are some suggestions for the collection and manipulation of the data.
  - ☐ The 'Travel to school factsheet: 2014' produced by the Department of Transport summarises the data collected in the National Transport Survey. You can use this for ideas on the type of charts and graphs that you might use on your dashboard.
  - ☐ Hyperlinks within the factsheet allow you to download an Excel spreadsheet with all of the data from the survey in it. Look for the links with the title 'NTS0613'.
  - ☐ You can use functions such as VLOOKUP to extract specific data, such as the results for a particular year.

ASSESSMENT ACTIVITY 2   LEARNING AIM   B

Discuss how data is used in decision-making in two different sectors

- Produce a dashboard for the data you identified on travel to school. The dashboard should have the following features.
  - ☐ Display overall data about the proportion of people using different methods.
  - ☐ Use relevant presentation methods to display the data, including tables, graphs, conditional formatting and pivot tables.
  - ☐ Use titles, labels, graphics and a range of formatting features.
  - ☐ Enable the user to select the display of data about specific methods of transport; for example, you could use a validation drop-down box to allow selection of the transport method to be displayed.
- The following are some suggestions for creating your dashboard.
  - ☐ You could divide the dashboard into two main areas; the top part could display static data summarising the data across all the transport types. For example, you could include a pie chart showing the proportion of people using each method plus the average distances, time taken and costs across all the methods.
  - ☐ You can add a pivot table to the top part of the dashboard. If you use the methods of transport as the row labels for the pivot table and then add the data about distance, time taken and cost to the values to be summed up it will provide a useful summary.
  - ☐ The lower half of the dashboard could display data relating to a particular type of transport.
  - ☐ You can use a validation list box on the dashboard to allow the user to select the transport method data to display in the lower half of the dashboard.
  - ☐ The selection the user makes in the list box can be used to pick up the data from a table in the data sheet using a VLOOKUP function.
  - ☐ You can use formatting tools (fonts, colours, shading and borders) to provide a consistent and professional-looking user interface for the dashboard.
  - ☐ You should make sure the charts and graphs you include in the dashboard have titles and axis labels.
  - ☐ You should bear in mind that in Learning aim C you will be asked to outline the trends, draw conclusions and make recommendations from your dashboard.

TAKE IT FURTHER

You could collect data about transport methods used by different classes in your school. This would allow you to compare methods used by students in different years.

Drawing conclusions

Having created a dashboard, you now must consider how the dashboard can be used to help users draw meaningful and accurate conclusions from the information presented.

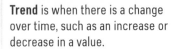
Trends

Spotting **trends** in lots of figures is difficult; however, it is much easier to spot trends on a graph. There are two main types of trend.
- An upward trend shows values increasing over time.
- A downward trend shows values decreasing over time.

Figure 2.50 shows an example of a graph of sales made in a retail company over a year in their three regions. The chart shows a downward trend, with sales falling across the 12 months.

KEY TERMS

Trend is when there is a change over time, such as an increase or decrease in a value.

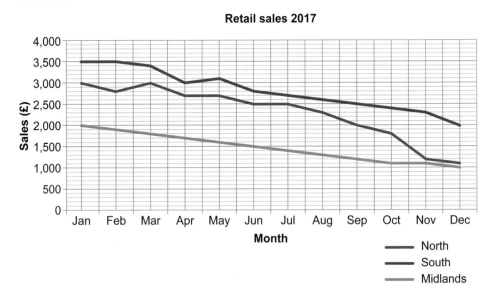

◘ Figure 2.50: What is the trend in sales across the three regions?

Note that not every month shows a fall in sales, but the overall trend is that sales are falling, in other words the sales at the end of the period are lower than those at the start.

Before reaching a conclusion about a trend, you need to make sure you are looking at enough data. If you were looking for evidence of global warming (that is, a trend in increasing temperatures over time), looking at temperature data for just a few years would not give enough information to confirm the existence of a trend in increasing temperatures. You would need to look at data across a much wider range of years, for example, 50 years instead of five years.

KEY TERMS

Pattern is a repeating change in the data over time.

Patterns

With some types of data you may be able to identify a **pattern** rather than a trend. One example of this would be seasonal patterns. Sales of some items depend on the season of the year (for example, more ice cream is sold in summer). The retail sector is a good example of where seasonal patterns exist. Clothing also has strong seasonal patterns with warmer winter clothes sold at the end of the summer and summer fashions coming into the shops early in spring.

Figure 2.51 shows an example of a graph where a seasonal pattern can be seen.

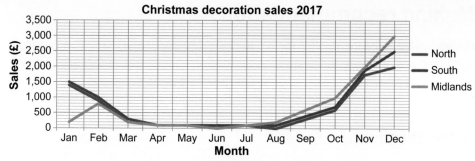

■ Figure 2.51: Some retail sales are dependent on the time of year

Other more complex patterns may also exist in data and might not be obviously connected. For example, the number of people travelling by car may increase when the weather is bad as cycling or walking is less pleasant when it is cold or raining.

Anomalies

Anomalies occur when some aspect of the data does not fit the overall trend or pattern. This may be because of an error in the data or it may be caused by unusual circumstances. Care should be taken to make sure anomalies do not affect the overall trends and patterns in the data. One way of helping to overcome the effects of anomalies is to ensure a large enough sample of data so that anomalies have little effect. An example of an anomaly might be snow in August or a surge in Christmas decoration sales in June.

Possible errors

Errors in data may come from many different sources. Human errors, such as typing mistakes, may cause incorrect data to be entered when the data is collected. As with anomalies, it's important that errors don't affect the trends or patterns in the data. In some cases it may be necessary to identify anomalies and errors in the data and delete them. You should also check the formulae you use in spreadsheets to ensure they are correct and use the correct cells.

The methods used to collect data and location or timing of the methods may also introduce **bias**. For example, if you carry out a survey on a hot and sunny day you are likely to get more positive opinions than if you carried out the same survey on a cold rainy day.

DID YOU KNOW?

Many large organisations, such as banks and supermarkets, collect large amounts of data about their customers. The collection and analysis of large volumes of data is known as big data. Analysing such large quantities of data can reveal patterns that can help organisations create advertising and marketing plans and develop new products.

KEY TERMS

Anomaly is when something differs from the normal or what is expected.

KEY TERMS

Bias is an external factor that may influence results.

ACTIVITY

1 Create a spreadsheet like the one shown or use the given spreadsheet at www.pearsonschools.co.uk/techawardDITsupport.

	A	B	C	D	E	F	G
1	Sales						
2		Sales volume					
3	Product no	Jan	Feb	March	April	May	June
4	AB10034	385	398	422	420	435	448
5	AB10035	425	410	402	3850	372	363
6	AB10036	695	670	652	645	682	697
7	AB10037	520	502	530	512	535	518
8	AB10038	620	632	625	635	6.4	645
9	AB10039	299	295	301	300	302	308

2 Using whatever methods you think appropriate, identify any trends or patterns in the sales for each product. There are also a couple of possible errors or anomalies. Try to identify them.

CHECK MY LEARNING

Explain the difference between:

• a trend and a pattern

• an anomaly and an error.

Give examples of each.

Making recommendations

Having looked at the information displayed in the dashboard and drawn conclusions about patterns or trends, the next step is to make recommendations that take advantage of what has been discovered. Conclusions describe what you have found, recommendations are suggestions about what should be done about it.

Using dashboards

To be able to make a recommendation based on a dashboard, the key requirement is that the dashboard contains sufficient information to enable an accurate recommendation to be made. If your family were thinking of going on holiday in May, Figure 2.52 shows the climate dashboard data for May for the location the data was collected for.

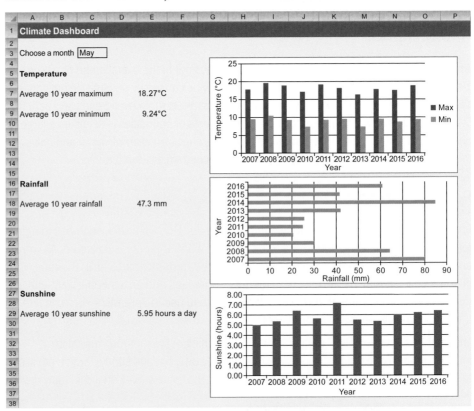

■ **Figure 2.52: What other information could be added to this dashboard?**

The temperature data is clear, showing the average maximum temperature is below 20 °C, so it will be warm without being hot. The rainfall data shows a wide variation, so people should be prepared for rain, possibly heavy rain. The sunshine data shows that there is an average of nearly 6 hours' sunshine each day. The dashboard therefore would allow us to make recommendations on the type of clothes to wear and the sort of activities that could be done while on holiday.

It is important to note that looking at monthly climate data over several years like this does not reveal any trends or patterns. What it does show, especially with the rainfall data, is that it's very unpredictable.

Another example is the dashboards many schools use to track student progress. Teachers can use these dashboards to identify students who may need support and to recommend interventions, such as catch-up classes or one-to-one coaching, to help them get back on track.

Targeting adverts

Many companies collect data on their customers. Supermarkets are a good example, with many of them using loyalty cards to collect detailed information about what their customers purchase. This data can be used to identify purchasing patterns, such as items that are often purchased together. These patterns can be used to target adverts at customers who are most likely to be interested in the products. The data can also be used to adjust product placements in supermarkets with products commonly purchased together moved closer to each other in the store.

Another possibility might be that patterns in the data reveal geographical differences in the number or amount of products sold. This might suggest that it would be beneficial to target adverts in the areas where take-up of the product is low as there is more opportunity to increase sales.

Deploying staff

Dashboards that show demand at various times can be used to make recommendations on the number of staff who need to be on duty at different times and on different days. In a customer service call centre (for example, of a bank, insurance company or mobile phone provider), the volume of calls is carefully monitored throughout the day, week, month and year. This can include data such as the number of incoming calls, the amount of time callers have to spend on hold and the length of calls. Typically, a call centre will use a dashboard to monitor this data and managers will review the patterns in the data to try to make sure the number of staff available to answer calls is adjusted to keep waiting times to a minimum.

Adapting transport schedules

Many types of transport, such as buses, trains and aeroplanes, run to a schedule. Scheduling is a complex process and needs to consider demand. A dashboard could be used to identify patterns in terms of the number of people who want to travel at different times and days. A dashboard can also help support decision-making in terms of the frequency and capacity of public transport at different times of the day and on different days.

■ Look at your local bus timetable. When does it run the most buses? Why do you think that is?

ACTIVITY

Some data follows that a bus company collected on the number of passengers who travel on different routes at different times.

Northchester Bus Company – average number of passengers travelling

Route		Time					
From	To	7 a.m.–9 a.m.	9 a.m.–11 a.m.	11 a.m.–1 p.m.	1 p.m.–3 p.m.	3 p.m.–5 p.m.	5 p.m.–7 p.m.
New Town	Southbury	2,467	2,315	2,105	1,986	2,539	2,128
Northchester	New Town	1,536	1,421	1,435	1,325	1,623	1,297
Southbury	Station	3,120	1,857	1,746	1,521	1,696	3,239

1 Use a variety of data processing methods on the data to identify any trends or patterns.

2 What recommendations can you make about the number of buses they should run at different times on each route?

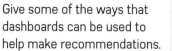

How presentation affects understanding

GETTING STARTED

In small groups, look at some of the dashboards you have created and discuss if the way they present data is clear enough for accurate conclusions to be drawn.

The way information is presented in the dashboard can have an impact on how that information is interpreted. Poorly presented information may make understanding what the dashboard shows difficult. How the information is presented may lead to it being misinterpreted.

There are several ways that presentation can affect the understanding of information.
● Information being misinterpreted – the way you present the data in a dashboard can have an impact on the way it is interpreted by the people who use that dashboard.
● Information being biased – bias can occur when the data is presented in such a way that it appears to support a particular opinion or show the information in a favourable light.
● Inaccurate conclusions being made – if the information in the dashboard is poorly presented, then it may lead to inaccurate conclusions being made.

Graphs and charts

One of the most common methods of presenting data in a dashboard is to use a graph or chart. There are a number of issues you need to consider when creating graphs or charts to avoid the results being misinterpreted.
● If the data contains values that are totalled up, don't include both the original values and the totals, otherwise this will result in a misleading chart. Include either the original value or the totals in the chart, but not both.
● A lot of data (for example, more than 10 rows) may result in a complex, difficult-to-read chart. If the chart editor doesn't have room to display the titles along the x-axis it will leave them out. However, once you enlarge the chart, the titles will appear as there will then be room to display them.
● Instead of enlarging the chart to correct this problem, it may be better to extract some subtotals from the data and chart only them rather than use all the data. Remember, one of the goals of creating a chart is to make the data easier to understand, so the chart should not be too complex.
● If your data contains blank rows or columns, the chart editor may include them in the chart it draws, which will result in a gap in the chart. It is best to remove any blank rows or columns before creating a chart.

LINK IT UP

To find out more about graphs and charts, go to lesson 'Presentation methods 1' in Learning aim B of this component.

■ What are the consequences if your graphs don't accurately represent the data?

Averages

Another example of presenting data is the use of averages. Statistic methods such as averages can be misused in a way that can cover up the true picture. For example, consider the following imaginary data.

Test results – out of 100, pass mark is 50

Student 1 – 99	Student 6 – 38
Student 2 – 29	Student 7 – 18
Student 3 – 32	Student 8 – 42
Student 4 – 95	Student 9 – 87
Student 5 – 25	Student 10 – 46

If you calculate the average of all the marks (add them up, then divide by the number of students) you get the result of 51. The average mark was above the pass mark, which sounds quite good. However, if you look carefully at the data only three of the ten students passed, but because they got high marks those marks compensate for the poor results from the seven students who failed. Note that in a dashboard the detailed data (such as the marks for individual students) may not be shown; only the summary data, such as totals or averages, might be shown.

Using the average exam score, a conclusion may be drawn that the class are doing reasonably well and don't need any additional support. However, the reality is that just a few students are doing well and everyone else needs support to get them through their exams.

ACTIVITY

Create a bar chart from the data of the student's test results.

Averages can be a good measure of a range of values. However, they don't give any idea of the spread of values across the range. Including a chart or graph with the averages can give a much better idea of the spread of values. For example, the bar chart you created of the students' test results in the activity clearly shows that the marks included a small number of very high marks but the majority of marks were below the pass mark.

ACTIVITY

1 Find examples of misleading charts; an internet search for 'misleading charts' will produce plenty of examples.

2 Discuss why they are misleading; for example, how the presentation of the chart makes interpreting it difficult.

CHECK MY LEARNING

Give five ways that information on a dashboard might be open to misinterpretation.

Learning aim C: assessment practice

How you will be assessed

Now that you have studied all the topics in Learning aim C, you need to use the dashboard you created for Learning aim B to show how you can draw conclusions and make recommendations based on the information displayed in the dashboard. You also need to consider how the presentation methods you have used impact on the conclusions and recommendations you have made.

CHECKPOINT

Strengthen
- Identify the trends and patterns that exist in your dashboard, and any errors or anomalies.
- Describe the presentation methods you have used in your dashboard.

Challenge
- Explain the conclusions you can draw from the information presented in your dashboard.
- Describe the recommendations you can make.
- Assess how the presentation methods you have used impact on the way the information is interpreted.

TIPS

You can start with simple trends, such as the most popular methods of getting to school.

Another trend you might want to investigate is how the distance pupils must travel to school is related to the method of transport they use.

To access the higher grades, you will need to analyse how your dashboard's presentation of data influences the conclusion drawn and recommendations made. An analysis involves a detailed examination of the dashboard's presentation methods, identifying its essential features and showing how they interrelate.

ASSESSMENT ACTIVITY 1 | LEARNING AIM | C

The dashboard you created for Learning aim B was meant to help the school investigate how students travel to school so that the school might be able to encourage the use of eco-friendly methods such as walking or cycling.

1 Explain the conclusions you have drawn and give recommendations from the dashboard.

2 Explain the trends that exist within the data in the 'Travel to school' dashboard you created for Learning aim B and draw some conclusions from it.

3 Give recommendations based on the conclusions you have drawn from the dashboard.

4 Explain the methods you have used to present the data and how those methods make it easy to understand.

TIPS

Look at how the use of different methods of transport varies across the different years in the school.

When explaining the methods you have used to present data, annotated screenshots will help to provide the evidence.

It is not easy to spot trends, so consider the suitability of the methods of presentation you have used on your own dashboard. Look at your dashboard with a partner and discuss the methods you have used and the trends or patterns within the data. Explain to your partner why you chose the presentation methods you did and how they make the data clear.

ASSESSMENT ACTIVITY 2 | LEARNING AIM | C

Assess how effective the presentation of data is in your dashboard.

- Write an assessment of how effective the dashboard is at presenting information.
- Assess how the presentation of the data affects the conclusions you have drawn from it and the recommendations you have made.

TIPS

Consider that the purpose of creating the dashboard was to help the school with its aim of encouraging eco-friendly methods of travelling to school.

The ease with which you were able to identify trends should tell you how effective the dashboard is at presenting the data.

The way you have created the dashboard may make identifying trends difficult. This is something you can include in your assessment.

You need to include an explanation of the link between the presentation methods you have used and the conclusions and recommendations you made. For example, if your dashboard has a pie chart showing the proportions of each transport method used, you need to say why you chose that presentation method and how it made identifying trends (such as more pupils take the bus to school than ride a bicycle) possible and how that supported your recommendations (such as the school needs to do more to encourage pupils to cycle to school).

TAKE IT FURTHER

Having looked at the way the presentation of data in your dashboard impacts on the conclusions and recommendations you can make, is there anything you would do differently with, or improve on, your dashboard? How can these changes be achieved?

03 Effective Digital Working Practices

Introduction

In this component you will explore how IT professionals work with digital solutions to integrate them into organisations and their activities.

You will draw on your understanding from Component 1 of how user interfaces for different systems are created and how projects are planned so that solutions can be developed. You will show your understanding of how data is used to make decisions and the types of threat that could affect the data, which you learned in Component 2.

You will develop your understanding of legislation and any regulations that are relevant to the development of an IT solution. You will also develop an understanding of security and digital safety, examining how threats and vulnerabilities could impact on the solution and the techniques that could be applied to reduce risk.

WHAT YOU WILL LEARN

In this component you will learn about:

A	Modern technologies and their impact on organisations
B	Threats to digital systems and how an organisation can manage them
C	Responsible, legal and ethical use of data
D	Planning and communication in digital systems.

Communication technologies

Most organisations use technology every day to gather and process information that can be used to help the organisation function. In this section you will be introduced to technologies that are used to help organisations exchange information, communicate and complete work-related tasks.

Ad hoc networks

Traditional networks are made up of several PCs, routers and other devices that are connected using cables and wires. These systems can be difficult to change because they are fairly fixed, for example cabling network nodes are often hardwired into buildings during construction. Modern technologies make it possible for organisations to work increasingly flexibly, allowing devices to be connected as needed. Connecting devices and systems in this way is called an **ad hoc network**.

◘ Table 3.1: Benefits and drawbacks of ad hoc networks

Benefits	Drawbacks
They are scalable, which means that more devices can be added at any time.	They are less secure. This is because they are more open and therefore are more likely to be accessed by attackers.
They are flexible, which means they can be temporarily set up at any time and in any location.	They have a reduced speed. There is a limit to the amount of data that can travel at one time.
They require limited setup. Devices can communicate instantly once a connection is established.	They often have no single device that has overall control, which means that the network can become unorganised.

Table 3.2 shows some examples of common types of ad hoc networks.

◘ Table 3.2: Key features of ad hoc networks

Ad hoc network	Key features
Personal area networks (PANs)	• Connects multiple devices that are nearby to create a small network • Allows exchange of files, images, documents, etc. • Devices typically use Wi-Fi or Bluetooth • Needs to pair devices using **PINs** before data can be exchanged • Limited range • Use of Bluetooth sometimes called a piconet
Open Wi-Fi	• Availability of Wi-Fi connections in public places, e.g. cafes, parks, train stations, coffee shops, etc. • Allows users to freely connect • Does not, generally, require passwords • May not be **encrypted** so communications may not be secure • Allows more flexible working patterns, such as remote working (working outside the office)
Tethering or personal hotspots	• Connects a device with a network connection to one without • Transfers data to and from the network using the device that has been tethered • Connects a notebook to a mobile phone with an internet connection, which is a popular use of this technique • Uses a wired tether (usually **USB**) or Wi-Fi to create a personal hotspot

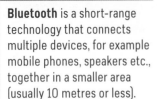

Security issues with open networks

An open network is one that anyone can access. You can search for them using a device, such as a Wi-Fi-enabled smartphone. Some open networks allow users to freely connect without entering a username or password. Connections that do not require a username or password are often **insecure** because they are not encrypted and you may receive a warning on your device before connecting to them.

Performance issues with ad hoc networks

You may encounter different issues when using an ad hoc network, including:
- poor or intermittent signal – an intermittent signal is one that comes and goes, often without warning
- limited range – Bluetooth connections have a limited range and the devices can often only connect if they are in the same room
- incomplete or interrupted data transfers.

Issues affecting network availability

Various issues can affect the availability and performance of both wired and wireless networks. These include:
- rural versus city locations – rural locations typically have fewer residents, so telecommunication companies may not invest in the same level of infrastructure (cell masts/towers etc.), resulting in poor network coverage
- developed versus developing countries – mobile networks may not be as advanced in developing countries due to lack of investment and logistical issues
- available infrastructure – services such as **streaming** a movie use a lot of a network's resources, which can place a strain on the system
- mobile network coverage – not all telecommunication companies in the UK (or even across the world) have the same levels of coverage, although this is slowly improving
- blackspots – these may occur where geographical features, such as hills and valleys, block wireless signals. Natural materials, such as thick stone and some modern building materials, can also make it harder for signals to be sent between devices on the network.

How can you use your device to find out if there is an open Wi-Fi connection in the area?

ACTIVITY

Work with a partner and create a presentation slide describing some of the network availability issues in the area where you live. You should aim to include the issues described above, where they are relevant.

CHECK MY LEARNING

Describe what is meant by the term 'ad hoc network'.

Give two security issues with open networks.

Explain the issues that can affect network availability.

Cloud storage

As an alternative to storing your files and folders on your PC or device, you can store them remotely. In this lesson you will find out about cloud storage.

What is cloud storage?

Cloud storage is where files created and used on one or more computers or devices are stored and managed remotely.

- The files are stored on **servers** so that they can be accessed via the internet.
- When you want to access the media, the data is **downloaded** or streamed to the device you wish to use it on. It remains in the file in the cloud unless you delete it.
- Data on your device can also be **uploaded** to the cloud.

Features and usage of cloud storage

Internet service providers often give users a cloud storage allocation as part of their phone or tablet contract. For example, iPhone, in early 2018, gave 5 GB.

- Users can choose to pay for more storage (or less if their needs change). This is an example of scalability.
- The alternative to using an online service from your phone provider is to use other services provided by third parties. Setting up this service with a provider is as simple as registering an account and providing the relevant details.
- Cloud storage is useful for storing backups of your files. Copies of the files are made on different servers so that they are protected if attacked or in the case of a natural disaster, such as fire or flood.
- You can also **synchronise** with the cloud. For example you could sync the photo library on your iPhone with the iCloud so that the photos taken are backed up and can be accessed from any device.

What is scalability?

Users have the option to change the amount of storage they can access and use. This is one of the key benefits of storing data in the cloud. If you need more, you can rent additional space. If you do not need the storage capacity you have allocated to you, you can reduce it and save money.

When is cloud storage available?

Files and media stored in the cloud can only be accessed when there is an internet connection.

- If the connection is broken, access will be terminated.
- The speed of the connection will also impact the speed at which files upload, download or stream.
- If there is a suitable connection, data and files in the cloud can be accessed 24/7.

◻ What do you store on the cloud?

What happens if your data is being stored in countries that do not have the same data protection laws as the UK?

Your data is protected in the UK and in the EU under the General Data Protection Regulations (GDPR), which came into force in May 2018. The US and EU have an arrangement called the Privacy Shield, which protects your data if it is held in the US.

The EU has released a list of countries outside the EU that it considers provide adequate protection for your data – for example, Andorra, Argentina, Canada, New Zealand and Switzerland.

How does cloud storage help users to complete tasks?

The main benefit of cloud storage is that data can be accessed from anywhere with an internet connection. Additionally, it can be accessed by anyone that has been given a username and password to enable them to access the folders and files. This allows users to continue to work on their files away from work and share access.

■ Table 3.3: Benefits and drawbacks of cloud storage

Benefits	Drawbacks
You can access your data from any device that has an internet connection and a web browser.	You cannot access your data without an internet connection. You also need a steady internet connection to ensure you can view your data without interruptions.
It is scalable. This means that you can purchase more storage space easily without having to physically install another storage server.	Although some cloud storage providers offer a limited amount of free storage space, additional storage space can be expensive.
The data and its security are managed by the cloud storage provider.	You have no control where or how your data is stored. You must trust that the provider is keeping your data safe and confidential.

LINK IT UP

To find out more about GDPR, go to lesson 'Data protection principles' in Section C of this component.

ACTIVITY

1 Work with a partner and investigate one of the online cloud storage services available.

2 Write down what services are provided for free and how much you would need to spend to increase your storage capacity. Are there any limitations or restrictions to the service, such as the size of files you can upload? Find out about their privacy policy and what rights you would have if you use their services. What devices could you use to access the data you store with the provider?

3 Share your findings with your class.

CHECK MY LEARNING

Give the key difference between data on your phone and data stored in the cloud.

Explain why it is a good idea to back up your files in the cloud.

Describe how cloud storage helps users to complete tasks.

Cloud computing

There are two main ways of accessing online applications. Web-based applications, which run entirely through browsers, and cloud-based applications where your local services and cloud service work together to provide a service.

Using online applications

When applications like Microsoft Office are installed onto a computer's hard drive they can usually only be accessed and used by the person sitting in front of the computer.

Software is now available that allows users to access their own PC from another machine, making their files and applications accessible from different places.

This is not the same as using applications that are stored and accessed through the cloud. Web-based applications are accessed via the internet and run in a web browser.

ACTIVITY

1 Use software, such as Word Online, and create a half page document. For example, write about your favourite TV programme, a sport you enjoy, or a game you play. Save the file to your local area and then open in the word-processing software you have installed on your PC. Make some changes to your document, such as:
   - reorder paragraphs
   - add some text
   - reformat headings
   - add images.

2 Discuss this activity with your class.

3 How similar were the two environments?

4 How intuitive was the online version?

☐ Table 3.4: Benefits of online applications

Benefit	Description
No installation	• Most online applications can be used entirely online without the need for content to be loaded onto a local machine. • This saves the technician time they would have spent installing the software on the machines.
Cost effective	• Organisations must buy licences. This means buying a copy of the application for each member of staff who will use it. • Using applications online means the organisation only pays for what it needs, and it is easy to add or remove users.
No need for updates	• If organisations buy their software and install it on their own machines, their technical staff will need to maintain and upgrade it. • If online applications are used, the software is updated and maintained by the provider.
Accessible from anywhere	• The software and files can be accessible from anywhere and at any time.
Direct access	• The application is directly accessible by anyone who needs to use it.

LINK IT UP

To find out more about collaboration tools, go to lesson 'Using modern technology when managing teams: communication and collaboration' in Section A of this component.

The key drawback of online applications is that you must have a reliable internet connection. There are several techniques you can use to make your internet connection and connection to the local network more stable and reliable.

1 Place your Wi-Fi transmitter high up and in an area free from clutter.

2 Use an extender to repeat the signal to other areas of the house that might otherwise be difficult to reach.

Application versions and features

Organisations make sure that their employees use the same version of software applications to ensure consistency of the features available to them. It also means that, within the cloud, employees can access and use files created by others (with permission), which maintains consistency.

Sharing a file with another user at the same time

By using software such as Google Docs™, two or more people can work on the same document file at the same time. For example, two colleagues in different places, one in an office in Birmingham, the other on a train between Manchester and Newcastle, can work on the same document. As shown in the image, the colour coding makes it clear who has added content to the file.

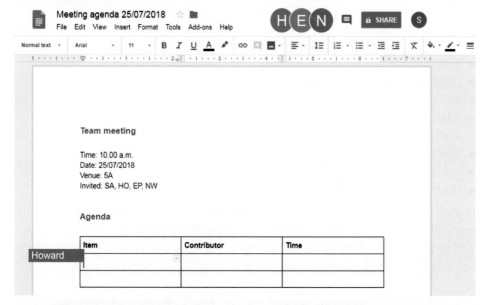

◼ The name of the person editing the document appears in real time. Why is this a valuable feature?

Collaboration tools

Software like Google Docs allows users to do a number of things.

- Add comments to documents – for example, suggesting document changes to a colleague. These comments can be deleted or hidden once the changes have been made.
- Track changes made to the document (who made the change, what the change was and when the changes were made). Some software uses different terminology – for example, Google Docs uses the term 'edit' and allows users to make direct changes to the document or to make suggestions about what could (or should) be changed. Users can accept or decline (refuse) changes that have been made to documents by others.
- Use services such as live editing – multiple users can work on the same document.
- Use chat facilities to discuss proposed changes to documents, plans or drawings before these changes are made in the file (these can be saved to show a history of document editing).

Selection of platforms and services

There are many different platforms available for an organisation's employees and **stakeholders** to use. Crossing platforms to use cloud-based technologies is sometimes difficult.

Platform selection

The most common platform types are shown in Table 3.5.

◘ Table 3.5: Common platforms

Desktop client	Notebook	Tablet	Smartphone

All these platforms can be connected to a network and make use of cloud technologies. However, they have different features that can affect available services, for example:

- screen size
- portability (how easy it is to move around)
- processing power
- RAM
- storage capacity (the amount of data a device can hold)
- user interface (keyboard, mouse, touchscreen, voice control, etc.)
- network connectivity speed
- operating system (Apple iOS, Microsoft Windows, Android, etc.).

In addition, each platform can use different services, which are accessed by the software applications available for that platform. For example, if you wanted an app that shared your location with your family but your family have a mix of Android and Apple devices, you would need to find an option that would be suitable for both platforms.

How platform and services selection affect cloud technologies

If an application is not available for a particular platform then the user will normally be unable to access the same cloud technologies, such as their cloud storage. For example, if you have written a document using Microsoft Word and then upload it to Google Docs, the appearance of the document may be different or some parts of the document may not be displayed.

Another issue to consider is that, even when applications are available for many platforms, the platforms can limit or change the quality of access to cloud technologies. As a result, a user's experience might be worse on certain platforms – for example, on mobile devices where wireless connectivity is poor or signal strength is low.

A complex application may not function well on a mobile device because of a lack of processing power or RAM. On a better-resourced desktop or notebook these issues may not exist. This creates difficulty moving between devices when accessing cloud-based technology. In some instances, such as Apple's iCloud Photo Library or Microsoft's OneDrive®, platform issues have been solved through careful design of the applications and their interfaces to give a seamless experience as illustrated in Figure 3.1.

1. User takes photograph on mobile phone

2. Image uploaded to user's cloud storage

3. Image downloaded and inserted into document on notebook

◘ Figure 3.1: How does this process provide a seamless experience?

Number and complexity of features

One key consideration when choosing a cloud platform is the number of features that it can provide and how complex they are. For example, an organisation may consider the following features to be important.

- Security methods – as data is stored in the cloud, you will need to consider how sensitive that data is and what security methods are provided by the cloud platform provider.
- Amount of storage space – cloud technologies usually allocate users a certain amount of storage space in the cloud. You therefore need to consider if you are going to need more storage space and the costs associated with this.
- Ease of use – users expect things to be simple to use. Having a platform that is easy to use will reduce the amount of training that is needed and allow employees within an organisation to be more productive.
- Frequency of updates – users may want to consider how often the cloud platform is updated. If there are regular updates then this can be good as you will frequently be given new features to use. However, this can also be bad because if there are lots of updates then this could increase the amount of **downtime** within an organisation while the updates are being installed.
- Accessibility – an organisation may have a range of different devices and therefore may need to consider if the cloud platform can be accessed across all of their devices.

Cost

Although many applications are downloadable for free, others need to be paid for. Paid-for applications may offer improved access to cloud technologies and services or be compatible with a broader range of cloud-based services.

An application's functionality and flexibility is often indicated by its cost. However, research and comparison of services and prices is always recommended. For example, SurveyMonkey is software used in market research, which anyone can use to create online surveys, and has various plan types, increasing in benefits the more you pay.

Interface design

Applications designed to perform the same function on multiple platforms must be suitable for different hardware devices – for example, keyboards or touchscreens, 22-inch screens or 7-inch screens.

Although programmers try to retain the same functionality on different devices, there are often some features that may be difficult to use or be entirely absent because of the platform's interface limitations. This might be because a screen is too small (so functions are not visible), there is no voice control (no access to voice command features), or there are issues about the availability of **geo-data** etc.

ACTIVITY

Select an application that uses cloud technology and is available on different platforms. Compare the different interfaces and functionality available. How do they compare? Which platform is best? Give reasons for your answers.

KEY TERMS

Downtime is a period when a computer and its services are unavailable.

Geo-data is geographical information that is stored in a way that it can be used by devices such as smartphones and tablets to provide data about your location.

LINK IT UP

To find out more about interface design, go to Component 1, Learning aim A.

CHECK MY LEARNING

Explain what is meant by platform.

Give three attributes that can affect a platform's available applications and services.

Give an example of using cloud technologies on different platforms.

Give three factors that might impact the use of cloud technologies on a mobile device.

ACTIVITY

Case study

Moov2gether is a national chain of estate agents that has offices and a website. Their managing director has been investigating how they can improve their digital working practices by making better use of cloud technologies while observing data protection principles and ethical concerns regarding their customers' data.

In groups, make a list of possible platforms and services that Moov2gether could use to improve their employees' work practices and their customers' user experience, while still observing data protection principles and considering ethical concerns.

Using cloud and traditional systems together

GETTING STARTED

Which services would you need to synchronise before they can be used on a new device?

Many services use cloud technologies to store important data, which can be synchronised between different devices.

Synchronising content over devices

Sometimes applications and files are located on an organisation's own systems or user's PC, or they could be in the cloud. Most organisations and many individuals use a combination of both. When you are using a combination of both, synchronisation is particularly important. For example, a salesperson has files stored on their work PC, which are then synchronised to their laptop and are available via a smartphone.

Another example of synchronisation over devices is using Apple's iTunes to manage the media on an Apple iPhone or iPad. A user can choose to automatically back up their device to the cloud, and to only sync ticked songs and videos (rather than all content) over Wi-Fi. If the user has several devices that access the same cloud content, all the devices would be updated.

Media (games, music and video) could be stored on your home machine or in the cloud. Synchronising the content of devices is often optional but is important if you want to access the same files on each device, and it is essential if you are working with documents to make sure you are always using the most up-to-date version.

◘ What services do you synchronise across your devices?

Online/offline working

Laptops are often issued to staff who work from remote locations, such as their own homes, at a customer's premises or when travelling. This allows them to access an organisation's systems while they are away from their normal business location (off-site).

Communications that may need to be shared include:
- a new order processed by sales staff
- information about work done by an engineer for a customer so that an invoice can be raised
- a technical manual for a device or installation to help a computer engineer with a repair.

◼ **When might it be useful to work remotely?**

Most laptops connect to the internet using Wi-Fi. If no Wi-Fi connection is available, it may be possible to tether laptops to smartphones. This way, the phone is being used as a personal hotspot, which allows the laptop to connect to the internet via the phone.

If no internet connection is possible, then the user will work offline and upload or synchronise the content with the relevant systems when an internet connection is available.

Managing notifications

The Windows 10 operating system has a Sync Centre with settings that allow users to sync files between devices. Users can set preferences (such as how often syncs should take place), view the results of a sync activity and take action if there have been any problems.

Managing a sync process requires the user to respond to notifications that are generated by the software managing the sync process. An example of a notification would be one that warns the user that the copy of the file they are synchronising may be older than the file that already exists on the system. In this situation, the synchronisation process will wait for action from the user.

Notifications can usually be configured depending on user needs. Some users switch off, or reduce the frequency of, notifications where the only required access is to confirm with a 'Yes' click.

LINK IT UP

To find out more about Wi-Fi, tethering and personal hotspots, go to lesson 'Communication technologies' in Section A of this component.

ACTIVITY

Watch a YouTube video about backing up and synchronising content between devices. Create a short, step-by-step guide that explains how to backup and synchronise media content between a PC and at least one device.

CHECK MY LEARNING

Explain why you should sync content between devices and systems.

Explain how a personal hotspot helps with synchronisation.

Choosing cloud technologies

There are several different factors that organisations will have to consider when choosing cloud technologies that will work for them and their situation.

Disaster recovery policies

Most cloud technology services offer backup services as part of their set-up costs. Sometimes these costs are included in the fees that the organisation pays to the provider over the length of a contract. On other occasions the organisations may be required to pay an installation fee up front.

Automatic backing up of data is usually carried out at quiet periods, such as outside of the organisation's working hours.

A disaster recovery policy is typically designed to set out the actions that will need to take place after a disaster, for example an attack or natural disaster, such as a fire or flood, to restore an organisation's services and processes as quickly as possible.

Cloud technologies can generally be relied on to:

- be unaffected by attack or disaster as they are physically located away from the organisation itself
- have appropriate nightly backups, particularly if there are many transactions each day, so that in the event of a disaster very little data is lost
- be protected by good security.

▫ **Table 3.6: Benefits and drawbacks of disaster recovery policies**

Benefits	Drawbacks
They can reduce the amount of time it takes to recover following a cyber security disaster.	It is not always possible to think of every single risk that could occur before an attack is carried out.
They set out the roles of each person so everybody knows what to do following an attack.	Once the policy has been created, it needs to be continually updated to ensure new threats have been accounted for.

Being able to rely on cloud technologies in this way makes disaster recovery much easier for many organisations and can be a key reason for their selection.

The impact of cloud technologies on data security

An organisation has a responsibility to ensure that its data is secure, particularly anything relating to its customers. When organisations make use of cloud computing solution providers to store their data, they must be assured that the providers are also taking data security seriously.

Most cloud computing solution providers, such as Google, Amazon® and Microsoft, will have several strategies in place to protect the security of their customers' information.

The largest cloud technologies service providers are experts in data, server and network security and are focused on keeping their customers' data secure. This is because any substantial security breach could damage their public image and lead to serious consequences for the organisation, such as loss of customers and legal action.

As a result, the cloud technologies service provider will employ a range of security measures, including keeping their digital systems protected at their large data centres, where many computers are located under one roof. They will also ensure they are controlling who has access to data and are storing data safely and in an encrypted format where necessary. Additionally, broken or outdated digital systems will be appropriately disposed of.

◻ **Did you base your cloud technology choice on security?**

These service providers also audit their security on a regular basis and typically meet the internationally agreed security standards for the sector. For example, security standard ISO/IEC 27018 gives guidance for service providers that process PII (personally identifiable information) and sets out controls that need to be implemented to manage known risks to the data. This is one of the safeguards that protects personal data and is an international standard.

In July 2016 the European Commission agreed that the EU-US Privacy Shield Framework is an acceptable method for EU companies to comply with requirements under its Data Protection Directive in connection with the electronic transfer of personal data from the EU to the US. This framework protects EU organisations when using US-based cloud technology storage, for example Google Cloud Platform™.

Compatibility issues

Compatibility usually isn't an issue for organisations when choosing cloud technologies from well-known providers. Most cloud technologies will use either Microsoft Windows or Linux, which are examples of well-supported and documented operating systems.

This should enable organisations to run any combination of popular applications and services without an issue.

ACTIVITY

Case study

Moov2gether is trying to decide which technologies to use to ensure that its data is secure and can be recovered quickly. Using what you know about the organisation, what would you advise? Work with a partner and write the text of an email message to the manager of Moov2gether detailing your suggestions.

DID YOU KNOW?

The most popular security standards relating to digital systems are created by ISO – International Organization for Standardization. Three certifications are particularly important:

ISO 27001 – covering systems, applications, people, technology, processes and data

ISO 27017 – cloud security

ISO 27018 – cloud privacy.

CHECK MY LEARNING

Describe how cloud technologies can support an organisation's disaster recovery policies.

Give three ways a third-party cloud technology provider keeps an organisation's data safe.

Give three important security standards that are internationally recognised.

Maintenance, set up and performance considerations

GETTING STARTED

Cloud technologies offer many benefits over traditional systems, but they do have their drawbacks. Identify three possible issues that organisations might have when using cloud technologies.

LINK IT UP

To find out more about dashboards, go to lesson 'What is a dashboard?' in Component 2, Learning aim B.

KEY TERMS

Virtual machines (VMs) are software applications that are designed to behave as if they are a whole computer. A larger computer will run several virtual machines, using the larger computer's resources, but behaving as if they are separate devices.

System administrator is a person who is responsible for a technology or series of technologies. They have to make sure that the systems are maintained, configured and reliable.

Organisations must be aware of possible drawbacks in relation to cloud technologies. This lesson explores several factors that should be considered.

How cloud storage solutions are maintained

Maintenance of cloud computing solutions is usually automatic because solution providers regularly update processes, which keep the **virtual machines (VMs)** up to date and make sure that the solutions stay healthy and secure. In addition, organisations may add their own services and updates as part of their security policies.

Most cloud computing solutions have web-based dashboards that can monitor activity levels, such as CPU usage, disk space and network communication. Additional settings can email the organisation's **system administrator** about potential problems, including high CPU usage, low available disk space etc.

Downtime

Downtime is usually limited on a cloud computing solution. Downtime of just a few minutes can be a serious issue for organisations that rely on a continuous 24-hour service, such as hospitals, power stations, banks or online retailers.

Downtime can be caused by:
- interrupted internet connectivity
- cyberattacks
- updates. When updates take place, cloud servers usually need to go offline, which means that users cannot access them. The disruption caused can be minimised by carrying out these updates during quieter times, such as during the night.

Setting up cloud service/storage

Cloud computing solutions have a reputation for being quick and easy to set up when you compare them to setting up a local server.

◾ Table 3.7: Requirements for setting up a server versus cloud storage

Setting up a server requires:	Setting up a cloud computing VM solution requires:
<ul><li>hardware purchase</li><li>hardware build or customisation</li><li>operating system installation and configuration</li><li>applications and services installation and configuration</li><li>device hardening to protect from external threats</li><li>test network connectivity.</li></ul>	<ul><li>selecting the cloud computing solution provider, e.g. Google, Amazon, Microsoft, etc.</li><li>creating an account and supplying payment information</li><li>selecting type of cloud computing solution required, e.g. storage, computing or both</li><li>selecting VM performance required, e.g. processing power, storage capacity etc.</li><li>selecting operating system and role of solution, e.g. web server, database server, storage server</li><li>deploying the device</li><li>performing additional configuration as required.</li></ul>

In many cases, a cloud computing solution is quicker to set up and run. Most providers also allow cloud-based solutions to be 'cloned' using a single button click on a web-based interface, creating an almost-instant duplicate of the original VM. This can be a useful way of backing up data and services to other locations.

Performance considerations

Cloud computing solutions are not noticeably lacking in performance or responsiveness when compared to local servers and can typically fulfil the same roles as a web server, database server etc. For example, when most employees start work at the same time there is a sudden demand on the computer's resources as everyone logs in. Many organisations will tell you that there are times of day when the computer system needs to manage more transactions.

Some cloud computing providers may limit certain functionality, such as preventing cloud computing solutions from being used to distribute **spam**.

Available devices, operating systems and communication technologies generally follow accepted standards, which are the agreed expectations of products or services. However, some cloud computing providers may use unique products or services that are not 100 per cent compatible and this can cause issues for data transfer.

KEY TERMS

Spam is electronic junk mail, usually sent with a commercial purpose.

Inbox (8)
Spam (99)
Trash (3)

◻ Why would cloud computing solutions want to stop spam?

◻ Table 3.8: Benefits and drawbacks of cloud technologies

Benefits	Drawbacks
• Technologies are generally secure 'out of the box'. • Technologies are kept up to date. • Automatic backups may be created as part of the plan. • Solutions can be duplicated easily. • Solutions can be re-provisioned quickly and without fuss. • Technologies may require less monitoring. • Technologies may require less manual intervention. • Disruption of service is generally rare.	• Some services and roles may not be allowed, e.g. mail servers. • A good internet connection is required. • Organisation's data is stored on the internet. • Pricing plans may be more expensive than expected. • Incompatible products or services may cause issues with data transfer.

ACTIVITY

Case study

The managers at Moov2gether are trying to decide whether to invest in a new server or to move to cloud technologies. What advice would you give to them? Compare the two alternatives. Remember to talk about maintenance as well as setting up the technologies.

CHECK MY LEARNING

Explain why downtime might be reduced with a cloud computing solution.

Give two potential drawbacks of using a cloud computing solution.

Collaborative technologies

Collaborative technologies enable staff within organisations to work together more effectively by allowing them to communicate and share information and documentation more easily.

Organisations make use of a wide variety of technologies and software to help employees communicate and collaborate, enabling them to work together on day-to-day tasks and projects. For example, employees in different locations could work together on designs for a new product, working in the same files at the same time.

The technologies available in the organisation will be carefully chosen to support the tasks that are being carried out. Employees will be given appropriate software, which will allow them to communicate and collaborate as required by their job.

The benefits of collaborative technologies

Table 3.9 gives some features of collaborative technologies and how they benefit organisations.

◼ **Table 3.9: Benefits of collaborative technologies**

Benefit	Description
Global and multicultural workplace	Communicating and collaborating using technology can help build relationships between people of different ages, gender, religion or culture. This leads to increased creativity and diversity in the workplace.
Inclusivity	This is one of the key areas where technology has made a real difference – with functionality to help those who have limitations or disabilities. For example, people with visual impairments can work on the same files as those with no impairment by using software that can enlarge the text, apply colour in a particular way or use specialist software that captures speech and converts it to text or reads text to the user.
24/7/365	You may have seen 24/7 logos on TV channels, on shop doors or on other facilities, such as petrol stations. This means that the service or facility is open 24 hours a day, 7 days per week. But what does the inclusion of 365 mean? It means 365 days a year – which means all day, every day, all year round. Examples of a 24/7/365 service include the BBC's News Channel and the emergency services or an online retailer where you can purchase a movie at 3 a.m. on a Sunday morning, then download and watch it immediately. Just as importantly, internet content is available 24/7/365, with users able to access pages at any time of the day or night.
Team flexibility	Teams who work in different locations, countries or time zones can benefit from using technologies that allow them to share information and to contribute to projects from remote locations and at different times of the day. An organisation's working day can be lengthened, for example where they need to provide support for customers. One team can finish their day as another team in a different time zone starts. In terms of projects, this would simply mean that work could continue on the project when one team goes home, leading to faster completion of projects. Teams can be made up of a variety of employees, for example some staff may be permanent employees while others might be casual staff, on short-term contracts or freelance suppliers who are self-employed.

When collaborative technologies are used, adjustments might need to be made to suit user needs. Collaborative technologies are chosen to suit employee activities and could include a variety of communication software, such as:

- interoffice chat programmes, for example, LiveChat® or Office Chat®, which are useful for answering business questions more quickly than through email
- conferencing software like GoToMeeting™, which is used to support meetings without employees having to travel and can bring together suppliers and freelancers.

◘ Why is conference software so important for organisations?

You should note that when designing solutions that include communication software it is important to check that the software is available for all platforms (to ensure it can be used on all relevant devices).

Projects are often team activities so software like Google Drive and Dropbox™ can be used to support document sharing, or FlockDraw™ where team members can edit images simultaneously in real time.

If several people are required to work on the same document, they could each save the document onto their computer, which would create multiple copies of the same document. It can then become difficult to see everyone's work. Also, if person A sends their document to Person B, then it could overwrite Person B's version.

A solution to these problems is to use **version control**, which can have the following features.

- Workflow – only one person can work on the document at a particular time. The person who currently has access will have edit access so that they can make changes. Everybody else will have read access so that they cannot make changes while another person within the team is making changes.
- History – a log of what has been changed and who has changed it is kept. Therefore you can see what changes have been made and then either agree with them or disagree with them. If you disagree with them, then the document can be rolled back, which will delete the changes you disagree with.

KEY TERMS

Version control records changes to documents and files over time so that all versions can be recalled if needed.

CHECK MY LEARNING

Give two examples of how collaborative technologies benefit inclusivity in the workplace.

Explain the term '24/7/365'.

Describe how collaborative technologies promote inclusivity.

ACTIVITY

Watch a YouTube video demonstrating collaborative software being used. Use this information to explain to the owner of an estate agency how they could use software to enable collaborative working between staff in different offices.

Using modern technology when managing teams: communication and collaboration

Modern technologies have made it much easier for managers to monitor the activities of their teams.

Tools for collaboration

There are many online tools that teams can use to promote collaboration. One such tool is called Basecamp®. This online tool has many useful features that teams can use to manage one or more projects at a time.

Each project has its own dashboard displaying key information.

- A *To-do* area is where tasks can be listed and allocated to members of the team, while any documents belonging to the project can be added to an area called *Docs & Files*.
- The *Message Board* feature is where updates or other news for the team are posted; *Campfire* is a chat room feature where members of the team can have casual chats about different aspects of the project.
- The *Schedule* is where key dates are listed, such as the deadlines by which tasks must be completed.

GETTING STARTED

Look at the features of chat software that you use on your PC or device. Write down how often you use the software in relation to your schoolwork and how often you use it for social purposes (for example, 60 per cent in relation to schoolwork and 40 per cent for social purposes).

LINK IT UP

To find out more about planning, go to lesson 'Use project planning techniques' in Component 1, Learning aim B.

To find out more about dashboards, go to lesson 'What is a dashboard?' in Component 2, Learning aim B.

❑ **What other useful collaboration features can you think of?**

Communicating as a team

Many organisations use inter-office chat programs to help staff in different departments or locations to have quick discussions without relying on email, phone calls or crossing the office to talk to a colleague in person.

▣ **How could online chat programs be useful for you when working on a class project?**

One of the main benefits of this software is that you can see which of your colleagues are online. It is therefore clear who can be contacted. Alternative settings include 'busy', 'unavailable' and 'offline'.

The key benefits of using collaboration and communication software to manage teams include:

- storing and managing relevant working files in a single location
- ensuring that the file being worked on is the most up to date (as there is only one working copy of the file)
- archiving previous versions of the file (and accessing them if needed)
- using features of the software to allow team members to work on files at the same time
- communicating with the whole team simultaneously
- providing group support, as well as support for individuals, by the manager
- saving discussions (in case they are needed later).

ACTIVITY

In pairs, create a presentation on a topic of your choice. You should use an online platform, such as Google Slides™. You should both work on the same presentation at the same time and not communicate verbally with each other while you are creating the presentation.

When you have completed this, discuss how easy you found this task, and the benefits and drawbacks this type of software may have for organisations.

CHECK MY LEARNING

Explain why dashboards are a useful tool for helping teams to work together.

Give three key benefits of using inter-office communication tools.

Explain why scheduling helps teams work better together.

Using modern technology when managing teams: scheduling and planning

GETTING STARTED

How do you make sure that you remember important events? Do you use a diary? Does your email software include a diary facility? Do you use it? If so, when and how? If not, how could it be useful to you?

There are many benefits to using scheduling and planning software, and project teams will use different features depending on the context of the project.

Scheduling and planning

When you create a new project in planning software you type in the start and end dates and it automatically calculates the number of days involved. When managing teams, you could use project planning software to allocate tasks and control the schedule.

LINK IT UP

To find out more about different planning tools, go to lesson 'Co-ordinating project tasks' in Component 1, Learning aim B.

◻ What are the benefits and drawbacks of online scheduling tools?

The processes for setting up a working team may differ between systems. Generally you can set up a working team by inviting team members using their email address. The team member is then notified and is given a **URL** and password to access the system. When you invite users you can assign a role to them. This will determine their level of access in the system, for example a Collaborator usually has edit access whereas a Participant would only have view access.

KEY TERMS

URL stands for **U**niform **R**esource **L**ocator and is the address of a page on the World Wide Web.

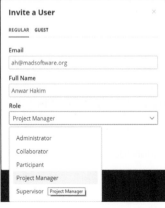

◻ What level of access do you think a Project Manager would have?

To add activities to the project you open the calendar function to the relevant month, click on the day and add the event. You can assign participants to the activity through a drop-down box.

Each participant then receives an email to notify them of additions or changes to the calendar. The notification centre can be configured to change the number and frequency of emails.

Using scheduling and planning software to manage teams

Table 3.10 shows the benefits of using scheduling and planning software to manage and work within teams.

◨ **Table 3.10: The benefits of scheduling and planning software**

Benefit	Description
Access	Files and folders can be stored in one place so that all members of the team can access them.
Tracking	Project managers can track progress and monitor the activities of the team members.
Version control/ archive	Older versions of documents can be archived to ensure that the documents used are always the most recent ones. The archive is a file of all the previous versions of documents.
Timelines and deadlines	Project deadlines and key milestones can be automatically synchronised with team member calendars.
Communication and collaboration	The software automatically allows for variations in time zones. This can enable workers in different time zones to see when they need to do tasks in their own time zone. For example, a deadline of Tuesday 5 p.m. in the UK would display as a deadline of Tuesday 12 noon in New York or Wednesday 1 a.m. in Tokyo.

LINK IT UP

To find out more on milestones, go to lesson 'Planning project timescales' in Component 1, Learning aim B.

ACTIVITY

Do you have homework for subjects on set days each week? Using scheduling and planning software and, if necessary, your email software's diary functionality, add and edit at least four events that reflect your homework schedule. Use the recurring function that automatically copies repeating events into the same day each week or month.

Explain the benefits and drawbacks of using software to schedule tasks in this way. Would you consider using scheduling like this in the future?

CHECK MY LEARNING

Give three benefits of using scheduling/planning software to manage project teams.

Explain how you could use planning software to manage your own activities.

Communication with stakeholders

Organisations use a wide selection of communication technologies to connect with their stakeholders, from their corporate websites to social media platforms such as Facebook®.

Technologies for communication

An organisation's stakeholders include customers, employees, suppliers and anyone else with an interest in the organisation.

A corporate website is one belonging to a company or organisation and communicates important information about the organisation, such as its main products and where they can be purchased.

A social media site is usually less formal and allows the organisation and its stakeholders (especially users such as customers) to communicate with each other, for example, by exchanging news and opinions.

Table 3.11 shows how organisations use different technology to communicate with their stakeholders.

◻ Here is a company's design for their corporate website. How would this be different to the company's social media site?

◻ Table 3.11: How organisations use technology to communicate with their stakeholders

Channels	Description
Websites	Provide a range of content, including information on products or services, prices, stock information and special offers so that customers can buy items online.
Social media	Organisations can communicate in a much more relaxed way, for example, customers can ask for advice about a product or for instructions on how to install software.
Email	More formal method of communication that has largely taken over from letters as the email is received almost instantly.
Voice communication	Online meetings are becoming increasingly popular, particularly where participants are located in different places. It brings people together without them being physically in the same room. Sometimes this can include live video as well as audio. This technology is often used to deliver training. The presenter can display presentation slides on the screen (screen-sharing) and the participants can hear the presenter speak. In most cases the participants use a chat window to ask questions and the presenter responds with their voice.
Live chat	Some organisations offer technical support and customer service via live chat functionality, where a text messaging app is used to support a conversation. Users almost always have to log into their accounts to access this feature.

How to choose the right communication channels

Organisations must think carefully about which communication channels they should use in different situations to share information, data or other media. Communications can largely be classified as either private/direct or public.

Private communications

Private communications are those between specific individuals, with the expectation that only they will be able to see the messages.

Types of information that an organisation would want to communicate privately might include:
- customer queries, such as order/payment information or requests for payment
- customer payment details, including account details and payment methods
- customer contact details, such as phone numbers or changes of address.

Public communications

With public communications the anticipation is that anyone can see the information. Information that the organisation might want to share more publicly includes:
- product information, such as special features
- price reductions and other special offers
- advice on using a product.

Some of the channels listed in Table 3.11 are more appropriate for public communication, others for private situations.

ACTIVITY

Look at the channels in Table 3.11. Which are public and which are private? Make a comparison table, placing each channel in the correct place. Share your answers with your class.

ACTIVITY

Case study

Moov2gether has many branches across the country. In each office there is a team of agents that looks after property sales in its local area. An important aspect of selling a house may be meeting clients outside normal working hours to carry out viewings, negotiate offers from potential buyers and keep homeowners informed of progress.

How could Moov2gether use modern technologies to communicate with their stakeholders? List five options and explain how they would use them. For example, emailing a purchase offer to a homeowner.

CHECK MY LEARNING

You have been asked by a teacher to help them use technology to inform all members of your year group about an upcoming school trip.

Knowing which technologies and platforms your fellow learners like to use, recommend three communication channels the teacher could use to advertise the trip.

Explain why you have chosen these channels. If you were to advertise it to parents, would the channels you choose be any different? If so, why?

Accessibility and inclusivity

Computers should be capable of being accessed and used by everyone, but some users have physical challenges that make aspects of computer use difficult or impossible. Technologies that help users overcome some of these challenges are becoming increasingly available.

Interface design

Organisations must think about how a website looks when it is viewed on different devices. This is because the screen size affects what is visible and how it is displayed. Websites that do not adjust for different devices are known as non-responsive websites.

One example is the Amazon website. Amazon's solution is to provide apps for different devices to make sure that their content looks its best on any device. They also have a mobile website that reflects the app design.

Interface layout

The layout of screens also contributes to inclusivity and accessibility of web content. For example, the content should be simply laid out with clear differentiation between different sections, with simple input and navigation controls that allow all users to easily manage their interaction with the onscreen environment.

Organisations must think about how a website looks when it is viewed on different devices. The screen size affects what can be displayed and how it is displayed.

Accessibility features

Adjusting fonts, colour and contrast are a few simple ways to increase accessibility, but these adaptations may not be appropriate for all users. Most operating systems have other accessibility technologies that can be applied to the user's own computer to make all software or websites more accessible.

Operating systems, such as Windows, have built-in accessibility features, such as magnifiers to enlarge the onscreen text, the option to change the colour schemes and even to use the computer without a display, mouse or keyboard.

▢ **What other accessibility features do you think are needed?**

ACTIVITY

Which colour combinations are recommended for users with dyslexia? Use the internet to explore the recommendations of the British Dyslexia Association.

There are many other tools that can be used to further enhance accessibility, such as screen readers, which read the content of the screen to the user. An example of this is NaturalReader®.

Software is also available that converts speech into text.

- The speech is captured through a microphone and converted into text on the screen. It includes products like Dragon®, Dictation Pro, VoiceNote II and Express Scribe.
- Before it can be used reliably it needs to be calibrated. This means that it must be taught how to interpret and manage accents, words said incorrectly, different pronunciations, too fast speech or words merged together. Without this calibration the software might not work efficiently.
- Other issues that may need to be considered are the environment in which the software is being used as background noise can cause interference.

ALT text is another tool that allows developers to add a text-based description of each image on a website for the benefit of blind or partially sighted users. You might expect this to be relatively straightforward, but unless the description is carefully considered, the description of the image components may not be relevant to the context of the image. In addition, you would need to decide which parts of the image are important and which are not.

LINK IT UP

To find out more about accessibility needs, go to lesson 'User accessibility needs' in Component 1, Learning aim A.

KEY TERMS

ALT text is alternative text that describes an onscreen image for users with visual impairments.

Inclusivity

Inclusivity is about different ways to involve employees who have useful skills to contribute, but who are not able to work in a traditional way, such as someone recovering from a hip operation who is unable to drive to work yet, but could work from home.

Organisations can allow their employees to work more flexibly permanently. This could be by allowing them to work hours that suit their childcare commitments or to choose working hours and locations that suit them.

ACTIVITY

Here are two images. Choose one and write descriptive text to support the image, making sure you include the components of the image. Share your description with your class.

CHECK MY LEARNING

Describe ALT text.

Give four examples of accessibility technologies or features.

How modern technologies impact on an organisation

GETTING STARTED

How does technology impact on your school?

Modern technology impacts on organisations in several ways, including cost, time, staff and security.

Infrastructure

The impact of infrastructure on an organisation has many factors, including:
- costing what is needed to buy and set up services
- training for staff
- implementing and testing time for the technology before staff use it in their work
- maintaining technology – if software is not updated it may not work correctly
- running costs of hardware, such as printer ink
- implementing a strategy to ensure that the organisation's data is backed up and secure.

Managers must weigh up the costs of the technology against the benefits it will bring. For example, issuing mobile phones to a sales team has a set up and ongoing cost (such as line rental), but the speed with which orders can be processed is a benefit for both the organisation and the customer.

■ Table 3.12: Benefits and drawbacks of technologies

Technologies	Description	Benefits	Drawbacks
Communication technologies (devices)	It is now common practice for managers to be issued with laptops, mobile phones and tablets.	Less paperwork to carry as files can be accessed electronically.	Can be intrusive as staff can be contacted day and night, which can impact on the employee's work/life balance.
Local platforms	Software installed and used locally.	May run faster than a web-based alternative.	Cannot be accessed outside the office.
Web-based platforms	Software installed and used online.	Can be accessed from anywhere.	May run more slowly than local alternatives if connectivity is poor or demand is high.
Availability	Because of the costs of technology, many organisations try to find different ways of using what they have, rather than simply buying more.		

Security of distributed/dispersed data

KEY TERMS

Distributed data is split into lots of bits and stored in different places.

Dispersed data is multiple copies of the same data in different locations.

Data that is **distributed** or **dispersed** can be stored over more than one server and network. The locations of the different bits or copies of the data need to be mapped so that the data can be found when it is needed. For example, an airline has a website in England that customers use to book tickets. The data for the tickets is processed in India. The data is then shared with check-in and arrivals desks at each airport in the world that the customer will visit as part of their journey.

■ Table 3.13: Benefits and drawbacks of distributed and dispersed data

Benefits	Drawbacks
• The data is less likely to be lost because it is not all in one place. • Security is greater because criminals would not know where the data is being stored. • The data can be accessed over different networks. • Greater reliability.	• There are more locations to keep secure. • Locations of data need to be tracked so that the system knows where the data is. • It can take a little longer to access data that is further away. • Additional software is often required.

24/7 access

Organisations that use technology are usually accessible 24/7. Tables 3.14 and 3.15 show the benefits and drawbacks for both customers and organisations of 24/7 access.

■ Table 3.14: Benefits and drawbacks for customers of 24/7 access

Benefits	Drawbacks
• Orders can be placed and accounts accessed at any time of the day or night. • No need to stand at the till to pay for your purchases as you can buy online. • Lower prices as there is more competition. • More choice as you can access a much wider range of products. • No need to spend money on transport or parking. • Able to check your bank balance and pay bills at any time of the day or night. • Ability to transfer money from one account to another without having to go to the bank.	• Usually you must wait until your purchase is delivered and pay extra if you want it delivered quickly. • You cannot see or touch the product before you buy it. • Security worries – is it a legitimate website? • You often must pay for delivery, or higher rates for faster delivery. • Returning items can be challenging and you may have to wait to receive a refund.

■ Table 3.15 Benefits and drawbacks for organisations of 24/7 access

Benefits	Drawbacks
• You can access more customers over a wider geographical area. Your potential customer base is anyone, anywhere in the world and you are only limited on where you are willing and able to ship products. • You may not have to pay the costs of having premises. Many online businesses do not have a presence on the high street. • Online businesses may be cheaper to set up. • You can collect information about your customers' browsing and shopping habits, which could enable you to improve how you target different types of customers with your different products.	• Many customers still like to visit a shop or business and speak to a person. • You have to make sure you build good relationships with customers as you will have more competition.

CHECK MY LEARNING ■■

Give three benefits and three drawbacks new technology could have on an organisation.

Give three benefits and three drawbacks of 24/7 accessibility for both customers and businesses.

Explain the main pros and cons in relation to the security of distributed/dispersed data.

ACTIVITY

Look around your classroom. How many PCs are there? How many printers? Use the internet and find out the price of a basic PC and printer. Work out the cost of the technology in the room.

How technologies impact the way organisations operate

Digital technologies have made communication and working together in organisations much more efficient and accessible.

Impact of technology on collaboration

The impact of technology on collaboration has many benefits but each comes with its own consideration.

■ Table 3.16: Benefits and drawbacks of collaborative technologies

Technology	Benefits	Drawbacks
File sharing	Using software such as Dropbox or OneDrive has enabled employees to work together and share development responsibilities and activities.	There is a need to make sure that employees are always using the most up-to-date version of a document.
Wikis	These are web pages that can easily be edited (for example, Wikipedia) by members of a team.	You need to check that information is correct, particularly if you are responsible for a commercial wiki.
Blogs	This is an abbreviation of web logs, which are often created about a specific topic.	They need to be regularly updated to keep their audience interested.
Chat systems	Interoffice chat systems are useful for helping staff access information or those seeking decisions quickly.	These systems can be time-wasting if they are used for social rather than business discussions.
Tele/video conferencing	Staff in different locations can attend meetings virtually rather than physically. This saves significant travel time and money and enables collaboration and decision-making.	A high bandwidth communication link is required to transmit and receive high-quality images.

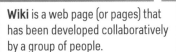

GETTING STARTED

How much school information do you access through your school PC? Can you see your timetable, information about school holidays or about transport? Examine your school's web pages or virtual learning environment (VLE) and write down five important categories of information you can access.

KEY TERMS

Wiki is a web page (or pages) that has been developed collaboratively by a group of people.

LINK IT UP

To find out more about the benefits to organisations, go to lesson 'Collaborative technologies' in Section A of this component.

ACTIVITY

Find out about online meeting software, such as GoToMeeting™. What does it do? How much does it cost? Are there any restrictions on the way you use it depending on the package you pay for? Create a one-page flyer explaining this software (if possible include images).

Technology and inclusivity

Technology has made it easier for organisations to be inclusive, employing staff:
- over a wide age range
- who may have health needs
- who may have additional needs, or
- who may come from other cultures.

In addition to the costs of technologies to support inclusivity, there may be other issues to be considered, such as accommodating hospital visits or enabling staff to observe their religious practices.

Technology and accessibility

In addition to the technologies already covered, many organisations are now supporting the use of wearable technologies. The benefit for staff is that they are easily accessible. They can receive phone calls and read emails without accessing their phones.

However, as many of these wearable technologies have sensors that can capture health and fitness information, some staff are reluctant to wear them as the organisation may have access to data that the employee might wish to keep private.

Organisations are required by law to make accessibility adaptations to the working environment if a member of staff has an accessibility or health-related issue.

Technology and remote working

More and more people are now able to access paid work that does not require them to go to a designated place of work.

The benefits to the organisation are:
- access to a wider and more diverse range of potential employees
- less office space needed if some staff work from home, resulting in cost savings.

The main drawback for organisations is that the employee is not on site, limiting the interaction between colleagues and opportunities for ad hoc meetings and impromptu discussions.

Some employers may choose to install monitoring software on the employee's computer to check the hours they are working and the activities that they undertake. This can be demoralising to employees who do not feel trusted.

■ Do you think wearable technology will become more common in the workplace? Why?

ACTIVITY

Case study

Moov2gether has decided to trial a remote working scheme. What infrastructure is required to support this type of working pattern? Create a single presentation slide with your ideas.

CHECK MY LEARNING

Give three examples of technologies that promote collaboration within an organisation.

Explain the benefits and drawbacks of remote working.

How technology impacts individuals

Devices like smartphones have changed the way we communicate and entertain ourselves. How often do you play music, videos or games on a handheld device when you are travelling in the car, on the bus or train? Do you stream music while you are working?

How would you have entertained yourself when travelling before devices became available? In the 1950s and 1960s you would probably have read a book, sung songs or played 'I Spy'.

In the 1970s, games companies developed 'travel' versions of board games to entertain people on longer journeys. The first personal music players became commercially available in the late 1970s.

Today's devices can quickly become overloaded with games and other apps and it is good practice to try to group apps together by category, such as information, retail, games or productivity apps used for work.

In addition to the fun aspects, using technology has now become common in the workplace and has made many aspects of work much easier, such as being able to access a work diary from anywhere. But there are other ways in which technology impacts the individual.

■ Do you listen to music on your phone? What other ways do you entertain yourself using your phone?

How technology impacts an individual's wellbeing

Technology impacts the way you feel about yourself and the world around you. Technology can impact positively on the wellbeing of individuals, but this is not always the case and you should be aware that for some people there can be negative consequences as well.

■ Table 3.17: Impact of technology

The impact of technology	What it really means	Benefit or drawback
Contact with others	You can talk to other people about things in your life that are going well or badly, but too much contact can be intrusive.	Benefit and drawback
Self-confidence	Being able to research things makes you more confident, if you are sure that the information is correct and reliable.	Benefit
Lack of confidence	Some of us need reassurance about what we are doing, and we need input from others to feel confident about what we are doing.	Drawback
Separation from a stressful environment	Technology means that you can escape into computer games, videos or music to remove yourself from stress.	Benefit
Control of your own schedule	People who use and carry electronic diaries or schedules often feel in more control of their personal and working lives because they know where they need to be.	Benefit
Ability to control your schedule to meet the needs of your family	Just as you need to control your own schedule, technology gives you the confidence that you can adapt your schedule to meet the needs of your family.	Benefit
Less time commuting to or between offices	Technology could make you more productive if you can work from home or you can be based in a single place and take part in virtual meetings.	Benefit
Loneliness	Just because you can talk to someone via a device or app does not mean that you are not lonely.	Drawback
Depression	People who work extensively on their own can become isolated and depressed because they are not interacting with others.	Drawback

Working flexibly and choosing your working style

If you can work flexibly, during hours that suit you and your family, this can improve your morale and reduce personal stress levels. But working flexibly does require employees to be self-disciplined and organisations may monitor your activity.

Do you prefer to work in the morning, afternoon or evening? Do you like to work on a PC, laptop or on a different device?

ACTIVITY

Shanaz is considering applying for a new job that requires her to use modern technologies to work from home.

If Shanaz is successful, at the start of each week she will be sent a task to complete. Shanaz will then have 7 days to complete the task at home and then send it back to her employer.

Write a letter to Shanaz discussing the positive and negative impacts this could have. Make sure you include:
- flexibility
- working styles
- impact on mental wellbeing.

◼ Do you use an electronic diary? What are the benefits and drawbacks of using one?

ACTIVITY

Case study

Moov2gether is concerned about the welfare of its employees who work remotely. Create a leaflet that can be issued to new staff advising them on how to recognise issues of mental wellbeing that may stem from the use of different working styles.

CHECK MY LEARNING

Explain how technology can make you more productive.

Give two examples of how your mental health can be negatively impacted by technology.

A: assessment practice

How you will be assessed

You will be assessed on your knowledge and understanding of this component through a test that will include a series of questions related to a scenario. The test is set and marked by Pearson.

Although the topics from the whole component could occur in any of the questions across the assessment, some examples of the types of questions that may be asked in relation to topics in Section A are shown here. Before answering the following questions, refer to the command words used at the end of the section.

CHECKPOINT

Strengthen
- Give recommendations for different cloud solutions for a range of situations.
- Explain the term 'impact' in relation to modern technologies.
- Give some positive and negative examples to illustrate your answers.

Challenge
- Describe the needs of different types of users.
- Explain how you demonstrate your understanding of the needs of organisations.

TIPS

When you answer questions, you need to make sure that you respond in the right way. You will find it helpful if you become familiar with the words examiners use to indicate the type of answer you should give.

Describe – when you describe, you need to give an account of something. When you describe an orange, you could talk about what it is or you could talk about its features – for example, an orange is a citrus fruit. Oranges come in different sizes and can be eaten by simply peeling them or the juice can be used to make drinks.

Discuss – when you discuss something you need to look at all aspects – for example, if you discuss people working from home you might look at some of the benefits and drawbacks. You might even say what you think about it.

ASSESSMENT ACTIVITY 1 **A1 MODERN TECHNOLOGIES**

You should be able to show that you understand how current and modern technologies are used by, and have an impact on, organisations and stakeholders. How is technology used to exchange information? To communicate? To complete work-related tasks?

Task 1

Tomasz Kowalczyk owns a software company that is expanding quickly. The company specialises in venue ticketing systems for theatres and cinemas. Tomasz has recruited an additional six software developers but he is facing a number of challenges, including running out of storage capacity, and is thinking about moving to a cloud storage solution.

a) Tomasz has been told that one of the benefits of cloud storage is scalability. Describe what this means.

b) To help his development team's productivity, Tomasz is considering moving to online applications. Describe two benefits of using online applications.

c) Describe what Tomasz will need to think about when designing applications and services that rely on cloud technologies so that they work on different platforms.

d) In relation to disaster recovery policies, identify two ways that cloud technologies can generally be relied on.

e) Describe what is meant by 'downtime'.

f) Discuss the different factors to consider when choosing cloud technologies. For each factor you should discuss why this should be considered.

Task 2

Midlands Moov2gether staff meet once a year for a regional meeting, which approximately 70 staff attend.

a) Describe how the organisation could use a PAN to share electronic files to support the meeting.

A new video advertisement has been created for the organisation and has been uploaded to the cloud. The managers intend to allow the staff to view the video on their devices during the meeting.

b) Explain the term 'streaming'.

Moov2gether has taken a cross-organisation decision to make more use of cloud storage but need to persuade staff of its benefits.

c) Describe the key benefits of cloud storage.

d) Discuss how cloud storage will help staff at Moov2gether complete tasks.

Task 3
The staff at Moov2gether are split into working teams and are asked to think about the organisation's disaster recovery policy.

a) Explain what should be included in the disaster recovery policy.

b) Give reasons why you have included the content you described in (a).

ASSESSMENT ACTIVITY 2 — A2 IMPACT OF MODERN TECHNOLOGIES

You should be able to show that you understand how technologies impact the way that organisations operate. You should be able to show both the benefits and drawbacks of how technologies can be used to manage teams and communication and allow stakeholders to access tools and services.

Task 1
Raeni Anderson has been promoted to Head of Sales, managing a team of 130 sales people who are based around the world. She has been asked to review the collaborative technologies that are being used in the organisation.

a) Give two examples of collaborative technologies to help Raeni's team operate. For each example explain two benefits.

b) Describe how the organisation might use a dashboard.

c) Raeni is reviewing the communication channels that the organisation uses to communicate with its stakeholders. Give two messages to customers that should be communicated using a private channel.

d) Evaluate the effectiveness of collaboration and communication tools and how effectively they can be used to manage teams of people.

Task 2
You are working for a local disability charity and you have been asked to prepare a guidance document for local employers about accessibility and the benefits of enabling home and remote working to attract a wider pool of talented staff.

a) Give two accessibility features that would be appropriate for a partially sighted employee.

b) Discuss the benefits and drawbacks of allowing staff to work from home.

c) Explain two ways in which technology can have a positive impact on a person's wellbeing.

d) Explain two ways in which technology can have a negative impact on a person's wellbeing.

Task 3
Technology News Spot is a global online publication that publishes its content electronically every two weeks.

The next publication will focus on the impact of modern technology on organisations and their stakeholders.

Explain the benefits and drawbacks of 24/7 access on an organisation's staff and on its stakeholders.

Explain – you need to show your understanding by justifying your reasoning – for example, when you explain the best things you did in class today, you need to say what they are and why you think they were the best.

Give – questions expect you to recall information – for example, give four ways you could get to school would require a response of 'I could walk, cycle or go by car or bus'. It does not require any further information.

Identify – you are expected to select the right pieces of information from a larger set of information. For example, here is a list of software: Windows, Microsoft Office, Linux, Outlook. Identify the operating systems in the list.

Evaluate – you are expected to review information then bring it together to form a conclusion, drawing on evidence, including strengths, weaknesses, alternative actions, relevant data or information. You could come to a supported judgement in relation to its context.

Why systems are attacked

You have already seen how increasingly reliant organisations have become on digital systems to hold data and perform vital business functions. Cybersecurity is the combination of policies, procedures, technologies and the actions of individuals to protect from threats both internal and external.

Reasons why systems are attacked

Many organisations have their digital systems attacked daily. The reasons why these attacks occur are varied and complex.

◻ Figure 3.2: Which reason do you think is the most common? Why?

- Fun/challenge – hackers may attack systems for the thrill, adrenaline rush or sense of personal achievement. They may view increased security as a technical challenge and enjoy trying to get past it. They may also get recognition from their peers when they successfully hack into systems.
- Industrial espionage – cybercrime has no effective borders so it is possible for organisations to have their **intellectual property**, for example, designs, business strategies etc., stolen through organised cyberattacks. These types of assets can be highly valuable, leading to cheaper, counterfeit (fake) copies of products being sold and the original organisation suffering a loss of income.
- Financial gain – a very simple motive: money. Extorting (obtaining something under pressure and force) money from victims of a cyberattack is common practice and in 2017 made news headlines when large organisations, including the National Health Service (NHS), were attacked by **ransomware**. It encrypts local files, making them inaccessible until the victim pays the attacker a fee to get the files decrypted.
- Personal attack – some attacks can be personally motivated, the most common by ex-employees holding a grudge against their former employer, perhaps feeling they have been unfairly treated or suffered a form of emotional distress.

- Disruption – any attack that prevents an organisation from operating normally causes operational chaos, loss of earnings and reputational damage, all of which can have lasting effects. Disruption can occur in many ways, such as defacing a website or **denial-of-service (DoS) attacks** which prevent servers from responding to genuine requests, which then prevents online sales. Sometimes disruption may not be financially motivated; it may be for social or political reasons and may not involve any data/information theft or corruption.

- Data and information theft – both have value as something that could be sold to criminal gangs or organisations for financial gain. This is done by stealing customer payment information (debit and credit card details, names, addresses, etc.) that is used to purchase goods illegally. Breaches of data and information are a major cause of identity theft.

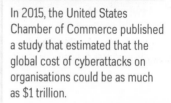

 Have you heard any news stories involving hackers? Have you seen hackers portrayed in any films or TV shows?

ACTIVITY

Case study

Earlier in the year Moov2gether experienced a serious attack on its digital systems. Create a wiki for the organisation's intranet that educates staff about the reasons why systems are attacked so that the staff are more aware of potential threats.

CHECK MY LEARNING

Give three common reasons for attacks on digital systems.

Give a common reason for a personal cyberattack on an organisation.

Give two types of common disruption an organisation might experience through a cyberattack.

Describe the type of personal data/information often stolen and sold to other criminals.

External threats to digital systems and data security

LINK IT UP

To find out more about ethical hacking, go to lesson 'Finding weaknesses and improving system security' in Section B of this component.

KEY TERMS

Social engineering is the act of getting users to share sensitive information through a false pretext (commonly known as 'blagging').

Phishing is a cyberattack that sends spam messages to try and trick people to reply with desired information.

Attacks on systems can come from system users or from others outside the organisation. This lesson explores a range of external attack methods.

Unauthorised access/hacking

Unauthorised access is where users attempt to gain access to remote systems without the permission or authorisation of their owners to do so legally. This type of behaviour is referred to as 'black hat' hacking.

Hacking that is legally performed by paid specialists testing the security of digital systems for a company is called 'white hat' or ethical hacking. Another form of this is 'grey hat' hacking where hackers test security without permission but don't exploit any vulnerabilities for personal gain.

Social engineering is also on the increase with criminals contacting users via email or phone, pretending to be a user's bank and asking the user to confirm information such as their username and password. The intention is to steal the ID information so that it can be used to commit fraud.

Phishing

Phishing is a form of social engineering and a very common form of cyberattack, arriving in a user's inbox as a spoof email, pretending to be from a legitimate company. 'Spoof' means that the email is a forgery but looks genuine, fooling the user into believing that it is from a legitimate source. The user is typically asked to click a link to visit a website and confirm some critical information, and it is usually said to be because of a problem with a recent order or a bank account.

Usernames, passwords and credit card numbers are the most commonly captured personal information. These can then be sold for profit to other criminals or used to illegally purchase goods or services.

◘ Why must you be careful when entering credit card details online?

On closer inspection the fraudulent email often contains obvious spelling and grammatical errors, which should raise suspicion; however, sometimes the deception is so good that it can fool even the cautious and alert.

Many internet service providers (ISPs) and email hosting companies (e.g. Google, Microsoft, AOL®, etc.) filter known phishing emails as part of their automatic spam filtering, but they can't catch everything. Attacks targeting specific organisations or individuals are called 'spear phishing'. Although email phishing is the most common form of attack, SMS texts and phone calls are also used.

Pharming

This is a type of cyberattack, its name a combination of phishing and farming. In **pharming**, a user is maliciously directed to a fake website thinking it is real and they then unwittingly enter confidential details such as usernames and passwords.

The cybercriminal then uses these captured details to log into the real website and commit further illegal acts, such as withdrawing money, purchasing goods, downloading personal files or sending fraudulent emails, etc.

◩ Have you ever been directed to a fake website? How could you tell that a website is fake?

KEY TERMS

Pharming is a cyberattack that uses malware to direct a user to a fake website that requests information.

Man-in-the-middle attacks

This is a form of cyberattack where the communication between two devices, for example, a user and a web server, is intercepted and potentially tampered with. For example, a man-in-the-middle attack took place in 2015 when a criminal gang stole €6 million by hacking into several European organisations to steal corporate emails, which were then used to request money. Once they had these they were able to monitor communications and intercept and take over payment requests, successfully diverting and stealing the money.

The use of encryption can protect against this form of hacking as any intercepted data cannot then be easily used, for example, online banking. There was also a suggestion from cybersecurity specialists that users would be safer if they did not use Wi-Fi.

LINK IT UP

To find out more about encryption go to lesson, 'Data level protection: device hardening and encryption' in Section B of this component.

ACTIVITY

Create a wiki that details external threats to digital systems and data, advising users on how they can protect against them.

CHECK MY LEARNING

Explain what a denial-of-service (DoS) attack is.

Identify the technology that helps prevent the spread of phishing emails.

Give two common forms of malware.

Internal threats to digital systems and data security

You have already learned about external threats and the motivations behind attacks on digital systems. But what does an organisation do if the threat comes from someone inside the organisation itself?

Internal threats

Although many threats to an organisation's digital systems and data security are external in nature, internal threats are also common.

Common internal threats can be seen in Figure 3.3.

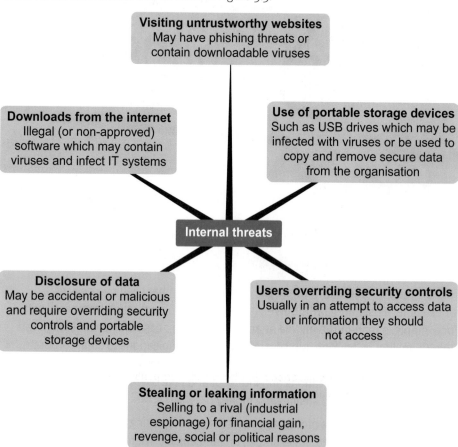

Visiting untrustworthy websites
May have phishing threats or contain downloadable viruses

Downloads from the internet
Illegal (or non-approved) software which may contain viruses and infect IT systems

Use of portable storage devices
Such as USB drives which may be infected with viruses or be used to copy and remove secure data from the organisation

Internal threats

Disclosure of data
May be accidental or malicious and require overriding security controls and portable storage devices

Users overriding security controls
Usually in an attempt to access data or information they should not access

Stealing or leaking information
Selling to a rival (industrial espionage) for financial gain, revenge, social or political reasons

▣ Figure 3.3: How many of the threats listed could affect you and the systems you use?

Although some internal threats occur because of accidents, mistakes or simply poor choices made by an organisation's employees, it is also possible that a disgruntled employee could do something malicious, particularly if they are leaving the organisation. For example, they could:

- delete customer records
- steal confidential information
- create fake invoices that will be paid to their own bank account
- install malware.

Protecting an organisation against internal threats is therefore just as important as protecting it against external ones.

Impact of security breach

Although improving data security is often expensive, the importance of protecting a digital system from internal and external threats should not be underestimated.

Unfortunately, a security breach can impact an organisation in many ways; some will affect its operations almost immediately, but others may do longer-term damage.

- Immediate impacts may include data loss, lost sales, downtime and a resulting reduction in **productivity**.
- Longer-term impacts may include damage to the organisation's public image, which could lead to financial loss and potential legal action.

Can you think of any organisations that have had their public image damaged as a result of a security breach?

ACTIVITY

Work with a partner and investigate potential threats that could occur if an employee attempted to override security controls and download files or applications from untrustworthy websites. What could happen to the organisation's systems? Discuss this in a small group.

CHECK MY LEARNING

Give four common examples of internal threat.

What type of device is commonly used to copy and remove data from an organisation?

Identity three longer-term impacts of a security breach.

Explain how security breaches could negatively impact an organisation's public image.

KEY TERMS

Productivity is a measure of effectiveness – how long it takes an employee to produce an item for sale.

LINK IT UP

To find out about acceptable use policies, guidelines and sanctions, go to lesson 'Acceptable use policies' in Section C of this component.

User access restriction

To prevent unauthorised access to systems and data, organisations implement both physical- and software-based security processes.

Physical security measures

This type of security is designed to prevent the user getting physical access to an IT system and its data or, potentially, stealing a digital system for its data. Table 3.18 gives the benefits and drawbacks of these measures and Table 3.19 shows some of the most common techniques used by organisations.

GETTING STARTED

It is likely that your access to a digital system has been restricted at some point. What user access restrictions are used in your school?

KEY TERMS

Swipe card is a plastic credit card-sized device, often with a metallic strip that contains information that is scanned by a sensor to verify the user's identity and access to a secured location.

◘ **Table 3.18: Benefits and drawbacks of physical security measures**

Benefits	Drawbacks
• Act as a deterrent and deter attackers. • Stop attackers from gaining direct and physical access to locations where data is stored. • Automatically and secretly call the police if an attacker is detected on-site.	• Often more expensive to purchase and install as they are physical objects and need to be manufactured. • Building work may be required. • Some methods of physical security, such as CCTV, do not stop data from being stolen.

◘ **Table 3.19: Benefits and drawbacks of common physical security techniques**

Security technique	Benefits	Drawbacks
Electronic swipe lock	• Prevents access to digital system. • Traditional key or electronic lock requiring PIN or **swipe card**.	• Both cards and keys can be lost, stolen or copied.
Secured device	• Uses steel cable and lock to secure mobile devices to heavy furniture. • Makes theft of devices very difficult.	• You have to use your device in a stationary position once you've secured it to an object.
CCTV camera	• Acts as a deterrent but also records potential threats. • Can be controlled through an organisation's network.	• Having CCTV will not actually stop data being stolen, but it may help investigators identify those who stole it.

Passwords

The use of passwords is a very traditional security measure to control access to digital systems. The benefits and drawbacks of passwords can be seen in Table 3.20. Most organisations include password creation and usage in their security policy and acceptable use policy.

There are other forms of password, such as patterns that can be drawn connecting a series of dots or gesture passwords, which can be used with touchscreen devices where the user draws a shape.

LINK IT UP

For more about passwords and password policy, go to lesson 'Defining security parameters: passwords' in Section B of this component.

◘ **Table 3.20: Benefits and drawbacks of passwords**

Benefits	Drawbacks
• They are simple and easy to use. • There are no costs involved as they require no specialist hardware to set up.	• They are only effective if users keep their passwords secret. • A strong password that meets all the password complexity rules can be hard to remember. • Specialist software can be used by attackers to try to guess a user's passwords. • Users can find it hard to remember lots of different passwords.

Using correct settings and levels of permitted access

Using correct settings is essential to make sure that users only have appropriate levels of access to a system. For example, you would not necessarily want junior staff to have access to the personal details and pay structures for managers.

One key aspect of creating user access restrictions is to think carefully about the levels of access a user needs to complete their job. If their access level is too high, security is put at risk. If their access level is too low, they may be unable to complete their everyday tasks. Finding the correct balance is crucial.

Biometrics

This type of user access restriction requires individuals to use part of their body to prove their identity.

Common biometric examples include:

- eye (retina or iris pattern) scan
- fingerprint identification
- hand geometry (shape of a user's hand)
- voice analysis
- facial recognition
- gait analysis (how a user walks)
- handwriting analysis.

◘ Does your smartphone recognise your fingerprint?

◘ Table 3.21: Benefits and drawbacks of biometrics

Benefits	Drawbacks
• Users don't need to remember lots of different passwords or keep updating them. • They are more secure because biometrics cannot be guessed, lost or forgotten. • They can take less management because users are less likely to be 'locked out' or need to have their user accounts reset.	• They can be more expensive as you need specialist hardware devices to set them up. • They can easily spread germs, e.g. if lots of users are using the fingerprint scanner then germs can be easily spread. • Some users may feel that it is an invasion of their privacy by having their biometric data stored.

Many arguments exist about the value of biometric authentication, but the processing capabilities of modern devices easily support biometrics security, such as fingerprint identification and facial identification, and often use these to replace or complement traditional PIN entry.

Two-factor authentication

Two-factor authentication (TFA or 2FA) is a popular form of multifactor authentication and is used when just a password or PIN is not considered sufficient. It works by asking the user to supply two forms of identification, see Figure 3.4.

PIN (something you **know**) + Biometric match (something unique about **you**) = TFA/2FA

PIN (something you **know**) + Swipe card (something you **have**) = TFA/2FA

◘ Figure 3.4: Why is a cash machine a good example of this?

◘ Table 3.22: Benefits and drawbacks of two-factor authentication

Benefits	Drawbacks
• It's more secure. You need to know and have something to gain access. This makes it harder for attackers to gain access. • Users can use items they already have to authenticate themselves, such as their mobile phones, so no extra equipment is needed.	• It is possible that some factors may get lost, e.g. you may lose your swipe card. • The recovery options that are used to reset your account are easy to get through, which could be exploited by attackers. • It can take longer to gain access, e.g. a code may be sent to your phone, which you are required to type in and which takes time.

CHECK MY LEARNING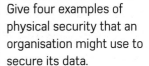

Give four examples of physical security that an organisation might use to secure its data.

Give an example of two-factor authentication.

Data level protection: firewalls and anti-virus software

Various hardware and software techniques can be applied to protect data stored in a digital system.

Firewalls

Firewalls can be hardware or software based. Firewalls work by using a set of rules that filter and reject unwanted or suspicious network packets arriving from a remote network.

Hardware firewalls usually exist by sitting between an external network and an internal connection – for example, the internet and a **local area network (LAN)**, such as that used by an organisation. Firewalls form the first line of defence in protecting digital systems from external threats such as cyberattacks and viruses.

A digital system such as a desktop computer can also host its own firewall service, blocking network data travelling in and out. Additional options may stop certain applications from sending and/or receiving certain packets of network data. They do this by creating a set of rules that determine which packets of data are sent and received, which is called an **access control list (ACL)**.

For example, you may be unable to access YouTube at school. Organisations frequently prevent their staff from accessing social media websites when they are using the organisation's machines, usually to prevent distractions from work.

Keeping an ACL regularly updated is a good way to manage threats to data.

◻ Table 3.23: Benefits and drawbacks of firewalls

Benefits	Drawbacks
They can stop attackers from gaining unauthorised access to a device.	Firewalls can block legitimate things like access to some websites that are completely safe and trustworthy.
You can customise the firewall settings to meet the needs of your organisation. For example, you could block all websites that are classed as 'untrustworthy'.	As a firewall has to read all data going into and out of a network it may use up a lot of computer memory. This can make the performance of a computer or network a lot slower.
Software firewalls are easy to install. There is usually a 'wizard' available to guide you through the setup.	Highly effective firewalls can be very expensive. Many have a yearly subscription, which can increase year on year.

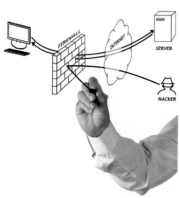

◻ Have you encountered any firewalls when using your school's computers?

Software/interface design

Modern software design aims to make applications easier to use, often including various tricks that can assist user inputs. Some techniques can improve security; others can cause issues.

Table 3.24: Common techniques to make applications easier to use

Obscuring data entry	A common technique to solve the **shoulder surfing** threat when using secure logins in a public place is to obscure the entry of sensitive data, e.g. passwords etc. The characters typed by the user are masked with anonymous placeholder characters, often asterisks (*) or circles. Email: a@b.com Password: •••••••• Login
Autocomplete	Autocomplete is a useful technique where an application (typically a web browser) will recognise a familiar input and start making suggestions from previous inputs. This can be a security risk, however, as on a publicly accessed IT system it can display other user's inputs, e.g. usernames, email addresses etc. Email: a / a@b.com Password: Login
"Stay logged in"	Web applications often use **session cookies** to keep a user logged in, even if they leave a page and later return to it. Again, although time-saving, this can be a security risk if a different user gains access to the IT system before the web browser is closed and the session cookie (containing the login information) is cleared.

Anti-virus software

Anti-virus software monitors a digital system, attempting to identify and remove malicious software through the unique digital signature in the virus before it can cause damage. Most viruses infect a digital system when the unsuspecting user opens infected email attachments. Complex worm viruses can even replicate themselves from device to device via the network.

In addition to ransomware, different types of viruses include:
- **worms**
- **Trojans**
- **rootkit**
- **spyware**.

Table 3.25: Benefits and drawbacks of anti-virus software

Benefits	Drawbacks
They can stop files that contain viruses from accessing your computer system.	Anti-virus software needs to be continually updated to ensure it can detect new viruses.
Some anti-virus software is free to download.	Anti-virus software is constantly scanning files, so it can use up a lot of computer memory. This can make the performance of a computer or network slow.
If a virus is not yet known, anti-virus software is able to monitor the behaviour of files to see if they are showing any virus characteristics.	Highly effective anti-virus software can be very expensive. Many have a yearly subscription, which can increase in cost each year.

 Do you have anti-virus software on any of your devices?

Data level protection: device hardening and encryption

Digital systems may have default settings or weaknesses that can make them (and their data) **vulnerable** to attack. The process known as 'device hardening' attempts to resolve these issues.

Device hardening

Several different techniques can be used to harden a device, including:
- installing a firewall
- installing anti-virus (and anti-spyware) software
- applying **security patches** and updates
- using encryption
- closing unused network ports
- removing non-essential programs or services
- restricting user access (called the principle of 'least **privilege**').

Procedures for backing up and recovering data

Backing up data on a regular basis (nightly, weekly etc.) is a sensible precaution. Backups can be created on an automatic schedule or manually, such as before a system update, just in case a problem occurs. Restoring the backup allows the digital system to recover from any potential loss or corruption of files needed to operate the computer system.

Backups held on magnetic tapes may be physically stored in a fireproof safe or sent to a separate secure location as an extra precaution. Modern security policies may favour cloud storage.

◻ What are the benefits and drawbacks of holding backups on magnetic tapes?

Encryption

It is common practice to encrypt data when it is stored and when it is being transmitted between IT systems.

plaintext **+** encryption algorithm + key **=** ciphertext

◻ Figure 3.5: What type of data do you think should be encrypted?

Encryption of stored data

Stored data is a popular target for cyberattacks, and whether it is stored in separate files or within a database, unencrypted (plaintext) data is considered insecure and a security risk.

One solution is to encrypt this stored data, targeting files and databases that contain sensitive information, such as medical records, bank details, user account credentials, etc.

It is also possible to encrypt complete disk drives, resulting in the need for a password before the operating system can decrypt the disk and load itself into memory. Encrypting complete disks is a useful technique that protects against data theft, which occurs when drives are physically taken from compromised IT systems, for example, in the case of a burglary.

Encryption of transmitted data

Vast quantities of personal data are transmitted from web browsers to web servers and back again, especially in web applications, such as social networking, online banking and e-commerce. Organisation web servers can use a digital signature (a small file that travels with the data) that can be transmitted to a web browser to prove its identity and encrypt data transmissions between them.

You can tell if a connection is secure when you see a padlock and the HTTPS (Hypertext Transfer Protocol Secure) prefix on a website address.

🔒 Secure | https://www.google.co.uk

LINK IT UP

To find out why it is important to encrypt data, go to lesson 'External threats to digital systems and data security' in Section B of this component.

 Visit some websites and check to see whether they have a padlock next to the address

 Table 3.26: Benefits and drawbacks of encryption

Benefits	Drawbacks
• Encryption scrambles data so that others cannot easily read it. • Using encryption ensures that organisations comply with data protection laws.	• Encryption does not stop data from being stolen. • Encrypting a large amount of data can take time. • Encryption methods need to continually 'evolve' and change as attackers find new ways to access data.

ACTIVITY

Investigate potential vulnerabilities in a digital system and apply device hardening.
- Identify known flaws or weaknesses.
- Research appropriate techniques to harden the device, for example, apply security patches.
- Apply the techniques to harden the device.
- Confirm the flaw or weakness has been removed.

CHECK MY LEARNING

Explain why it is important to use encryption when transmitting data.

Give three benefits of using a digital signature when transmitting a file.

Give three techniques that can be applied to harden a device.

Finding weaknesses and improving system security

Organisations have a responsibility to secure their IT systems to protect the personal and sensitive data they store and process. Assessing the security of IT systems objectively can be difficult to do, so sometimes external help is required, for example, calling in a cybersecurity, networking or hardware specialist, depending on the problem.

Ethical hacking

Ethical hacking is a process where an individual or a team of penetration testers are asked by an organisation to simulate an attack on its IT system to highlight any weakness and vulnerability. This process is often used in sensitive sectors such as finance, insurance, health and energy.

Initially, the hackers will be given little information about the system and will, through extensive probing, identify weaknesses and exploit them to see if sensitive data or services can be accessed.

Sometimes introducing a single vulnerability into a system can lead to further issues appearing in other parts of the system.

Ethical hackers are described as white hat hackers or grey hat hackers.
- White hat hacker – an IT specialist who is invited to discover vulnerabilities in a system or application, and report them to the organisation or author.
- Grey hat hacker – an IT specialist who discovers vulnerabilities in a system or application, typically without invitation, but does not exploit them for personal gain (although they might make the information publicly known).

▣ Table 3.27: Benefits and drawbacks of ethical hacking

Benefits	Drawbacks
You can see if the security of your network is able to withstand the skills of expert attackers.	Hiring professionals with the skills to carry out ethical hacking can be very expensive.
It can help to find 'loopholes' (insecure areas) in your network security in order to make it better.	It depends on the trustworthiness of the ethical hacker. Some may abuse their position.
The security of a system can keep evolving when loopholes in the network security have been found.	Some people may view ethical hacking as an invasion of privacy if others are able to view their data.

Penetration testing

Popularly known as a 'Pen' test, this is the systematic process used by ethical hackers to determine the security of an IT system. Ethical hackers avoid disrupting the business while performing their penetration testing, so may conduct tests at non-peak times, such as outside normal business hours.

The following areas are frequent vulnerabilities that ethical hackers uncover when attacking a system:
- unpatched operating systems and applications
- web applications that have not been well programmed, which has left them insecure
- data that has not been encrypted

- poor security practices, such as allowing users to use weak passwords and not setting correct privileges.

Many penetration testing software suites are automated processes that can be used to examine an IT system and collate detailed reports. Although penetration testing can be expensive, it is typically cheaper than the fines that an organisation could receive for having poor standards of data protection.

Sometimes weaknesses in the IT systems are caused by employee behaviour – for example, poor passwords, insecure workstations etc.

The findings are presented to the organisation as a formal report, including recommendations that may resolve the issues found.

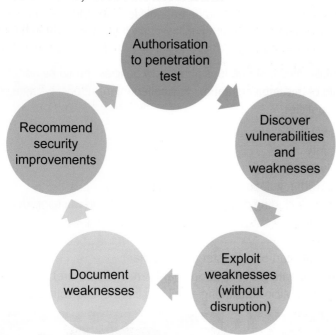

◘ Figure 3.6: Stages of a penetration test

This report is then used by the organisation to harden its security, addressing the issues found. This may include raising awareness, implementing training to improve work behaviours and creating better security. The process may then be repeated until the organisation is sufficiently confident in its systems; no system is 100% secure. Any significant change in IT systems in the future, for example, introducing a website, will typically require fresh testing.

ACTIVITY

Case study

Moov2gether has hired an ethical white hat hacker to perform a penetration test of its digital systems.

1. Create an email that the managing director can send to staff to explain what this process is about, how they may be affected and what they hope this activity will achieve.

2. In groups, discuss how users may feel if their accounts are hacked into – even though it is for a genuine reason.

3. Identify the pros and cons of this type of testing.

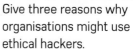

CHECK MY LEARNING

Give three reasons why organisations might use ethical hackers.

Give an example of how organisations use penetration testing to find weaknesses in a system.

Security policies

To make sure that all employees in all locations follow the same code of conduct in issues such as security, organisations create policies that set out the responsibilities of staff. These policies detail how staff are expected to behave and what procedures they should follow in the event of a disaster. In this lesson you will find out how organisations plan for unexpected events.

Who takes responsibility for what?

In relation to an organisation's data and IT systems, all organisations have designated individuals who are responsible for different policies. Most policies are implemented by IT and technical staff, although the policies may have been written by IT managers who regularly review the policies.

IT managers make recommendations about how policies should be updated and take ownership of this implementation. In smaller organisations, a single person may manage these policies.

Examples of security policies include:

- system security
- data security
- compliance (with regulations and legislation)
- environmental (including disposal of old equipment and waste products such as printer cartridges)
- disaster recovery
- data recovery (as part of a disaster recovery plan)
- infrastructure (updating and replacing hardware and software)
- responsible use policies (including email and internet use policies.

◘ **How have you disposed of your old devices?**

Staff with any concerns about these policies or the way in which they are being implemented should contact the named person responsible for the policy. Everyone is expected to work in line with the organisation's policies.

How to plan for disaster recovery

Policies exist to increase the robustness of IT systems and data and to plan for what should happen in the event of a disaster. Disasters can come in many forms, such as:

- theft of data (having systems hacked or having laptops or devices stolen)
- virus or other malware infection
- data loss (accidental deletion or intentional sabotage)
- fire or flood
- mechanical failure of equipment.

To make sure that the organisation can become operational again as quickly as possible, a detailed plan is created.

> **DID YOU KNOW?**
>
> According to https://breachlevelindex.com/ there are currently 58 data records that are lost or stolen every second.

◘ **Table 3.28: Disaster recovery plan**

Consideration	Description
Identifying potential risks	Identify potential risks to the system and how each risk will affect the computer system and data.
Who is responsible for which actions in the event of a disaster	Staff are given specific recovery tasks to avoid anything being duplicated or forgotten. The actions are linked to a job role rather than a named person (in case that person leaves).
What staff should and should not do	Ensure that all staff know the procedures even if they do not have any direct tasks.
How the systems will be backed up (including what will be backed up, how often and which media will be used)	Ensure that regular backups are taken. Some systems may need to be backed up hourly – others may be daily or weekly – critical data (without which the organisation cannot function) should be backed up most often. Decide where the backups will be stored and which media will be used to store the data, for example the cloud, removable devices such as tapes etc.
A timeline to establish how quickly the systems will need to be back up and running	After a disaster not all operations will be needed immediately. A plan should be made to define how long the organisation can be without each system. Critical systems must be identified and will need to be recovered first. This will create a timeline detailing the actions required.
An alternative location for operation (hardware, software and personnel)	After a catastrophic event the organisation may need to move quickly to another location. Hardware, software and personnel should also be available (along with the backups) so that the organisation can function again quickly.

ACTIVITY

Your teacher will give you some examples of policies to examine. Work with a friend and use a highlighter to highlight the key points.

Compare similar policies – do they have the same key points?

Discuss your findings with your class.

CHECK MY LEARNING

Describe the key components of at least two types of policy and why they are important.

Explain why disaster recovery policies are essential and which systems should be prioritised.

Defining security parameters: passwords

As you have seen in this component, various modern technologies can be used to protect against common internal and external threats that an organisation might experience. However, setting sensible security parameters is another useful precaution. A parameter is a set of rules to be followed or behaviours that need to be demonstrated.

Password policy

Organisations that take data security seriously typically have a comprehensive password policy that they ask employees to follow. Where practical, the organisation's software and system settings should support this policy. The policy typically covers both the creation and protection of passwords.

Creation of passwords

Passwords should be suitably complex (this is often referred to as their strength).
- Complexity is increased by: greater password length (in characters), the combination of upper- and lower-case characters, numbers, punctuation and other symbols.
- Passwords SHOULD NOT use words found in a dictionary, familiar names (family or pets) or be easy to crack.
- Using initial letters from a memorable phrase, mixing lower- and upper-case letters and numbers is useful for creating complex passwords, for example, 'My very first cat was named Simon!' becomes Mv1cwnS!

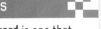

Table 3.29: Features of password strength

Password strength	Description	Examples
Weak	An obvious password using either standard letters or numbers, often personal to the user (for example family name, birthday) so can be easy to guess.	PASSWORD, 123456
Medium	Makes use of a combination of letters and numbers but could use more special characters and less recognisable words to make it more difficult to guess.	LiverPool5
Strong	Makes use of special characters, numbers and upper-/lower-case letters, making it very difficult to guess.	A?vEr8gS!

Protection of passwords

Passwords are our first point of defence for our files and personal information.
- **Default passwords** should be quickly changed as they are often commonly used and vulnerable.
- Passwords should be regularly changed, for example, every three months.
- Passwords should never be written down.
- Passwords should never be shared with anyone (inside or outside an organisation).
- Users should be aware of phishing schemes, which is where users may be asked to confirm sensitive information, such as their passwords, simply to steal the information.

Usually an organisation's software will prevent the creation of passwords that:
- don't match the organisational policy
- have been used before or are in a dictionary.

To judge the complexity of a password it is possible to use an online checker. Given a set of policy requirements it can assess the password's conformity and strength and explain any deficiencies, such as insufficient upper-case characters. Think carefully about how you use and manage your passwords.

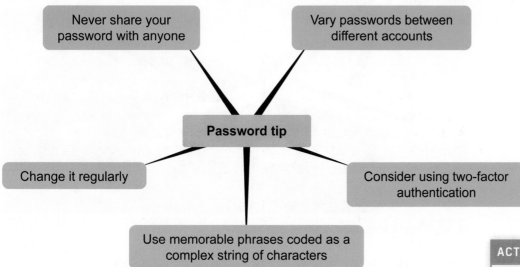

 Figure 3.7: How many of these rules do you follow?

Defining security parameters: policies

Have you ever wanted to use software that is not installed on your digital system? At home, this may not be a problem, but in the workplace it could cause potential problems. In a small group, identify one useful software application that could be installed on your digital systems and justify your choice.

Organisations are often made vulnerable by the installation and use of unapproved software by its employees.

◻ What might employees be trying to install?

Why is there an acceptable software policy?

Unapproved software could contain malware that might infect the organisation's systems, network etc., or it may conflict with the hardware on the digital system and with other software (operating system, other applications etc.) on the digital system.

To counter this threat, an acceptable software policy is created, which explains what will be done to help prevent any attempted installation and use of unapproved software.

Installation

- Users are usually forbidden to install unapproved software or updates.
- Users may ask for approval for new software or be asked to select from an approved list.
- Users may need support from their manager or another department for their request to be considered.
- Users will need to justify why this new software is required for their job.

Security policy statements may state the following.

- You may *not* install software on digital systems used within the organisation.
- All software requests *must* be justified and approved by a manager and then sent to the IT department or Help Desk in writing or by email.
- New software *must* be selected from the IT department's approved software list unless no match can be found that meets your needs.

How an acceptable software policy is enforced

It is usually the role of the operating system to apply appropriate safeguards that prevent the installation of software if the user does not have sufficient administrative rights. These safeguards are part of the device hardening carried out by the organisation's IT staff, such as administrators.

Different types of users may need (and be granted) greater or lesser rights on a system to perform their jobs.

However, other techniques can be used to prevent against unwanted installation of software. These include:
- CCTV monitoring of employees
- **software audit** of digital systems.

Use of unapproved software

The use of unapproved software is also typically disallowed by an acceptable software policy and may result in disciplinary action, such as a verbal or written warning, against the employee even if they did not install it.

Again, most operating systems can prevent the use of certain software applications and these form part of any device hardening strategy that an IT department might use to protect the organisation from malware and potential external threats.

The acceptable software usage policy reinforces the need for the installed software to be used responsibly and legally. It typically also prohibits the unauthorised duplication of the software for home use unless this is permitted by the software's licence.

LINK IT UP

For more about device hardening, go to lesson 'Data level protection: device hardening and encryption' in Section B of this component.

KEY TERMS

Software audit is a manual or automated process that lists the name, version and installation date of all software found on a digital device. The process may be carried out remotely, for example, across a network, or in person.

ACTIVITY

Working on your own, conduct a software audit on a digital system.

Identify which software has been installed.

Identify any potential risks from this software.

CHECK MY LEARNING

Identify the risks of installing and using unapproved software.

Describe how an acceptable software policy might be enforced.

Describe what a software audit is.

Give two reasons why employees are not automatically allowed to duplicate software for home use.

Actions to take after an attack

After an attack it is crucial that an organisation and its employees have a very clear idea of the actions to take to resolve the situation and reduce the likelihood of it happening again.

GETTING STARTED

In the event of an attack, what actions would you prioritise?

Write down your ideas and share them with your class.

Actions performed after an attack

Organisations often follow a pre-defined set of actions after an attack has occurred. These are shown in Figure 3.8.

1. Investigate 2. Respond 3. Manage 4. Recover 5. Analyse

■ Figure 3.8: Actions carried out after an attack

Investigation

The organisation will investigate the nature of the attack. It will want to establish the following.

1 The type of attack – for example, malware, network attack, data theft, phishing, etc.

2 The severity of the attack. This could be defined as Level 1 (low risk) to Level 5 (severe risk). A severe risk could be a serious breach of data and/or complete disruption of services. The complexity of an organisation's response to attack is usually linked to the severity level.

3 Which processes or services in the organisation are affected.

4 When it happened.

The information gathered at this point is vital to help the organisation determine how to respond, manage and recover from the incident.

LINK IT UP

To find out more about some different types of attack, go to lesson 'External threats to digital systems and data security' in Section B of this component.

■ Why is it important that the organisation identifies the type of attack?

Response

The type of response will vary depending on the severity of the attack. An organisation will typically inform:

- stakeholders (employees, shareholders, customers, suppliers, business partners, etc.)
- appropriate authorities (law enforcement including police, National Crime Agency, **Data Protection Controller**, etc.).

Notifying stakeholders, such as customers, is important as data breaches might include confidential details (usernames and passwords) that customers might use for other services. Although informing stakeholders may lead to a damaged public image, not telling authorities could result in legal action and potential fines. It is also important that interested parties are kept updated as more information becomes available from the ongoing investigation and as efforts to manage and recover continue.

How is the response to the attack managed?

The priority is to isolate the problem by containing the threat as close to the source as possible. This can be done by disconnecting an infected digital system from a network or blocking unauthorised network traffic by using a firewall.

The organisation's management of the response will be appropriate to the nature and severity of the attack as shown by the initial investigation.

How does an organisation recover?

The organisation will have a separate disaster recovery policy that it will follow in the event of an attack. It will detail the employees responsible for specific tasks, the expected timeline and the **remedial action** involved.

Longer-term remedial action may include changes to policy, procedures, investments in new hardware and/or software, increased device hardening or better employee education and training.

What needs to be analysed?

After recovery has occurred, analysis would focus on the following.

- What went wrong.
- How it happened (internal or external threat).
- How it could have been prevented.
- How effectively the organisation responded to the attack, especially in terms of its response and management of the situation.
- What lessons have been learned.

As a result, it is likely that the organisation will update its policies and procedures as well and make effective changes to the security parameters that protect its digital systems.

ACTIVITY

Working on your own, research recent cyberattacks on large organisations and summarise the organisations' responses to stakeholders. As part of your research you should find out how the attacks were investigated, how the organisation responded and how it analysed the experience to learn lessons to improve future actions.

KEY TERMS

Data Protection Controller is the named person in an organisation who takes responsibility for the safety and security of the organisation's data.

DID YOU KNOW?

Current data protection legislation states that it is a legal requirement for organisations to notify the authorities of a serious data breach.

KEY TERMS

Remedial action is an action taken to fix something that has gone wrong; a remedy.

LINK IT UP

To find out more about disaster recovery policy, go to lesson 'Security policies' in Section B of this component.

CHECK MY LEARNING

Give five actions that are likely to occur after a cyberattack on an organisation.

Give three examples of an organisation's stakeholders.

Identify the key questions that should be asked during an organisation's analysis after it has recovered from an attack.

B: assessment practice

How you will be assessed

Although the topics from the whole component could occur in any of the questions across the assessment, some examples of the types of questions that may be asked in relation to topics in Section B are shown here. Before answering the following questions, refer to the command words at the end of lesson 'A: assessment practice' in Section A of this component.

CHECKPOINT

Strengthen
- Give three reasons why systems are attacked.
- Identify three examples of internal and external threats.
- Describe how you can stay up to date about physical security measures.
- Describe what you can do to improve your knowledge about IT policies and practices.

Challenge
- What do you need to do to show your understanding of the terminology used?
- Describe what you can do to stay up to date about physical security measures.
- Identify three ways to demonstrate your understanding of system weaknesses?

ASSESSMENT ACTIVITY 1   B1 THREATS TO DATA

You should be able to demonstrate an understanding of why systems are attacked, give examples of attacks and how they occur and show that you understand the impact of breaches in security and how these can affect the organisation and its stakeholders.

Task 1
Tomasz Kowalczyk's software company has been suffering from a range of security concerns over recent months. You have been asked to investigate.

a) There have been suggestions that attempts were made to steal the company's customer data. Explain what this could be used for.

b) Describe what is meant by the term 'pharming'. What is it and how can you protect yourself and the company against it?

c) Explain two internal threats that might have affected the organisation.

d) Discuss the different internal and external threats that organisations should be aware of and methods they can use to reduce the risks that they pose.

Task 2
Khamisha Shah is a specialist accountant who manages the accounts of many well-known individuals in the entertainment industry.

She is concerned about her clients' data and has asked you about some key security issues.

a) Give four reasons why systems are attacked.

b) Explain each of the following terms:
- malware
- phishing
- denial-of-service attacks
- pharming
- man-in-the-middle attacks
- hacking.

ASSESSMENT ACTIVITY 2 · B2 PREVENTION AND MANAGEMENT OF THREATS TO DATA

You should be able to talk about different measures that can be used to protect digital systems and to show that you understand the purpose of features and functionality used to protect systems.

You should also be able to show how the impact of threats can be reduced.

Task 1

There have been suggestions that Tomasz's company needs to improve security using a range of methods.

a) Explain the term 'biometrics'.

b) Give an example of two-factor authentication.

c) Evaluate the different cyberattack prevention methods that can be used to reduce cyberattacks and how effectively they protect data.

d) Discuss how a firewall protects a system.

e) Describe device hardening.

f) Tomasz is thinking about employing a white hat hacker. Explain how Tomasz's company could benefit from the services of white hat hacking.

Task 2

Khamisha has asked you to advise her on two-factor authentication.

Discuss two strategies that make use of different combinations of technologies that Khamisha could implement. Justify your choices.

ASSESSMENT ACTIVITY 3 · B3 POLICY

You should be able to show that you understand the idea of policies such as security policies, acceptable use policies, what they are for and how these are implemented within organisations.

Task 1

To complete your work for Tomasz on cybersecurity he has asked you to help him develop policies to give guidance to staff about what to do in the event of a disaster.

a) Give four examples of the types of disaster the organisation could face.

b) Explain two considerations to make sure that the organisation will be up and running again quickly in the event of a disaster.

c) Give an example of a complex password.

d) Give reasons why Tomasz should ban the use of unapproved software on the organisation's systems.

e) Describe three actions the organisation should take immediately after it discovers that its systems have been hacked.

Task 2

Khamisha is thinking about developing an acceptable software policy for her staff.

a) Explain why Khamisha should develop an acceptable software policy and give two examples of what she should include.

b) Discuss the purpose of the sanctions section of an acceptable software policy.

SYNOPTIC QUESTION

Arnold would like to collect and store data about people's TV viewing habits. He plans to use a primary data collection method to collect this data. He then plans on storing this data on his computer.

Discuss the different data protection principles that Arnold should follow.

TAKE IT FURTHER

The government publish data security incidents. Check out the most recent data. Search for 'data security incident trends' at https://ico.org.uk.

KEY TERMS

Synoptic question is a question that tests your knowledge from across the whole course. Synoptic questions allow you to show your understanding of concepts from all three components and apply your learning to realistic contexts.

TIPS

Think about the data protection principles that are relevant when Arnold:

a) collects the data

b) stores the data

c) uses the data.

Sharing data

Every single day organisations generate, process and store large amounts of data using a range of technologies. To make sure that the organisation manages this data lawfully and uses its technologies in the right way, they have to think about how the data is used and shared and how it disposes of technologies that staff no longer use.

Accessing shared data

Mobile devices can be used to share information about you, such as your location, and many of us like to 'check in' on social media when we visit places. You should always think very carefully about allowing your technology to reveal where you are, and generally you should switch off this feature for your own protection.

How are you able to check in to specific locations? The real-time geo-data from your smartphone or other mobile device is used to track your location via **GPS** so that you can share it. The data is useful as it enables you to quickly find places of interest nearby, for example a bank or a particular shop or restaurant.

The same data is used by organisations to:
- send you advertisements for services and events close to where you are
- provide relevant travel updates.

One of the most important ways in which location-based services contribute to security is in fraud prevention. Your location can be matched with the place where your bank or credit card is being used. If the two do not match, it may be an instance where someone else is using your payment card without your knowledge.

Transactional data

Many things that you do generate transactional data, such as buying something, using a bus ticket or adding a diary entry. Data that is generated by one part of an organisation is almost always used by another part.
- Sales data might be analysed so that manufacturing can be adjusted (making more if sales are high or less if sales are low).
- Stock data might be analysed so that any stock that is not selling very well can be sold at a discount.
- Staff holiday information might be used to plan manufacturing activities (if staff are on holiday then temporary staff might be needed to keep production going).

Cookies

Web applications often use session cookies to keep a user logged in, even if they leave a page and later return to it. Cookie data is used by organisations in many ways. One of the most useful is sharing data that enables a server to deliver web content that is tailored to your needs.

Data exchange between services

Where data is shared between different services it may have to be transformed into a different format or configuration so that it can be used at the destination.

GETTING STARTED

Whatever you do online you will be sharing data. You may choose to share data about you, but other data might be shared without your knowledge. What data do you knowingly share with others?

KEY TERMS

GPS (Global Positioning System) is a navigational system that uses data transmitted by satellites to calculate the location of the GPS-enabled device.

■ Have you used your phone to find local places of interest? What were you looking for?

LINK IT UP

To find out more about session cookies, go to lesson, 'Data level protection: firewalls and anti-virus software' in Section B of this component and 'Data and the use of the internet' in Section C of this component.

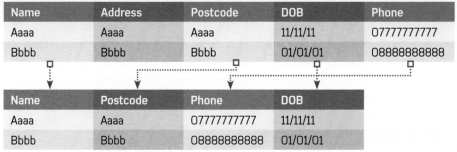

Name	Address	Postcode	DOB	Phone
Aaaa	Aaaa	Aaaa	11/11/11	07777777777
Bbbb	Bbbb	Bbbb	01/01/01	08888888888

Name	Postcode	Phone	DOB
Aaaa	Aaaa	07777777777	11/11/11
Bbbb	Bbbb	08888888888	01/01/01

- The name is still in the same position in the table.
- The postcode has moved columns because the address had been deleted.
- The date of birth and the phone number have changed places.

Using shared data

Table 3.30 shows the benefits and drawbacks of using shared data.

◻ **Table 3.30: Benefits and drawbacks of using shared data**

Benefits	Drawbacks
Sharing diaries helps teams to coordinate activity.	Users must make sure that they are not breaching any copyright.
Collaborating on projects means more ideas.	Data must be protected by law.
Work can be shared in real time, so projects can be completed more quickly.	Data can be sabotaged by damage or changed.
Sharing music on a family network means you only pay once.	Sometimes data gathered for one reason might not be entirely relevant in a different context.
Using existing data reduces the costs of collecting new data.	Data moving from one system to another can lose integrity (which is why the movement of data is tracked).
More information means better decisions.	Data must be downloaded from trustworthy sources to make sure it is not infected.

Using shared data responsibly

It is important that data is shared and used responsibly. Both individuals and organisations should act in ways that ensures that the use of data meets legal and ethical requirements.

Legal

There is a legal framework that sets out the requirements to protect data in the Data Protection Act, which became the General Data Protection Act in May 2018. Failure to protect data may result in a heavy fine.

Privacy

Would you want information about your medical condition, your religious beliefs, your sexual orientation or your political views shared with others? There is a duty of confidentially in the UK, which reinforces our right to privacy. Personal information is also protected under the law. Did you know, for example, that NHS professionals are not allowed to view the records of the members of their own family? If they do, they risk being disciplined or fired.

Ethical

Just because data is available does not mean you should use it, particularly if you know that it was collected for a different reason. To behave ethically, organisations should seek the permission of the **data subject** to share the information.

The impact of technology on the environment

The technology we use every day impacts on the environment in many ways – from the use of non-renewable resources, such as precious metals that are used in the manufacture of technology, to coal used to generate electricity to power technology, to the old technology that requires special disposal methods.

Making, using and disposing

Manufacturing and using computer technology generates waste products. According to www.recycling-guide.org.uk a PC is made from the following.

Plastic	23%
Ferrous metals	32%
Non-ferrous metals	18%
Electronic circuit boards	12%
Glass	15%

A computer can contain up to 2 kg of lead, which is a poisonous metal. Some of the materials are increasingly rare and are becoming more valuable, such as copper, which is used in computer cables. In 50 years' time, supplies of copper will become so scarce that manufacturers will have to use an alternative or stop making electronic devices.

Although there is some variation between models, according to www.energuide.be/en, using a desktop PC uses an average of 200 watts. As of early 2018, if you use your computer for 3 hours per day across an average 30-day month and with a kWh priced at about 13p, this means that running your computer for one month costs approximately £2.34.

Running a laptop is cheaper – about 94p for a month, based on the same factors as the PC.

ACTIVITY

Use the running costs calculator at https://www.ukpower.co.uk/tools to calculate how much it costs to run the computers in your classroom. Your teacher will tell you how many hours per day the computers are likely to be active.

Now use the information and find out how much it would cost to run all the computers in your school for a day and for a year.

You will need to find out how many IT rooms there are and you may need to make some assumptions about how many computers are in each room.

Disposing of computers and their **consumables** should be taken very seriously as it's important to limit the use of non-renewable resources. This is why the disposal of computers and other electrical products is governed by law.

ACTIVITY

Working in small groups, find out about Tech Recycle and Aim to Recycle. Make notes on the following.
- What do these organisations do?
- What services do they provide?
- What can organisations, such as schools and businesses, that sell computer equipment do to reduce the impact of technology on the environment?

Upgrading and replacing

One of the most difficult decisions organisations face is deciding whether to upgrade or replace their technology when it slows down and reaches the end of its useful life. It may take longer for programs or websites to load or the organisation may be running out of storage. Alternatively, there might be new technology that the organisation wants to use to make it more efficient or more profitable and there are many strategies it can use to make this happen.

Replacing components may be the solution.

Replacing memory will make the computer run faster – but you need to consider whether this will impact other components, such as the **motherboard**. Hard drives are also easy to upgrade if your computer is running out of storage, which is done by opening the computer and installing a new hard drive.

The alternative is to replace the whole system. Whole systems tend to be replaced when it would become more expensive to replace all the necessary components than to buy a new system.

KEY TERMS

Motherboard is the main electronic circuit board that all the other computer components, such as memory, processor, graphics card etc., plug into.

◻ Table 3.31: Benefits and drawbacks of technology

Benefits	Drawbacks
Electronic communication can mean that less paper and ink are used. This reduces the number of trees that need to be cut down.	Digital devices consume electricity when they are in use and when they are recycled. This means increased burning of fossil fuels.
Digital devices can be used to monitor the environment, enabling better predictions to be made about the weather.	Old computers are not always easy to dispose of. Parts are not always recycled, resulting in more waste going to landfill.
Industrial processes can be computer controlled rather than human controlled, which is more efficient and less polluting.	Some countries illegally send e-waste to third world countries. People in these countries are exposed to toxic substances when trying to extract the metals.

Usage and settings

There are many usage settings that can be adjusted to help reduce the impact of technology. They include the following.

1 Use the auto power-off setting on your computer to close and switch off if the computer has not been used for a period of time (maybe 30 minutes or 1 hour). Alternatively, set a regular power-off command in your operating system.

2 Use power saving settings on devices to reduce screen brightness, which saves power and means your device will last longer between charges.

3 Do you really need to print a hard copy of your document? If not, then provide it as an electronic version to save paper and ink.

◻ What is your brightness setting on your device?

CHECK MY LEARNING

Give three usage settings that can be adjusted to help reduce the impact of technology.

Identify the main reason for upgrading rather than replacing digital systems.

Explain at what point most organisations replace rather than upgrade their digital systems.

ACTIVITY

Check your school's recycling and energy saving activities, such as switching off lights and computers or recycling.

Work with a partner and create an information leaflet for new Year 7s that explains everyone's responsibilities.

Equal access to information and services

Laws exist that set out requirements for the way systems are created and protected and how data is managed. In addition, there are some less formal guidelines that organisations can agree to observe, but which are not enforceable by law. You are going to explore a range of these laws and guidelines to see how they influence the behaviour of organisations.

Benefits to individuals

If you have ever travelled with a device such as a phone or tablet you may well have experienced differences in your connectivity and connection speed in different places. In some rural areas the signal is poor and you may get an intermittent connection or even no connection at all. This is certainly true in parts of Scotland, the outer islands and the hilly areas of northern England and Wales.

◘ Why is your phone signal poor in some areas?

Many people would argue that this is unfair as you will still be paying the same for your phone or tablet contract regardless of the connectivity you experience. You do have choices about which provider you use and your selection may include assessing the coverage for your area and the areas you visit most to make sure that you choose the best option for you.

Benefits to organisations

To be competitive, organisations need access to lots of information so that they can make the right decisions.
- Information about their competitor's prices helps them to make sure that their own products are being sold at the right price.
- They can search for new suppliers to keep costs down.
- Improved communication means that the organisation can respond more quickly and provide a better customer experience.
- Improved financial management helps organisations identify and resolve financial problems that may have been hidden in paper-based systems.
- Access to information makes planning more efficient.

Organisations tend to have better services than individuals, but they generally pay more for their connections than individuals.

GETTING STARTED

Choose a website and compare how long it takes for the page to load on your PC and on a device such as a smartphone or tablet. Which is faster? Which version do you find easier to use? Why? How would you feel if only the version you prefer the least were available to use?

LINK IT UP

To find out more about issues affecting network availability, go to lesson 'Communication technologies' in Section A of this component.

Benefits to society

Information helps to break down social barriers and bring communities together. Social networking, for example, makes it possible for us to stay in contact with friends and family more easily.

Being able to find out about other countries, cultures and religions helps to make us more understanding of each other.

Improved access to information also makes countries work better together, for example, in the development of environmental or political agreements. With better sharing of health information, we are beginning to see improvements in tackling poverty in some communities in the world.

Table 3.32 gives some specific examples of technologies that have benefited organisations, individuals and society.

◻ Which social media sites do you use?

◻ **Table 3.32: Benefits of technology**

Technology	Benefits for organisations	Benefits for individuals	Benefits for society
Email	Fast communication with customers and other stakeholders.	Faster and cheaper than letters, no need to find a post box and it is easy to include photographs or other images with no printing required.	Easier to keep in touch with friends and family in a way that is not restricted by time (as a phone call would be if the contact lived in another time zone).
Online information	Competitor information, such as pricing, is easily accessible. It is also easier to stay up to date with regulations and laws that affect organisations.	Research is much easier with more information at your fingertips, which has a positive impact on education.	Access to a wide variety of information and online courses, such as degrees or other certificated training.
Online shopping	Brings an organisation's products and services to a wider market.	Convenience for individuals who can shop 24/7 and access a wider range of products and services. This often means more competitive prices.	An online business does not require the same financial model as a high street business and can be easily set up.
Online chat	Many organisations approve of office-based chat systems through which staff can ask each other questions and share information.	Online chat brings people closer together and can help those who are lonely.	Chatting online helps build communities and enables people in society to find and connect with others who share similar interests.
Media access and download facilities	Access to libraries of images, animations, music and video footage that can be used in marketing campaigns.	Downloading media, such as music and games, at any time of day and which is sometimes cheaper than you might pay in a shop (and some are free).	Accessibility to worldwide media and internet radio from around the world in addition to the usual paid for download services.

ACTIVITY

Interview a local small business. How reliant are they on information? What sort of information do they need to access to function, but that they do not generate within the organisation?

Work with a partner and create a questionnaire that you can use with a small business and share your findings with your class.

CHECK MY LEARNING

Explain why you think online shopping benefits society.

Explain how chat systems benefit organisations.

Explain how individuals benefit from services such as online chat and online shopping.

Legal requirements and professional guidelines

Organisations must work within a legal framework that covers their use of digital technologies, data and information. Details of these are provided in Table 3.33.

GETTING STARTED

We all must live in line with the law. In our work we may also come into contact with professional guidelines and accepted standards. Ask your teacher to give you an example of one law, one professional guideline and one accepted standard that they must work with in school.

□ Table 3.33: Legal and professional requirements

Legislation	Professional guidelines	Accepted standards
• Laws are created to make individuals or groups behave in a specific way. • They are updated and reviewed regularly. • Laws are enforceable. • If you break a law you could be punished with disciplinary action, you could be fined or you could even be imprisoned.	• Professional guidelines are usually focused on a single profession (for example, the banking industry or the health sector). • Guidelines are based on actions that have been agreed by the key organisations or sector bodies. • Only enforceable if a 'licence' to practice is involved – for example, a medical licence can be withdrawn, which would prevent a doctor or nurse from working in the sector. • Organisations that do not follow professional guidelines risk their reputation.	• Accepted standards are ways of doing things that are generally agreed to be examples of best practice. • They are often developed over time and can be influenced by a range of factors, such as emerging technologies. • They are not enforceable in law.

The legal requirements

In the UK there is a range of legislation that organisations must observe in relation to **discrimination**.

Organisations (and even individuals in some circumstances) that discriminate can be prosecuted under the law.

Legislation that could impact on an individual's ability to access information and services includes:
- race relations regulations
- equality laws
- discrimination legislation.

Examples of ways in which access to services or information could breach legislation include:
- provision of web content, such as commentary or images, that could be considered offensive to a group or individual
- failure to provide accessibility tools for an employee
- provision of content only in a format that is not accessible to some groups or individuals.

KEY TERMS

Discrimination is the unfair treatment of individuals (or groups) based on factors such as race, age, gender or disability.

LINK IT UP

To find out more about accessibility needs, go to lesson 'User accessibility needs' in Component 1, Learning aim A.

Professional guidelines/accepted standards

The access to information and services and the most important guidelines and standards are focused on web content. WAI (Web Accessibility Initiative) is a family of standards that includes the four principles of WCAG (Web Content Accessibility Guidelines) shown in Table 3.34.

◘ **Table 3.34: Four principles of WCAG**

Perceivable	The user should be aware of the content through their senses.
Operable	The user must be able to interact with and operate the interface in some way.
Understandable	The user must be able to understand the operation of the interface and the information it contains.
Robust	Must be robust and able to cope with a wide variety of users accessing it using assistive technologies.

ACTIVITY

Work with a partner and choose two different websites. Use the simplified checklist to compare each of the sites in relation to the requirements of WCAG.

Website 1   **Website 2**

☐   Each of the images and buttons has an ALT alternative.   ☐

☐   Input forms have text labels to provide information about the expected inputs.   ☐

☐   Tables are used for tabular data with column and row headings as appropriate.   ☐

☐   Colour has not been used as the only way to separate different areas of content.   ☐

☐   The page can still be read when the size of the text is doubled.   ☐

☐   Blocks of text are not more than 80 characters wide.   ☐

☐   All page functions can be accessed using just a keyboard.   ☐

☐   No content flashes more than three times per second.   ☐

☐   Each page has a descriptive page title.   ☐

☐   If the way that a word is pronounced is vital to it being understood, the pronunciation is written immediately after the word or can be accessed using a link or glossary.   ☐

☐   The website has enough instructions for the user to be able to complete and submit forms.   ☐

CHECK MY LEARNING

Give an example of discrimination.

Give three examples of how legislation is different to accepted standards.

Explain the four principles of WCAG.

Net neutrality

GETTING STARTED

Search YouTube for 'What is net neutrality and how could it affect you? – BBC News' and watch the resulting video. How would you feel if your ability to choose was taken away?

You probably use the internet at various points during the day, particularly if you use social networking, email, web browsers or play games online. Your ability to pick available products and services is currently your choice and is not filtered or influenced by the organisation that provides your internet connection. This is known as 'net neutrality'.

What is net neutrality?

The connections that individuals and organisations use to navigate the internet are provided as a service by various internet service providers (ISPs).

A basic principle of the internet is that all data is treated equally. What this means is that ISPs do not block, tamper with, speed up or slow down any data transfers based on source, destination or type of internet data. This concept is commonly called net neutrality.

DID YOU KNOW?

Net neutrality has been an important topic in the United States of America recently as President Trump has tried to overturn net neutrality regulations.

The UK

In the UK, different ISPs are able to offer a range of packages that limit overall internet speeds but the ISPs can't actively prioritise speeds for certain types of data, for example, streaming video services (such as Netflix™, Amazon etc.) or block access to rival websites because they have been paid to do so by a commercial competitor; nor can they charge customers more for accessing particular websites.

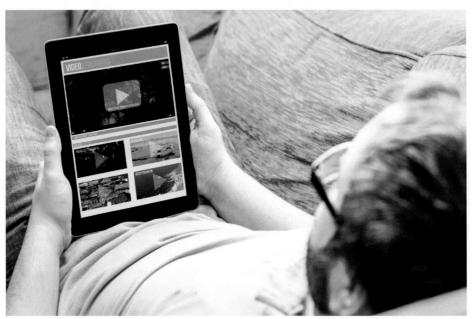

◼ Why would video streaming services benefit from faster data?

ACTIVITY

By 2015 the majority of UK ISPs had voluntarily signed the Open Internet Code of Practice, which supports full and open internet access. Find out what this means and identify at least six organisations that signed up to the code. Compare your answers with your class.

Net neutrality is seen to be beneficial to organisations, particularly new 'start-up' businesses that can compete on the same basis with larger and richer commercial rivals. It means that their users can choose which products and services to use rather than be limited to choices provided by their ISP.

But what would happen if net neutrality were removed? Figure 3.9 shows the possible positive and negative impact on organisations.

Good

Better (and more reliable) services may be possible

ISPs could subsidise free internet for more people from greater profits

Block illegal use of peer-to-peer (P2P) technologies which allow sharing of copyrighted material

ISPs can charge content providers more for resource-hungry traffic such as gaming, video etc., allowing more investment in their networks

Bad

User choices may become limited, e.g. search results filtered to clients paying ISPs

Smaller organisations may not be able to compete or innovate with larger rivals

Free speech through social networking could be blocked or filtered

Greater monitoring of users' online activities, sold to advertisers etc.

◻ Figure 3.9: Do you think it's a good idea or a bad idea to remove net neutrality?

ACTIVITY

Use the internet to investigate the following questions.

1 How does the potential loss of neutrality affect the ability to provide equal access to services and information?

2 Does this affect an organisation's ability to behave in an ethical manner?

3 What is the potential impact on an individual's rights under data protection legislation?

4 Work with a partner and write notes about your findings.

ACTIVITY

Case study

As a relatively recent start-up, Moov2gether is concerned that its rivals may receive preferential treatment if net neutrality agreements are relaxed in the UK.

Create a short document that helps employees to understand the potential impacts on the organisation if this should happen.

CHECK MY LEARNING

Explain net neutrality.

Explain the Open Internet Code of Practice.

Give three disadvantages of losing net neutrality.

Acceptable use policies

Most organisations create and enforce an acceptable use policy (AUP). The AUP is designed to document the ways in which an IT system (network, website and services) can be used and to provide a list of restrictions and potential sanctions that can be applied if rules are broken.

Acceptable use policy

AUPs can apply to internal users or external customers, for example, a commercial organisation may have one AUP for employees (users) and a different version for its customers. An AUP will also cover employees who access an organisation's network from another location when working from home or when working away.

The purpose of an AUP

An AUP is a key part of an organisation's broader information security policy and is one way of reducing potential internal threats (both accidental and malicious) and external threats. The AUP document therefore acts as both a set of guidelines and a warning.

Contents of an AUP

Although AUPs vary from organisation to organisation, they often have similar sections to those listed in Table 3.35.

◘   **Table 3.35: Sections of an AUP**

Scope	• States who the document applies to, such as employees, customers etc. • States what the document covers. • States when the policy came into effect.
Assets	• States what is covered by the document, such as equipment, documents, email communication and knowledge. • Often includes sensitive business information and intellectual properties.
Behaviours	• Acceptable behaviours that an organisation might expect from its employees, including: honesty, loyalty, confidentiality, collaboration, respect of peers, respect of data protection principles, etc. • Unacceptable behaviours that an organisation does not want, including coercion, harrassment, attempts to gain unauthorised access, breach of data protection, abuse, isolation, etc.
Monitoring	• How the organisation monitors employee behaviour. • Monitoring may be electronic, such as the use of electronic passes, internet history, network traffic, CCTV footage, recorded telephone calls or manual (such as incident reports, appraisals etc.).
Sanctions	• How the organisation deals with breaches of the AUP. For example, what it does if an employee is found to have behaved in an unacceptable way. • It should define the processes and potential sanctions (i.e. consequences and punishments) that can be applied. These may be minor (verbal or written warning) or, in extreme cases, termination of employment or legal action.

I have read and agreed to these terms.

Signature: *Felipé Franklin*

Date: *10/04/2018*

I have read and agreed to these terms.

Date: 10/04/2018

◘   **Written and online AUP agreements**

An AUP must have a section confirming that the employee/customer has read the policy and agrees to its rules. Consent is typically shown using an acknowledgement. On a written document this is often a handwritten signature; for online forms a checkbox you can click on is often used. In both cases the date of the agreement is also recorded.

Written AUPs are often countersigned by a person in a position of responsibility within the organisation, for example, a manager. The manager also signs to confirm that the employee's signature is genuine (a little bit like a witness).

■ **Table 3.36: Benefits and drawbacks of AUPs**

Benefits	Drawbacks
Users know what is expected of them and if they sign it then they have agreed to follow the code of conduct.	Users may not like the introduction of a new code of conduct as they may find it restricting.
It holds users accountable for their actions and acts as a contract for disciplinary action when users have not followed it.	Users may feel that you do not trust them if you set out exactly everything they can and cannot do.
It is more likely that users will use the network for more legitimate purposes.	An AUP is a voluntary agreement and therefore has no legal standing.

Use of social media for business purposes

Social media and business boundaries have become increasingly blurred because organisations now understand the power of social media and use it in a targeted way to convey their own message. For example, social media has become a popular method for commercial organisations to advertise their products and services. Businesses may use **third party cookies** or paid advertising to target users that have visited similar websites or used search terms related to their type of business.

Popular social media platforms, such as Facebook, often allow businesses to run simple promotions to their users based on the organisation's advertising needs and budgets. These are very effective because they can precisely target the right audience, such as advertising pet care products on a popular blog about funny cat videos.

Popular video bloggers (vloggers) may be paid to promote certain products as part of their presentations, typically as a source of income. For some vloggers, this money is one of their main sources of income. They are often required by the social media platform to acknowledge that they are being promoted by businesses to do this. Even so, their endorsement is often influential and enables the business to reach a large and receptive audience.

Impact of digital systems on professional life

The portability and ease of use of modern digital systems has continued to blur social and business boundaries. Popular examples include:
- checking and responding to work emails at home and outside normal working hours
- using career-style social media platforms, such as LinkedIn, to network and job hunt.

Organisations can also use social media platforms to recruit new employees and may also use them to uncover details of inappropriate behaviour by job applicants. Some organisations may also include inappropriate use of social media in their AUP as an unacceptable behaviour.

KEY TERMS

Third party cookies are text files that may be downloaded to your system without your knowledge while you are visiting a website. They contain information about the sites you have visited.

LINK IT UP

To find out more about cookies, go to lesson 'Data and the use of the internet' in Section C of this component.

CHECK MY LEARNING

Explain what an AUP is and its purpose.

Give examples of the sanctions an employee may face if they breach an AUP.

Explain how social media can be used for business purposes.

Give examples of how digital systems can impact on an individual's personal life.

ACTIVITY

Case study

Moov2gether employs staff in different roles within the organisation. For example, they have administration staff who upload property details and take them down when the properties are sold. They also keep in contact with potential buyers and inform them of new listings.

Area managers at Moov2gether who look after several branches need to monitor the branches and the activities of the staff.

Explore some different roles in Moov2gether and suggest occasions where each member of staff might use social media or digital systems for personal or professional activities.

Data protection principles

GETTING STARTED

Data about you is stored in many different places. For example, your school holds data about you, as do your doctor and dentist. What rights do you have to access this data and possibly change it? Find out and share your findings with your class.

Think about your own personal data: your name, address, contact details, medical history, education history.

Did you know that the Data Protection Act exists to protect your information and the way information about you is used? In May 2018 new regulations were introduced that manage the way that data is captured, processed, stored and protected.

◘ **What data would your doctors hold on you?**

Even though the UK voted in June 2016 to leave the European Union, aspects of UK law will continue to be based on laws that were required as part of our EU membership. One such law is likely to be the EU General Data Protection Regulation (GDPR) introduced in May 2018. The GDPR has led to additions to the principles of the Data Protection Act (additions shown in italics).

LINK IT UP

To find out more about the right to be forgotten, go to lesson 'Data and the use of the internet' in Section C of this component.

LINK IT UP

To find out more about data collection and the quality of information, go to lessons 'Data collection' and 'Quality of information and its impact on decision making' in Component 2, Learning aim A.

Capturing data

- Data must only be captured for a specified purpose.
- Data must be adequate and relevant *and limited to only what is necessary* in relation to the purpose for which it was collected.
- Data must be accurate and kept up to date *with errors quickly erased (known as the right to be forgotten) or rectified. Organisations will have to produce forms that are clear and enable data subjects to give informed consent using plain and clear language.*
- *It must be easy for data subjects to withdraw consent.*

Processing data

- Data must be processed in line with the rights of data subjects.
- Data must be processed fairly and lawfully *and in a transparent (clear) way.*
- Data captured for one purpose must not be used for a different purpose, *although processing it for archiving in relation to public interest, historical or scientific or statistical purposes will not be considered incompatible.*
- *Data must be processed in a secure manner.*
- *Data belonging to EU citizens must be processed in line with the GDPR even if the organisation processing the data is not in the EU.*

Storing and protecting data

- Data must not be kept for longer than is necessary.
- Organisations must take appropriate action to prevent unauthorised or unlawful processing of data.
- Organisations must act to prevent accidental loss, destruction of or damage to data.
- Data must not be transferred to another country that does not have adequate protection legislation to protect the data.
- Individuals have the right to find out what data is being stored about them *and under new regulations they will have the right to find out whether data is being held about them and where and why this is occurring.*
- *If data has been breached (for example, hacked) organisations will have to notify customers of the breach within 72 hours – this means informing customers without an undue delay.*
- *All data being stored about individuals should be anonymous, unless knowing the identity of the data subject is necessary to make sense of the data.*

Penalties and actions

- *Breaching the requirements of the GDPR can result in a fine of up to 4% of the organisation's turnover, or up to €20 million.*
- *It will be necessary for all new systems to be designed to fulfil data protection requirements.*

Ultimately, the intention of the GDPR is to tighten data protection laws and give individuals more control over how organisations use their personal data.

◘ **Table 3.37: Benefits and drawbacks of data protection**

Benefits	Drawbacks
Those who break the data protection laws face going to prison or paying a fine.	Data protection laws are difficult to enforce. Lots of smaller organisations hold personal information but do not always follow data protection laws.
Individuals now have rights over the data that organisations store about them.	Conviction rates are low, which may indicate that organisations are breaking data protection laws without being prosecuted.

ACTIVITY

Case study

The managing director of Moov2gether is aware of the changes in data protection law and has asked you to create a blog for the company's internal internet pages (intranet) that explains the key principles of the 2018 GDPR legislation to its employees.

CHECK MY LEARNING

Identify as many of the key data protection principles as you can in three minutes.

Data and the use of the internet

Organisations have a responsibility to ensure they behave in a legal and ethical fashion. The growth of the internet has challenged the idea of personal privacy and users often leave a much larger **digital footprint** than they imagine.

Right to be forgotten

There is a legal concept known as the 'right to be forgotten'. It means that an individual is free to pursue their life without being treated unfairly because of a specific action taken or comment made in their past. In terms of data, the EU has adopted the 'right to erasure'.

In practical terms, this can result in an individual asking an organisation to remove any copies of, or links to, information held about them. In addition, the organisation should tell third parties who may also have copies or links to erase them. Large fines can be applied if the organisation's data controller is not seen to have taken all reasonable steps to meet this requirement.

Appropriate and legal use of cookies and other transactional data

Using online services results in a user leaving a digital footprint, often containing personal information that organisations can sell to other organisations that may wish to use the information, such as to support targeted advertisements. This data can be stored and accessed in several ways.

Cookies

A cookie is a block of data that is typically created by a remote web server and stored temporarily in the memory of the user's device or for longer periods in a text file.

Cookies were created to be used by web designers to legitimately store memorable data about a user's interactions with a website, such as remembering user preferences, the contents of their shopping basket or whether the user is logged in etc. These are often called first party cookies, used and created by the same website domain, and are generally seen as harmless.

◘ Cookies are used to remember the contents of an online shopping basket. What else could cookies be used to remember?

GETTING STARTED

Think about your online activities: the websites you visit regularly, the social networking sites you like. What information can others see about you on your social media pages?

What type of digital footprint are you creating? Write some notes and compare your answers with a partner.

KEY TERMS

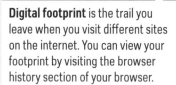

Digital footprint is the trail you leave when you visit different sites on the internet. You can view your footprint by visiting the browser history section of your browser.

DID YOU KNOW?

Each cookie has a lifespan – some cookies 'die' (are erased from the device's memory) when the web browser is closed – this is known as a session cookie. Other cookies are persistent and stay on the user's device until a specific date and time is reached.

However, enterprising websites often create cookies that can be used by advertisers to track a user's online activities, helping partners to display advertising offers closely reflecting the user's browsing habits and core interests.

These tracking cookies (or third party cookies) can be blocked or deleted by downloadable tools and web browser plug-ins and extensions to preserve a user's privacy.

The EU's legislation on cookies, known as the 'cookie law' or, more correctly, the ePrivacy Directive, requires that users give consent before a website can store and access information on their personal device. This usually appears as a cookie consent banner on the organisation website's main page. Figure 3.10 shows an example of how this might appear.

This site uses cookies. By continuing to browse the site you are agreeing to our use of cookies. Read our Cookie Policy to find out more. ☒

Agree

 Figure 3.10: Have you ever seen this on a website you've visited?

Organisations also collect transactional data, which is stored digitally. For example, an online purchase would include personal information, delivery address, item details, date and time of purchase, a unique order ID and tracking data for delivery. This data also has to be stored and processed legally and ethically.

ACTIVITY

Explore the data being stored by popular websites you visit. You need to use a web browser to view cookie data being stored by the site.

Identify the cookies as being first party or third party.

CHECK MY LEARNING

Give three examples of how legal and ethical constraints limit what organisations can do with the data they collect via cookies.

Explain the term 'right to be forgotten'.

Explain what a tracking cookie is and why it is used.

Explain the term 'transactional data'.

Intellectual property

Organisations need to protect their own intellectual property (IP), including brand names, logos and product designs, to prevent other organisations from using them. There are three common ways in which this can be achieved: registering a **trademark**, by applying for a **patent** or by **copyrighting** it.

Why intellectual property is important

Intellectual property applies to anything:
- that is copyrighted
- that is trademarked
- that is the subject of a patent.

Copyrighted materials and trademarked materials are often easy to identify because of the symbols for copyright © and trademark™.

Patents are rights given to a product that has been invented. The patent has a life (number of years during which it applies) and during this time no other person or organisation can replicate the product. Once the patent has expired, other businesses can copy the product.

KEY TERMS

Trademark is the recognisable design, words or symbols that have been legally registered by a company or individual for a company, product or name.

Patent is the exclusive rights granted to a person or organisation for a specific idea, design or invention.

Copyright is a legal right protecting the use of your work. There are different rules about how and when your work could be used and how long copyright is retained.

ACTIVITY

Case study

Moov2together is rebranding their business. Work with a partner to design or create a new logo for their estate agency.

Once completed, attach the logo to an email and send it to the senior managers, explaining what will need to be done to protect the logo from being copied by competitors.

DID YOU KNOW?

The first known English patent for an invention was granted by King Henry VI in 1449. King Henry VI gave a patent in the form of a letter to John of Utynam for a method of making stained glass windows.

How to protect intellectual property

Protecting intellectual property could mean registering patents, design rights, copyright or a trademark. The most commonly protected property includes:
- music
- artistic works
- designs
- logos
- inventions
- discoveries
- literature and other publications
- software/programming code.

When the patent is registered a search is made to make sure that the idea has not already been patented (if it has, you could be breaking the law by trying to patent it again).

◻ Check the inside page of a book. Do you see a copyright notice?

Plagiarism

When you are studying you may need to explain something to answer a question in your coursework and you may choose to copy information from a book or the internet. For example, you might be asked to explain a cookie and then copy the information directly from this book. If you do this without saying that it is a direct copy from the book or internet it is called **plagiarism**.

If you do copy from the internet or a book, you must say where the information has come from.
- When acknowledging text taken from a book you should include (author, year of publication, name of publication, name of publisher).
- In the case of the internet, you should include (author (or 'unknown' if not known), date accessed, URL of the website).

KEY TERMS

Plagiarism is copying someone else's work or intellectual property without acknowledging them, claiming it as your own.

Using other people's intellectual property

There are legal and ethical considerations if you want to use someone else's intellectual property.

If you do need to use other people's intellectual property, such as an image, there are some common actions you should take.
- Ask the owner of the property for permission to use the image (to be given permission may involve you paying a fee).
- An alternative is to license the content, which means paying to use it for as long as you need to use it. The original owner maintains ownership.
- Acknowledge the owner of the image when you use it.

Using the image without permission or acknowledgement could lead to:
- being asked to stop using the image
- being taken to court
- having to pay a fine and compensation to the owner of the image.

Why is it so important to acknowledge the sources you have used?

ACTIVITY

Case study

Moov2gether is aware that another company is trading online under a very similar name and using a company logo that customers are mistaking for theirs. Write a short document in your own words to explain how Moov2gether's IP can be legally protected.

CHECK MY LEARNING

Explain the term 'patent'.

Give three examples of intellectual property that an owner might want to protect.

Explain the term 'plagiarism'.

Describe the main actions you should take if you need to use someone else's intellectual property.

The criminal use of computer systems

Criminals represent a very real threat to computer systems used by an individual or organisation, and in general.

How criminals use computer systems

There are four main areas of common criminal activity as explained in Table 3.38.

◻ Table 3.38: Technology crimes

Area	Activity
Unauthorised access	This is where criminals target a system and identify its security weaknesses. They then access the unsecure system to identify a profile they can use and change the privileges to give them better access to the system.
Unauthorised modification of materials	Criminals who have managed to access a system find content to change. They change files, such as documents, web pages, or download files to give them access to other systems, or to divert money to other bank accounts.
Creation of malware	Malware, such as viruses, is written by criminals to be used to infect systems, either to cause damage or to steal money or information. The malware can be modified to take different actions on different systems after it has infected them.
Intentional spreading of malware	Malware is spread through infected files. The files can be spread via the internet or even via USB devices. Often, malware is spread through user ignorance (such as finding a USB and opening it on your computer to see what is on the device – this will infect your machine).

How malware can be spread

Malware is usually spread through users unknowingly downloading and opening infected files (documents, applications etc.) and having insufficient protection on their computer system.

The most common pattern of infection is shown in Figure 3.11.

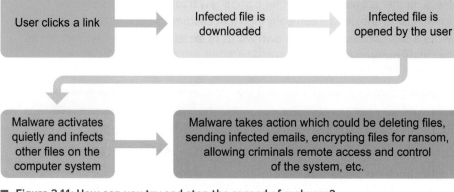

◻ Figure 3.11: How can you try and stop the spread of malware?

Because most malware infects and duplicates silently on a computer system, many users do not know their computer system has become infected and will unknowingly pass the malware onto another user, for example, by sharing infected files.

EFFECTIVE DIGITAL WORKING PRACTICES

Popular routes for the spreading of malware include:
- social networking sites
- internet chat rooms
- infected websites
- illegal **peer-to-peer** (P2P) network downloads of copyrighted material
- use of software 'cracks' to illegally register commercial software
- email attachments
- following malicious links.

◼ Following this link is a common way of spreading malware. Have you ever had this message appear on your devices?

KEY TERMS

Peer to peer (P2P) is a way of explaining two systems that are connected and have the same rights and privileges.

Cracks comes from the expression 'crack the code'. This is usually a software program that removes the need to register the software to be able to use it.

DID YOU KNOW?

Anti-virus software protects in four common ways:
1. Checking downloaded files (or newly added) files for malware.
2. Checking files when they are opened.
3. Checking email attachments.
4. Running a regular scan of the complete computer system for malware.

ACTIVITY

Case study

Moov2gether is concerned that its data and systems may have been compromised maliciously by some person or organisation using the username and password of two employees who have left the organisation. Work in a small group to discuss what Moov2gether should do to resolve the situation.

For example:

1 What should Moov2gether have done when the employees left the organisation to avoid this weakness?

2 What guidance should it give to IT staff to ensure that this does not happen again?

3 What guidance should it give to Moov2gether staff to reduce the likelihood of further infections or access by criminals using other means?

CHECK MY LEARNING

Give the four most common criminal uses of computer systems.

Describe how malware can be spread.

Give at least three popular routes for spreading malware.

C: assessment practice

How you will be assessed

As with Sections A and B, the questions you will be asked will be related to one or more scenarios.

Although the topics from the whole component could occur in any of the questions across the assessment, some examples of the types of questions that may be asked in relation to topics in Section C are shown here. Before answering the following questions, refer to the command words at the end of lesson 'A: assessment practice' in Section A of this component.

CHECKPOINT

Strengthen
- Check that you can explain 'intellectual property'.
- Check that you can name the key principles of the Data Protection Act.

Challenge
- Learn some of the data protection principles in each category (data collection, data processing, data storage).
- Remember to gather examples that you can use to illustrate your answers.

ASSESSMENT ACTIVITY 1   C1 RESPONSIBLE USE

You will need to show that you understand how data can be shared responsibly. In addition, you should be able to demonstrate an understanding of the environmental impact of digital systems.

Task 1

As Raeni Anderson's team are spread over multiple locations around the world she has decided that she needs to give her staff advice about how data is shared across the team. In addition, the company is environmentally aware, and she feels that her staff need guidance about the environmental impact of their activities. Here are some things that she must consider.

a) Describe the different methods that Raeni can use to track the movements of her staff.

b) Explain three benefits and three drawbacks of using shared data.

c) Describe how an ink cartridge could be recycled.

d) Give two examples of settings that can be used to adjust or to reduce the impact of technology on the environment.

e) Discuss the positive and negative impacts that different digital devices have had on the environment.

Task 2

Allie-Beth Kurz owns a sandwich shop in central London.

Johann has been working for a marketing company that has been doing customer research for a national chain of sandwich shops and he has offered his friend Allie-Beth access to the data and its findings.

Allie-Beth is tempted as the research data will not cost her anything and would help her to identify ways of expanding her business.

a) Give four benefits and four drawbacks of accepting the data that Johann has offered her.

b) Describe any legal implications of using this data.

ASSESSMENT ACTIVITY 3 — C2 LEGAL AND ETHICAL

You should demonstrate your understanding of legislation and how it impacts on the way that organisations use and implement digital systems. You should also show that you understand the wider implications of using technology, data and information and how to behave ethically.

Task 1

a) Describe two benefits and two drawbacks of net neutrality.

b) Give four examples of behaviours that organisations might expect from its employees.

c) Identify three principles about storing data (not capturing or processing).

d) Give a reason why cookies are used by organisations.

e) Describe what is meant by the term 'plagiarism'.

f) Describe how malware infects a computer.

g) Discuss the different legal and ethical uses of intellectual property. You should include permissions, licensing and attribution in your answer.

h) Evaluate the effectiveness of data protection principles on the security and privacy of personal data.

Task 2

Your local police force has asked you to create a series of information sheets for local small businesses to highlight how computers can be used for criminal activity.

Discuss the four most common areas of computer-based criminal activity. Describe what the activity involves and give an example in each area.

TAKE IT FURTHER

The Internet Society has several useful tutorials on digital footprints. Use the internet and find a tutorial. What are the key points raised in the tutorial? How can you make sure your own digital footprint is protected?

Forms of notation

LINK IT UP

To find out more on planning tools, go to lesson 'Basic project planning tools' in Component 1, Learning aim B.

All organisations need to know what technology they own – what it is and where it is. Some organisations create lists, others create diagrams that show the technologies and how they are connected. Diagrams are very useful for communicating complex ideas. In this lesson you will look at some examples of **notation**.

Which is better – text or diagrams?

In this lesson you will explore a range of notation diagrams. You will be able to create them and interpret them to help explain systems and system design. The following are some commonly used diagrams.

- Film-makers and animators usually use storyboards to provide a record of a sequence of actions in a film or animation.
- Programmers use flow charts to map the logic of a system and data flow diagrams to demonstrate how data will be processed via a program.
- Database developers use data flow diagrams to explain how different data is connected and how data is stored or processed.
- Computer technicians use system diagrams to explain the technologies and interfaces that make up an organisation's systems.
- Project teams and application developers use many of the diagrams listed to outline and detail how the processes in an application or a solution will work because solutions may be programmed, need a database, or need some sort of hardware and/or software.

ACTIVITY

At its simplest, a storyboard can explain a series of actions without any words. Work with a partner and write out exactly what is happening in this sequence. Make sure you include all the important information, such as the components, timings and actions, as the text version should have no visual clues.

An example of a diagram you will see in industry is an **information flow diagram (IFD).** These diagrams show how information flows around a system between people or functional areas of the organisation. Figure 3.12 is a diagram that represents the information flow that is needed to resolve an IT fault. Notice that there is no information about data storage, the technologies used, how the information is generated or what software was used. This is just about the different components of information that the system handles.

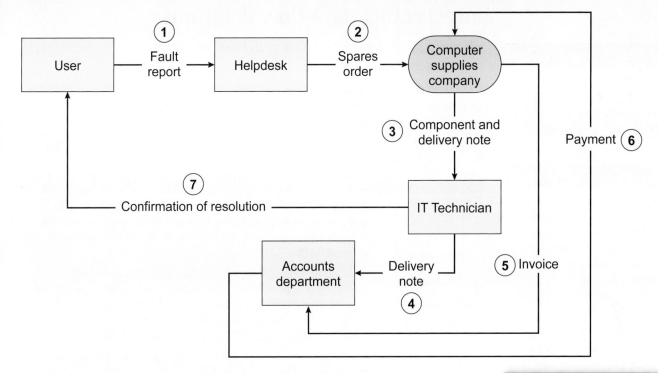

☐ **Figure 3.12:** Is this information flow diagram easy to follow?

As text this would look something like the following.

1 User reports the fault to the helpdesk.

2 The spares order is sent to the computer supplies company.

3 The computer supplies company send the component and a delivery note.

Developing systems

Organisations constantly monitor their own systems and activities to make sure they remain as efficient as possible. They also stay up to date with scientific and electronic developments to see if any emerging technologies might provide new opportunities. If they identify that changes to existing systems are needed, or would simply be of benefit, this becomes a project.

Before a new system can be developed, the components and processes in any existing system need to be recorded. This is because sometimes some or all of the components or processes may be incorporated into the new version of the system. They need to establish the following.

1 What the current system consists of (for example, its hardware, software and how it is connected to other components or systems).

2 What processes or actions the system carries out.

Planning a new system also means recording what the developed system will be designed to do, and the best way to do this is to create diagrams to be used in the development. The diagrams will show the following.

1 What the new system will consist of (what hardware, software) and how different components will be connected.

2 What processes or actions the new system will carry out.

The alternative to using diagrams to record the system would be to use text.

Interpreting data flow diagrams

It is important that organisations understand their data – how it is generated, how it is processed and how it is stored.

Data flow diagrams (**DFDs**) are used to explain how data is processed by an existing system and how it could be processed by a future system. Table 3.39 shows the components found in DFDs.

◘ Table 3.39: Components in data flow diagrams

Component	Description
1.0 / Process	A process box indicates that something is happening to data. This could be processing a customer invoice, creating a new membership at a gym, ordering a sandwich, checking stock. Each process has a different number.
M1 or D1 / Data store	A data store is where the processed data goes after it has been processed, or where it is taken from before a process takes place. If the data store is a physical file like a diary or an address book, it is numbered with an M in front (which stands for manual). If it is an electronic data store it is numbered with a D in front (which stands for digital).
Entity	An entity is a person, organisation or a group that is interacting with the process.
→	The arrow shows which way the data is flowing.

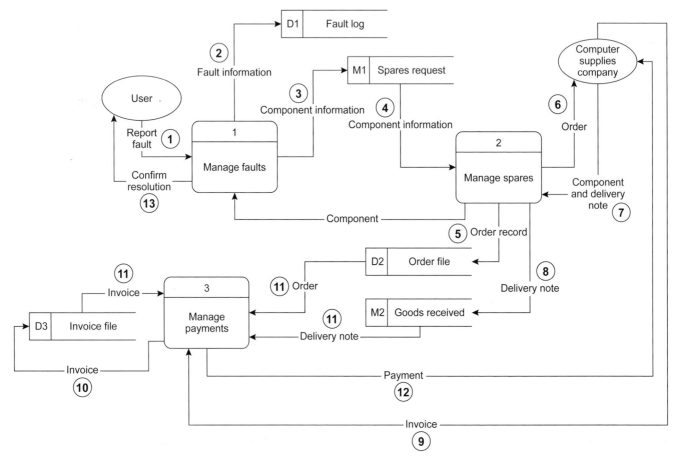

◘ Figure 3.13: Do you prefer the information in this format or presented as text?

Written as text this diagram would be represented as follows.

1 The user reports a fault to the MANAGE FAULTS PROCESS.

2 The fault information is recorded into digital store D1 – the fault log.

3 Component information needed to fix the fault is recorded on a spares request form, which will be stored in manual file M1.

4 The MANAGE SPARES PROCESS uses the information on the spares request form to create an order.

5 A copy of the order is then sent to the digital store D2 – the order file.

6 The order is sent to the computer supplies company.

7 The delivery note and component are received by the MANAGE SPARES PROCESS from the computer supplies company.

8 The delivery note is placed in the manual file M1 – goods received.

9 An invoice is received from the computer supplies company.

10 The invoice is placed in the invoice file.

11 The MANAGE PAYMENTS PROCESS takes the order from the order file, the delivery note from the goods received file and the invoice from the Invoice file and raises the payment.

12 The payment is sent to the computer supplies company.

13 The user is informed that the problem has been resolved.

As you can see, Figure 3.13 has three processes (manage faults, manage spares and manage payments) and five data stores (three digital – fault log, order file and invoice file – and two manual – spares request and goods received). These stores and processes were not defined in the IFD.

The reality is that most of the processes in this diagram are more complicated than they appear in the DFD because there are more actions that are taking place, but these are not wholly relevant to the overall fault resolution activity.

■ **Table 3.40: Benefits and drawbacks of data flow diagrams**

Benefits	Drawbacks
They show what and who the system interacts with. This includes the internal and external entities.	Some data flow diagrams can be very complex and difficult to understand.
You can quickly see how data moves through a system.	Different data flow diagrams use different symbols, which can lead to confusion.
It helps in defining the boundaries of the system.	A DFD does not show the hardware or software required to operate the system.

CHECK MY LEARNING

In relation to data flow diagrams, explain what an entity is.

Describe why the direction of the arrows is important.

Explain the difference between a data store marked M and a data store marked D?

ACTIVITY

Case study

This diagram has been provided by Moov2gether to explain one of their key processes.

Make some notes about what this diagram is telling you. Remember to look at each of the components and how they are connected.

Explain the diagram to a partner.

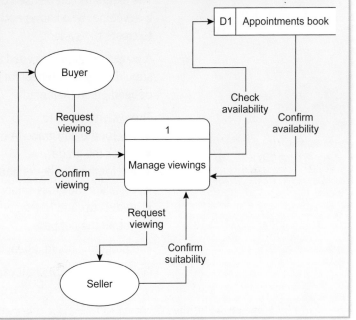

Interpreting flow charts

Have you ever tried to record the steps of something you have done? You could use text and write down one step at a time. But what do you do if you have to repeat an action, or what do you include between two actions?

So far you have considered how data and information flows can be captured and recorded using diagrams. Systems developers use flow charts to record the activities that happen in a process. These diagrams have several components.

☐ **Table 3.41: Components in flow charts**

Component	Description
Terminator	Terminators show where a process starts and ends.
Process	A process shows that an action is taking place. Examples are a calculation or sending information to data store.
Decision	A decision box is used where a selection needs to be made, based on a condition. It means that one action happens rather than another. A condition is a statement that can be tested. For example, 'Did the user press Y or N? If Y, do this, if N, do that.' There can only ever be one input to and two outputs from a decision box.
Data	Data shows inputs into the process or outputs from the process.
→	Arrows link the components together in the direction of the flow of activities.

Using these symbols and the concepts of selection (decisions) and iterations (loops to make actions repeat), diagrams can be created that represent how processes really work.

These diagrams can be used to represent actions in existing systems or record the designs and planned actions of new ones.

The diagrams can be used by developers to create the system and, if drawn correctly, a developer who knows nothing about what the system is supposed to do will be able to create the system.

A wages solution is needed to process staff wages. This means that the solution should be able to repeat for multiple staff. Staff are paid one of two pay rates depending on their grade.

The system needs to:
- ask for the pay grade (A or B)
- check the grade
- ask for the number of hours
- calculate the gross salary based on the hours and grade
- deduct tax and NI (National Insurance)
- output the net pay.

The program should repeat if another wage calculation needs to take place.

Figure 3.14 is a flow chart explaining the wages solution.

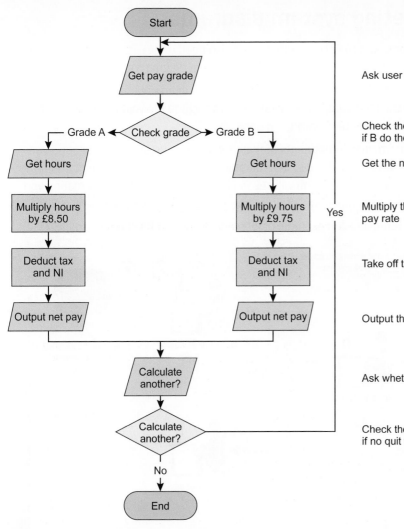

The flow chart shows the following steps with descriptions:

- **Start**
- **Get pay grade** — Ask user for the pay grade of the employee
- **Check grade** — Check the pay grade, if A do the left hand side, if B do the right hand side
  - Grade A side:
    - **Get hours** — Get the number of hours worked
    - **Multiply hours by £8.50** — Multiply the number of hours by the relevant pay rate
    - **Deduct tax and NI** — Take off tax and National Insurance contributions
    - **Output net pay** — Output the net wages for the employee
  - Grade B side:
    - **Get hours** — Get the number of hours worked
    - **Multiply hours by £9.75** — Multiply the number of hours by the relevant pay rate
    - **Deduct tax and NI** — Take off tax and National Insurance contributions
    - **Output net pay** — Output the net wages for the employee
- **Calculate another?** — Ask whether another wage needs to be calculated
- **Calculate another?** (decision) — Check the answer – if yes go back to the start, if no quit the program
- **End**

■ Figure 3.14: Can you follow this flow chart?

■ Table 3.42: Benefits and drawbacks of a flow chart

Benefits	Drawbacks
It shows the order in which tasks are completed within a system.	Some processes or tasks are so complex it becomes difficult to represent them clearly in a flow chart.
It can be used to give a generalised overview of a system or the functions that it carries out.	If a change needs to be made to a system, the flow chart might need to be redrawn.
It can help a person or organisation to see where the problems are within a system.	People need to understand what the flow chart is for and what the symbols mean. It can be confusing until you are familiar with the symbols.

ACTIVITY

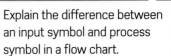

Work with a partner to create a flow chart for the following scenario.

A solution is needed for issuing club membership cards. The level of membership is based on a member's age. If 18 or under, the member is classified as a junior, if over 18, the membership is adult.

Draw the flow chart.

CHECK MY LEARNING

Explain the difference between an input symbol and process symbol in a flow chart.

Describe what a terminator is used for.

Explain what a decision box checks.

Interpreting system diagrams

Physical systems and their components may also need to be captured in a diagram. This lesson explores how this could be done. System diagrams are often less formal.

System diagrams can represent several components in an organisation's system. It will often include the technologies involved and may include the volumes of data – but only if the volumes are unusually large or small.

There are no particular components that are required in a system diagram and you will see lots of variations. But a system diagram should tell you something about the system and the way it works. You will see in Figure 3.15 that there is information you have not seen on any other type of diagram.

This diagram represents an example of a technical support function for an ISP.

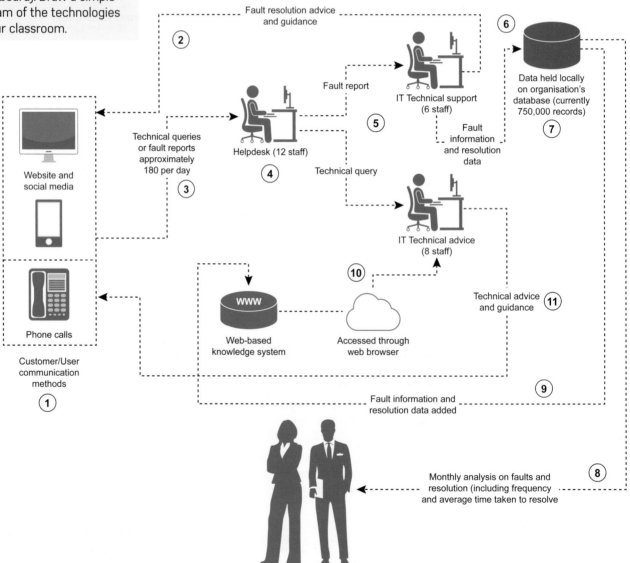

■ Figure 3.15: What is each area of this system diagram telling us?

1 Customers or system users can use three different communications methods when they contact the organisation: phone, handheld device, such as a tablet or smartphone, or a computer (via a web page or social media).

2 How to fix a fault or other guidance goes back to the customer/user via the same methods.

3 Technical queries and fault reports (about 180 per day) are dealt with first by the helpdesk.

4 The helpdesk has 12 staff.

5 The helpdesk redirects the communications by sending fault reports to the six staff in IT technical support or to the eight staff who provide IT technical advice.

6 Fault information and the resolution of faults are recorded in a database.

7 The database currently holds 750,000 (current) records.

8 Data from the database is sent to managers each month detailing the faults reported, how they were resolved and how long it took to resolve the problem.

9 Fault information and how these were resolved is added to a cloud-based knowledge system.

10 The IT technical advice staff draw down the information from the knowledge system through a web browser to use it to resolve technical queries.

11 The technical advice is fed back to the customer/user via the same methods that generated the query.

ACTIVITY

Case study

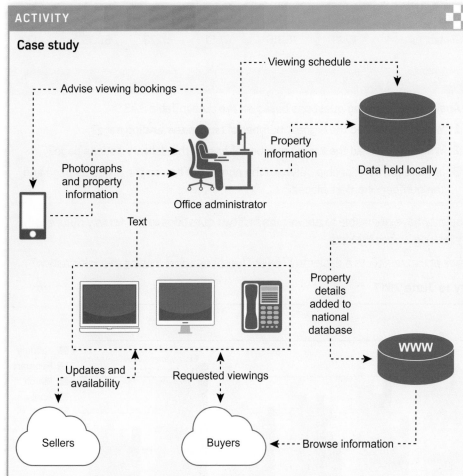

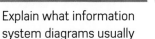

This system diagram represents the minimum technologies used in each of the branches of Moov2gether. Explain to a partner what the technologies are and how they are being used.

CHECK MY LEARNING

Explain what information system diagrams usually contain.

Describe how system diagrams help you understand a system.

Tables and written information

Displaying information in tables is often an ideal way to organise information. In this book you will have seen tables used many times, but are tables always appropriate?

Tables

Consider the following data in Table 3.43.

◻ Table 3.43: Hits data on organisational website

	January	February	March	April	May	June
Landing page	18,882	17,116	18,666	15,157	16,159	21,101
Product information	16,443	16,997	17,847	14,632	15,710	18,463
Order page	14,694	16,005	16,841	13,547	15,067	17,996
Payment options	9,598	8,152	15,461	12,685	14,612	17,614
Delivery options	6,189	10,717	12,656	11,487	12,922	14,456
Personal account	10,823	9,599	8,465	11,659	14,654	16,546
FAQs	16,859	18,101	15,463	14,656	14,651	14,565
Contact us	8,070	6,316	7,651	9,222	8,006	7,123

ACTIVITY

Answer the following questions based on the data in Table 3.43.

1　Which month had the highest number of hits on the landing page?

2　Which month had the lowest number of hits on the delivery options page?

3　Is there any relationship between the number of hits on the products page and the number of orders placed?

You may have been able to answer the first two questions in the Activity quite easily by looking across the data.

Look at Figure 3.16. Is it easier to answer Questions 1 and 2 using this information?

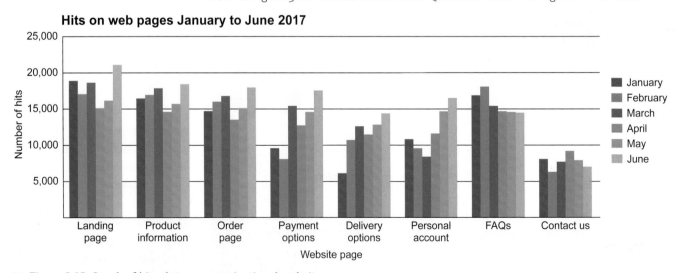

◻ Figure 3.16: Graph of hits data on organisational website

Is Question 3 easier to answer by looking at Table 3.43 or Figure 3.16?

The answer to Activity Question 3 is no – there is no direct relationship between the number of views on the products page and the number of orders made (for example, look at June with the highest number of hits on the products page and fewer orders placed in comparison with the month before).

However, if we extract the two relevant rows of data and create an additional chart it is very easy to see.

Written information

When you are documenting systems, written information will also be needed. This can be in the form of an **executive summary**. Sometimes you need to add text descriptions to tables, charts or diagrams to give them context.

Extensive documents explaining systems will have two key additional components that help the users of the documents navigate them.

Creating data flow diagrams

The best way to learn about data flow diagrams is to create them. Creating a data flow diagram of a process within an organisation requires you to use different shapes for specific components.

Project – Myla's fancy dress shop

Myla owns a fancy dress shop on the High Street and provides an online service, dispatching items via a courier. She has a wide range of outfits that can be rented, including clown costumes, costumes for pirates, fairies, soldiers, Vikings, Romans, princesses, police, firefighters, astronauts and a range of superhero costumes. These costumes are for adults and children.

In addition, she sells accessories, such as masks, gloves, braces, wigs, hats, bracelets, glasses and moustaches.

To operate her business, there are five key processes that happen each day:

1 enquiries

2 sales

3 payments

4 dispatch

5 returns.

A data flow diagram that represents these processes would look like this.

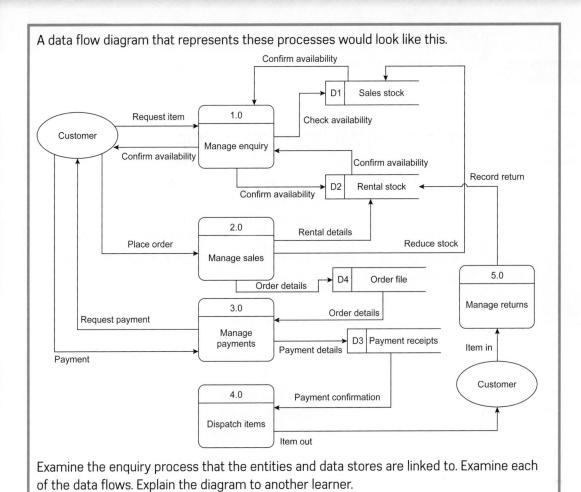

Examine the enquiry process that the entities and data stores are linked to. Examine each of the data flows. Explain the diagram to another learner.

ACTIVITY

Work with a partner and draw a data flow diagram to represent the following doctor's surgery scenario.

- A patient requests an appointment.
- The appointment availability is checked in an appointments diary.
- An appointment is offered to the patient.
- The appointment is confirmed in the diary.
- The patient is told that the appointment has been made.

Share your solution with your teacher or class.

LINK IT UP

To find out more about the different components of data flow diagrams, go to lesson 'Interpreting data flow diagrams' in Section D of this component.

CHECK MY LEARNING

Your teacher will give you another example of a data flow diagram. Remember, it may appear to be slightly different as it may use alternative symbols – but the basic principles are the same.

Examine each of the processes and write out how they are interacting with the other components that they are linked to.

Answer the following questions.

Can a data store be directly linked to another data store?

Can an entity be linked directly to a data store? Why?

Creating flow charts

Creating a flow chart is like walking through a sequence of actions. Think back to the example for the wage calculator and the membership card generator.

GETTING STARTED

Creating a flow chart for a process requires you to use different shapes for specific components. Can you remember what they are?

LINK IT UP

To find out more about the different components of a flow chart, go to lesson 'Interpreting flow charts' in Section D of this component.

ACTIVITY

Describe what this flow chart is showing you.

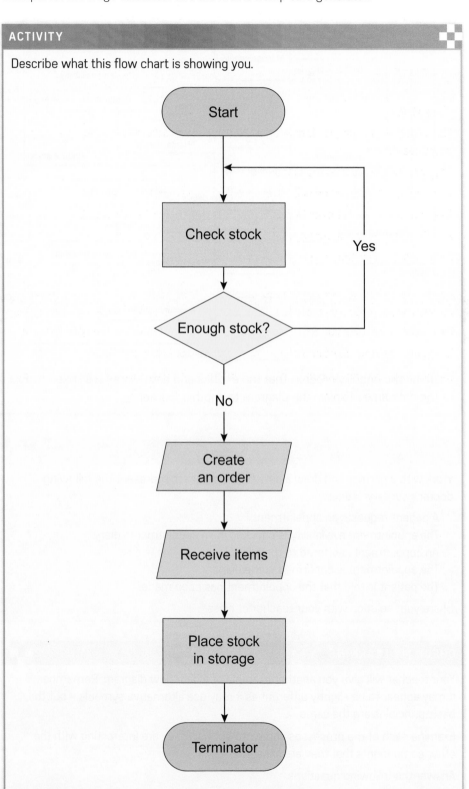

Work with a partner to interpret the diagram and share your interpretation with your class.

Have you ever used a cashpoint?

If not, your teacher will provide a link to a simulation.

Once you understand how a cashpoint works, draw a flow chart that explains the process of inputting and validating your card and displaying your balance on screen.

Case study

Moov2gether is trying to decide on a fee discount structure to encourage more customers.

They are looking to give fee discounts.

All commercial properties will attract a 10% fee discount.

Residential properties over £200,000 will attract a 6.5% fee discount.

Residential properties under £200,000 will attract a 2% discount.

Draw a flow chart that demonstrates this fee structure.

Your teacher will give you a further scenario and ask you to draw a simple flow chart.

Complete the flow chart and share your solution with your teacher.

Explain how flow charts can help you understand the way a system works.

D: assessment practice

How you will be assessed

When being assessed for this section as part of your externally set assessment you will be expected to produce or interpret one or more diagrams.

In a similar way to the examples you have already seen, you will be provided with a scenario and some information, and asked to produce one or more diagrams. You will be told which type of diagram you will need to create.

Before answering the following questions, refer to the command words at the end of lesson 'A: assessment practice' in Section A of this component.

CHECKPOINT

Strengthen
Make sure you know the difference between:
- data flow diagrams
- flow charts
- system diagrams.

Check that you can use the right components in the right diagram.

Challenge
Decide how you will check that you have included everything in the diagrams you work with.

ASSESSMENT ACTIVITY 1 | **D1 FORMS OF NOTATION**

You will be expected to be able to show how textual and diagrammatical communications can be used to explain digital solutions. As part of this you will need to demonstrate that you can interpret and create diagrams.

Task 1

You are working for PPDS Leisure Centre and your manager has given you a data flow diagram and asked you to explain the information and booking process for members.

Here is the diagram.

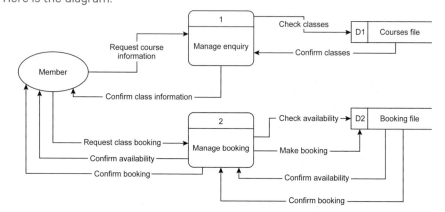

a) Describe the processes involved.

b) Discuss the suitability of the diagram and how effectively it represents the processes involved in the system.

Task 2

Alternatively, you could be asked to interpret a flow chart about an exercise class booking.

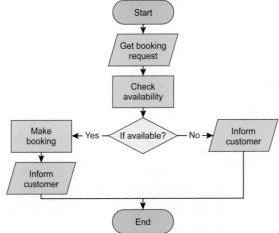

a) Describe the diagram.

b) Evaluate the different forms of notation and how effectively they represent the data, information and systems within an organisation.

Task 3

EG Power and Utilities provides domestic gas and electricity services to residential homes in the UK.

Customers must provide gas and electricity readings on a regular basis so that the company knows how much to charge them.

Each time a gas reading is entered, the value is checked against the existing value on record. If the new value is higher than the value on record, the new value is accepted and recorded in the file.

If not, it is rejected and the customer has to input the value again, until the new value is bigger than the old value. When the gas value is correct, the customer receives confirmation.

Each time an electricity reading is entered, the value is checked against the existing value on record. If the new value is higher than the value on record, the new value is accepted and recorded in the file.

If not, it is rejected and the customer has to input the value again, until the new value is bigger than the old value. When the electricity value is correct, the customer receives confirmation.

Draw a data flow diagram and a flow chart for this scenario.

SYNOPTIC QUESTION

Poppy is about to start managing a new project that requires her to plan and design a new user interface. Before she does this, she needs to collect information about the user interface that is being used.

Describe how Poppy could make use of different forms of notation when collecting information about the current user interface.

TAKE IT FURTHER

Practise your diagramming techniques, using both software and drawing them freehand (as you will not have access to diagramming software during the assessment).

Glossary

Absolute addresses do not change when the formula is copied. They are created by including a $ sign in front of the column letter and/or row number.

Access control list (ACL) is a list that tells the network which data can be sent and received.

Accessibility is about how devices are designed for people with disabilities to use with ease.

Ad hoc network is a type of wireless network that does not rely on fixed hardware such as routers in wired networks.

ALT text is alternative text that describes an onscreen image for users with visual impairments.

Anomaly is when something differs from the normal or what is expected.

Bias is an external factor that may influence results.

Bluetooth® is a short-range technology that connects multiple devices, for example mobile phones, speakers etc., together in a smaller area (usually 10 metres or less).

Breadcrumbs is the term used to describe a user interface component that makes navigation easy and instinctive.

Bugs are flaws in computer programs or systems.

Cell is an individual box on a worksheet.

Central Processing Unit (CPU) is central to every PC and device. It's the computer's brain and without it a PC cannot function.

Cognitive needs cover a wide range of disabilities, including developmental delays, learning disabilities, brain injuries and dementia.

Constraint is a limitation or restriction that you face while completing a project.

Consumables are items such as ink cartridges, paper, toner, cleaning products, maintenance tools and cables.

Copyright is a legal right protecting the use of your work. There are different rules about how and when your work could be used and how long copyright is retained.

Cracks comes from the expression 'crack the code'. This is usually a software program that removes the need to register the software to be able to use it.

Dashboard is a display of important information, using visual and other methods of presentation.

Data is a collection of numbers or text that is stored and processed by computer systems.

Data flow diagrams (DFDs) are made up of four key components. Different versions of these diagrams may use slightly different symbols, but the meaning will still be the same.

Data models are a way of showing the relationships between data and investigating the possible outcomes of change.

Data Protection Controller is the named person in an organisation who takes responsibility for the safety and security of the organisation's data.

Data subject is an individual whose personal data is being stored.

Default password is one that is automatically allocated when your account is set up. Users are always advised to change default passwords on first use.

Delimiting is the use of one or more characters to separate one data item from another.

Denial-of-service (DoS) attacks attack a remote computer by making it unable to respond to legitimate user requests.

Digital footprint is the trail you leave when you visit different sites on the internet. You can view your footprint by visiting the browser history section of your browser.

Discrimination is the unfair treatment of individuals (or groups) based on factors such as race, age, gender or disability.

Dispersed data is multiple copies of the same data in different locations.

Distributed data is split into lots of bits and stored in different places.

Downloading a document or file to your computer or device means it can be used when you are not connected to the internet.

Downtime is a period when a computer and its services are unavailable.

Encrypted means that information or data has been converted to a type of code that cannot be understood without a translation key.

Engaged is a term used to describe how involved someone is in a task and how much attention they are paying to it.

Executive summary (sometimes just called a summary) is a description of the important points of the document.

Fields divide data up into groups of all the same type, such as people's names or their phone numbers. Typically, the fields make up the columns within a table of data.

Firewall is a device that protects an IT system (or network) from unauthorised access by blocking 'bad' network traffic.

Form controls include buttons, tick boxes and option boxes to enable the user to enter information.

Function is a type of formula that carries out a calculation. Spreadsheets have many different functions than can be used.

Geo-data is geographical information that is stored in a way that it can be used by devices such as smartphones and tablets to provide data about your location.

GPS (Global Positioning System) is a navigational system that uses data transmitted by satellites to calculate the location of the GPS-enabled device.

Haptic relates to a sense of touch. Haptic outputs recreate the sense of touch by applying forces to the user.

House style refers to a set of rules that an organisation follows on all their documents to ensure they are all consistent.

Icons are small computer graphics. This is usually an image representing an application or file.

Infographics combine several methods of presenting complex information, such as graphs, diagrams, images and tables, in a brief, clear and visual way.

An **information flow diagram (IFD)** is a diagram that shows how information flows around a system.

Insecure connections mean that other users would be able to intercept the data being transmitted between your device and its destination. This could include your login credentials, bank account details, email addresses, etc.

Integers are whole numbers with no fractional part; for example, 15.

Intellectual property is an idea that you invented that belongs to you, for example, an image that is copyrighted.

Intuitive means easy to understand. In this context a user should be able to understand and interact with an interface instinctively.

Invalid data is incorrect or unsuitable.

Iteration is a new version of a piece of computer hardware or software.

Iterative methodology is when one set of requirements are analysed, designed, implemented, tested and evaluated before continuing to the next set of requirements.

Keyboard shortcuts are combinations of keystrokes or a sequence of keystrokes which commands the software.

Local area network (LAN) is a network based on geographical location, such as an office or a school.

Macro is a small program that carries out instructions to perform a particular task, for example, it can be used to automate spreadsheet functions.

Malware is a malicious form of software that is transferred to, and then executed on, a user's machine to damage or disrupt the system or allow unauthorised access to data.

Milestones are stages of a project by which time something should have been developed for a stage when a decision will be made.

Motherboard is the main electronic circuit board that all the other computer components, such as memory, processor, graphics card etc., plug into.

Motor needs relates to users who have limited function in their movement, muscle control or mobility.

Navigate/Navigation is how a user works their way around the software.

Nodes represent different tasks that will be completed within a project. They will often contain the task number or letter.

Notation means using symbols to represent something. In IT this means using diagrams to represent a range of ideas.

Operating systems control the whole operation of a computer system such as mobile phones or tablet computers.

Patent is the exclusive rights granted to a person or organisation for a specific idea, design or invention.

Pattern is a repeating change in the data over time.

Peer to peer (P2P) is a way of explaining two systems that are connected and have the same rights and privileges.

A **peripheral device** is defined as a computer device, such as a keyboard or printer, that is not part of the essential computer (i.e. the memory and microprocessor). These auxiliary devices are intended to be connected to the computer and used.

Personal area network (PAN) is a computer network used for data communication between devices.

Personal hotspot is using a phone's internet connectivity when connected to a device to access the internet from the laptop.

PERT stands for Program Evaluation Review Technique.

Pharming is a cyberattack that uses malware to direct a user to a fake website that requests information.

Phishing is a cyberattack that sends spam messages to try and trick people to reply with desired information.

PIN is an acronym meaning personal identification number.

Pixels are the smallest dots that make up the screen on our devices. An image is made up of millions of pixels.

Plagiarism is copying someone else's work or intellectual property without acknowledging them, and claiming it as your own.

Platform is the name given to the computer (hardware) and operating system (software) on which applications can be run.

Predetermined defines something that is set in advance such as a drop-down list.

Privilege is a set of rules that allows users to use specific components or access data folders or files.

Productivity is a measure of effectiveness – how long it takes an employee to produce an item for sale.

Productivity software is software that is made up of a suite of different programs such as Microsoft Office or the Google Drive Apps.

Project methodology is a term used to define the phases and processes that should be completed within a project and the order that they are completed in.

Prominent means to stand out easily and be particularly noticeable.

Qualitative information is information that describes qualities that cannot be represented numerically.

Quantitative information is information that describes information that can be measured and best represented by numbers.

Random-access memory (RAM) stores the files that the device has open and stores the information from any applications in use.

Ransomware is a form of **malware**, usually infecting unprotected digital systems occurring when users open malicious email attachments.

Record is one complete set of fields. Typically, the records make up the rows within a table of data.

Relative addressing is where the cell in a formula changes relative to the row and/or column where it is copied.

Remedial action is an action taken to fix something that has gone wrong; a remedy.

Replication is the process of copying something.

Rootkit is a collection of tools or programs that allow an unauthorised user to obtain undetected control of a computer system.

Security patches are additional settings or program codes that fix vulnerabilities in applications, operating systems and device firmware, and are usually downloaded from the manufacturer.

Sensors detect and respond to the environment around them. They can be responsive to heat, light, sound, movement or patterns.

A **server** is a computer that manages lots of processing requests, delivering data between machines that are connected in a local network.

Session cookies are data stored by the web browser until it is closed.

Shoulder surfing is obtaining sensitive personal information from a user by literally looking over their shoulder while they use digital devices such as computers, cash-dispensing machines etc.

Social engineering is the act of getting users to share sensitive information through a false pretext (commonly known as 'blagging').

Software allows users to complete tasks or to create something. There are different types of software to control hardware and applications such as word processing.

Software audit is a manual or automated process that lists the name, version and installation date of all software found on a digital device. The process may be carried out remotely, for example, across a network, or in person.

Spam is electronic junk mail, usually sent with a commercial purpose.

Spyware is software that is installed on a device without the user's knowledge. It can gather information about their computer activities by transmitting data secretly from their hard drive.

Stakeholders are those with an interest or investment in a business or organisation and who are affected by changes, decisions or financial concerns, such as employees and suppliers.

Streaming data is sent to your device in a continuous flow when the device is connected to the internet. When streaming a movie you are watching it at the same time as the movie file's data is being downloaded over the internet.

String operation is editing (manipulation) that is carried out on a **text string**.

Swipe card is a plastic credit card-sized device, often with a metallic strip that contains information that is scanned by a sensor to verify the user's identity and access to a secured location.

Synchronising is when files held on two devices are updated to make sure that both devices have the same content.

Synoptic question is a question that tests your knowledge from across the whole course. Synoptic questions allow you to show your understanding of concepts from all three components and apply your learning to realistic contexts.

System administrator is a person who is responsible for a technology or series of technologies. They have to make sure that the systems are maintained, configured and reliable.

Task dependencies are the previous tasks that should be completed before a new task can start. For example, Task B depends on Task A and therefore Task B cannot start until Task A is fully complete.

Tethering is where a smartphone acts as an access point, allowing other devices to connect to it using wired or wireless connectivity, in order to share its mobile broadband connection to the internet.

Text string is a sequence of characters; for example, the password 46*lKpQE is a text string of eight characters.

Third party cookies are text files that may be downloaded to your system without your knowledge while you are visiting a website. They contain information about the sites you have visited.

Tip text is text that appears on the screen when the user hovers over an item.

Trademark is the recognisable design, words or symbols that have been legally registered by a company or individual for a company, product or name.

Trend is when there is a change over time, such as an increase or decrease in a value.

Trojans are types of malware disguised as legitimate programs.

Uploading a document or file to the server means it can be accessed by you (and others with access), although your device will need to be connected to the internet.

URL stands for **U**niform **R**esource **L**ocator and is the address of a page on the World Wide Web.

USB stands for Universal Serial Bus. It is a standard for connection sockets on computers, connecting devices such as mice, keyboards, printers, external hard drives, etc.

User interface is a piece of software that allows users to interact with their devices.

Valid data is correct or suitable.

Validation involves testing that the input data conforms to certain rules.

Verification involves entering data more than once to ensure the entries are the same.

Version control records changes to documents and files over time so that all versions can be recalled if needed.

Virtual machines (VMs) are software applications that are designed to behave as if they are a whole computer. A larger computer will run several virtual machines, using the larger computer's resources, but behaving as if they are separate devices.

Vulnerable describes a flaw or weakness in the design, implementation or configuration of a system. Known vulnerabilities can be exploited by 'black hats' to attack a digital system.

Waterfall methodology requires one whole task or section to be completed before another task begins. All the project requirements are analysed, then designed, implemented, tested and evaluated at the same time within each stage.

Wiki is a web page (or pages) that has been developed collaboratively by a group of people.

Worksheet is the table of cells within a spreadsheet. The collection of worksheets in a single spreadsheet file is called a workbook.

Worms are small computer programs that can spread to other programs.

Index